GOD
END-TIME UPDATES
THE GUARDIANSHIP
OF FRIENDS

ANTHONY A EDDY

Strategic Book Publishing and Rights Co.

Copyright and Publishing

Strategic Book Publishing and Rights Co., LLC

USA | Singapore

www.sbpra.com

For information about special discounts for bulk purchases, please contact Strategic Book Publishing and Rights Co. Special Sales, at bookorder (@) sbpra.net.

Hardcover ISBN: 978-1-68235-348-6

Paperback ISBN: 978-1-68235-347-9

13. "GOD End-Time Updates The Guardianship of Friends"

A Part of 'The End-time Psalms, or Works, of God' as named by God, or 'The End-time Homilies of God' as named by man - in being 'Religious discourses which are intended primarily for spiritual education rather than doctrinal instructions'.

For Searches or Overviews visit www.thewebsiteofthelord.org.nz

GOD End-time Updates

I, The Lord Jesus, offer friends the guardianship of one another,
with the everlasting keys to friendship of excellence,
the keys to be sustained by ample polishing,
to be sorted and very carefully kept.

The Guardianship of Friends

ensures the benefit of linking arms for all who would be friends,
seeks the kind and the loving to meet as 'tis their custom.
All who would participate in a time of preparation,
to farewell mortality, as eternity so beckons.

Anthony A Eddy

(Scribe)

*"With Friendship in Unity
is The Power revealed"*

Order— Received

Contents— Alphabetical

Contents— Category

I, The Lord Jesus

And I hear The Lord Jesus saying,
"I,
>   The Lord Jesus,
>>   am at home in My surroundings,
>>   am at home within the time frame deemed to be available for Grace,
>>   am at home with all the friendships as established over ages,
>>>   now waiting for the changes with the updates.

I,
>   The Lord Jesus,
>>   know the friendships of the past within mortality,
>>   know the fleeting instant friendships of the present,
>>   know the circumference of friendships as gathered in the wings,
>>>   awaiting the invitation to proceed onto the stage of life.

I,
>   The Lord Jesus,
>>   choose to dwell within the remembrance of man,
>>>   within the friendliness of man,
>>>   within the laughing and encouragement as friendships are developed,
>>>>   as friends come to understand what they are being offered,
>>>>   as friends await the movements,
>>>>>   which will result in their being ever grateful:
>>>>   for all they have received,
>>>>   for all with which they have been blessed,
>>>>   for the ingrained fall of wisdom as the tongues contribute,
>>>>>   as fluency is obtained,
>>>>>   as wonders are experienced and shared,
>>>>>   as the patterning of that prepared for welcoming;
>>>>   in readiness for a change in lifestyle when the trumpet sounds:
>>>>>   an approaching at the fulfilling of the promises,
>>>>>   as grace is seen departing,
>>>>   with the surprises of the lifelines now advancing—
>>>   now released into the new reality of man within the realms of God.

I,
>   The Lord Jesus,
>>   summon up the wind of uniting friendship,
>>   summon up the wind of close companionships,
>>   summon up the wind which brings the rain:
>>>>   whether in season or in the time of need.

X

I,

    The Lord Jesus,

        know the need for rain within a garden,

        know the need for rain upon a crop in growth,

        know the need for water in a trough from where the stock do drink.

I,

    The Lord Jesus,

        know well the water of life as scattered in the approaches to a desert,

                as buried in a well where lifting is required:

                    to a height from where it can flow and nourish,

                as pumped by the wind where distance is important,

                where locations accept the pipes for quenching thirst,

                where quantities are measured,

                    to be made available,

                    to satisfy the thirsty and the shrivelled,

                        the wilting and the collapsing,

                        the dying and the desperate.

I,

    The Lord Jesus,

        know well the power of prayer,

        know well The Father's care,

        know well the needed fare.

I,

    The Lord Jesus,

        remember well the price of succouring,

        remember well the price of teaching,

        remember well the price of reaching,

        remember well the price of offering and sacrifice.

I,

    The Lord Jesus,

        see man in all his garbs of posturing,

        hear man in all the levels of the sincerity of his voice,

        observe man in his approach to,

                or his departure from,

            the path of righteousness within his Freewill quest for peace or war.

I,

    The Lord Jesus,

        can summon The Family of God,

        have no need to question the intent,

        can implant the visions as required for amendments and repair:

      in situations where the presence of the demonic needs attention and expelling,

                both from the thoughts and the actions of Freewill.

I,

The Lord Jesus,

    am rounding up the evil strains in man,

    am breaking forth the hand of friendship and of trust,

    am leading man to follow in My footsteps as they construct the way,

        as the way is opened,

        as the way is known,

        as the way is fed with encouragement for Faith at the havens,

            is structured by Grace along the way.

I,

The Lord Jesus,

    can heighten and decrease as impulse demand requires:

    can bring to pass that which has been loosed,

    can prevent that which has been bound.

I,

The Lord Jesus,

    leave the footprints of preparation,

    leave the footprints of consolidation,

    leave the footprints of determination.

I,

The Lord Jesus,

    bring glory to The Father,

    testify to Him of the publishing in declaring of what issues,

            or does not,

            from the tongue of man;

  am silent when the lies are heard in attacks upon the truth:

        where ignorance is not to blame,

        where wisdom is nowhere to be heard.

I,

The Lord Jesus,

    shelter and protect the innocent and the admirable,

        the fixed in acknowledgment and objectives,

        the certain and the decisive,

            in their preparation for a destiny of choice.

I,

The Lord Jesus,

    will greet and welcome as honouring is deserved,

    will assist and introduce the known to the unknown,

    will uphold and validate the ways and means unto Salvation:

        for all those within The Multitudes,

            who would seek and accept My teachings,

            as spread across the centuries,

            and sometimes not without great cost.

I,
The Lord Jesus,
know The Father's Will,
know The Father's Love,
know The Father's intent for His children of adoption.

I,
The Lord Jesus,
have prepared shelter and protection from the storms of life,
as arising from the demonic and depraved,
the evil and infested,
the selfish and the greedy.

I,
The Lord Jesus,
say to man this day with his listening ears,
'Come and Behold,
Visit and Discover,
Prepare and Be Ready for what is to be found within:
The Eternal Garden of Your Living Loving GOD.'"

Godly Intent for Understanding The Importance Inherent in The Number of Lines of Dictated Text per Stanza

And I hear the Lord Jesus saying,
"1 line: A declaration.
2 lines: A two-way option.
3 lines: From The Father, The Son, and/or The Spirit: as The Three-in-one.
4 lines: As and for a partial affirmation awaiting completeness.
5 lines: For and under Grace arising from The Cross.
6 lines: For and of fallen Man.
7 lines: From and of Heaven in perfection.
8 lines: For and of a new beginning; or 2 x 4.
9 lines: 3 x 3.
10 lines: Multiples of 5.
11 lines: 5 + 6.
12 lines: Multiples of 6."

A line not completing with indicative punctuation carries on to the next line.

My Content Study Aid

_____

_____

Preview to Freedom

And I hear The Lord Jesus saying,
"Preview to freedom is the first sight of the dawn,
    is the first trip away from family,
    is the encouragement of discovery,
    is faith exposed to testing,
    is righteousness assailing all which should retire,
    is grace and truth united in the heart and lungs of man.

Preview to freedom is a wonder to behold,
    is an entrée to an answer,
   which satisfies the quest for:
      the reasoning of man,
      the existence of man,
      the why the when the how within the life of man,
   which satisfies The Freewill now exercised by man,
   which keeps the accountability of man in the forefront of his actions,
   which releases the mindset of his inclinations to the visiting of maturity.

Preview to freedom opens doors for viewing the external,
   opens windows for participation in the great outside,
   tracks the pathways to idyllic surroundings,
    where the waterfalls do play as they caress the stones,
      which give them life and vigour.

Preview to freedom is a function of the living space,
   is a function of the climate,
   is a function of mobility,
   is a function of the purse,
   is a function of the will of man,
   is a function of the majesty of measurement,
   is a function of existence within the climes of The Earth.

Preview to freedom brings a sense of rejoicing,
   brings a compulsion to visit,
     to see,
     to understand,
    that which dwells beyond the current horizons of man,
   where differing ways of life with language,
  present themselves for inspection in accordance with the national culture:
      arising,
       if permitted,
      from the exercising of Freewill.

Preview to freedom lies down the road of testing and overcoming,
of seeking and establishing,
of valuing and preserving—
of all which has been gained.

Preview to freedom sees situations where freedom is not valued until it has been lost,
where scrabbling after what was once known,
no longer lingers in the woods or landscapes,
where dwellings once existed on land,
which brought forth the rewards for effort and
of knowledge,
now has been captured via the use of force,
which leads into disaster,
with an incumbent loss of life and the freedom
of the day.

Preview to freedom should encourage a worthwhile valuation,
should put a prize upon attainment,
should feed the situation with the nourishment of truth.

Preview to freedom breeds willingly among the hives of bees:
where organisation is explicit and rewarding;
where the queen is highly valued and protected;
where preparation is required for times when food is scarce,
as climate turns its back on the sunlight,
as the floral abundance is filled with activity,
prior to the opportunity passing into history,
with the storehouse equipped and full for the rainy days.

Preview to freedom declares the ways of bees should be imitated by man,
should see his larder full to overflowing by his effort in the sunshine,
when the days are long,
should see his wisdom establishing the means,
for nurturing the children of the family,
as he strives to fill the reserves—
as needed for the time of trials,
as needed to fill the sanctuaries with neither debt nor hindrance,
as needed to ensure all is available,
is at hand,
without the need to beg.

Preview to freedom should observe and adopt:
for as the needs do change,
so the bees do swarm:
to find another niche acceptable and promising,
with a surplus space unchallenged,
with obvious availability.

XV

So man should accommodate the lifestyle of the bees—
                              to move when needed for the replenishment of resources,
                              for the benefit of the family,
                              for gaining knowledge of his God:
                       to seek to acquire wisdom by request,
                       to learn of the gifts of Pentecost;
           of how and why such are intended to be used within the provisioning of God.

Preview to freedom is a prelude to the stars,
                       is a prelude of much interest to God,
                       is a prelude introducing eternity with its eternal life,
                              with its gathering of families and individuals where appropriate,
                              with its being adopted into The Family of God,
                              with its preparation of a dwelling place as promised,
                              with its wider of the widest scopes,
                                     where discovery is laden with fresh knowledge,
                                            arising from the scenes and voyaging,
                                                   which neither tire nor bore.

Preview to freedom encircles but does not impound,
                       cherishes but maintains the circulation,
                       values but does not minimize inspection,
                       trusts but does not know deceit,
                       highlights but does not exaggerate,
                       tells but does not lie,
                       continues but does not stall.

Preview to freedom suggests and promotes,
                       encourages and lifts,
                       envisages and displays.

Preview to freedom is not a myth among the monsters,
                       is not a dilemma without solution,
                       is not a promise without fulfilment.

Preview to freedom is a starburst in the spirit,
                       is the explosion of the mind in capability,
                       is the newness of revival,
                       is the gateway to independence,
                              where violence is shuttered as a discard,
                              where love and peace are the profiles of eternity,
                              where invitations to join are sincere and waiting for achievement,
                              where the dreams,
                                     the aspirations of man,
                              are transitioned into an eternity with The Living Loving God.

Preview to freedom is an accompanied journey without end."

XVI

Dedication

'Lord, I have heard of your fame;
Lord, I am in awe of what you have done.
Through all generations you have made yourself known,
and in your wrath you did not forget mercy.'

Ref.: Habakkuk 3:2,
The Revised English Bible

Acknowledgements

We thank and appreciate the proxy ministries coming forth

with The Blessings and The Healings and The Counselling

from and with

The Will and The Power and The Authority of God.

There are nine parts within this end-time series which The Lord has named either as 'The End-time Psalms of God' or 'The End-time Works of God'. These may probably be better known by man in his naming as 'The End-time Homilies of God' - in being 'Religious discourses which are intended primarily for spiritual education rather than doctrinal instruction'.

There are also four later companion books which The Lord has named as 'The Flowers of God', having prefixed the titles with 'GOD End-time Updates ...'

Introduction

Jesus sees the content here as a series of flowers and has so named them. The End-time Flowers of God in these last four books are The Companion books in a similar style and layout to The End-time Psalms of God in the first nine books. These Divinely originated unfolding Flowers have waited for many centuries to bloom. Again, they mostly consist of Truth Statements intermixed with counselling and are presented for serious contemplation as to their ramifications and how we approach them in the conclusions we may draw. For they are filled with great significance for these present times and the future they may unveil.

I testify here to one and all that these Flowers from God are not of my naming, writing nor instigation. These Flowers each stand alone but willingly accompany the three preceding books to take the reader up a staircase for feeding from the closer proximity of Heaven, from which only God Himself can bring to our attention. On the original individual documents the scribe has begun each Divine Flower with the words: 'And I hear The Lord Jesus saying,' "...". This is the true stated origin of the content of this book both by testimony and by claim of Jesus Himself for Books 10, 11 and here in the completion of Book 13, while The Father Himself is the initiator of Book 12.

Here in Book 13 there is a change of title of address requested by Jesus on page 50 where 'The Lord Jesus' is changed to 'Jesus' from thereon at His specific request. This is in reflection of a closer level of friendship, with a lowering of formality, in the dictation companionship process and relationship.

The style of the book preserves the very few scribal comments in italics; while double quotation marks " " denote and enclose the content of a Divine origin. British spelling is used for reasons of national culture. Layout simplifies ease of reading and personal study which allows usage of spare space within the printed book. A concordance or a thesaurus has not been used at any stage prior to, during, or after the receiving of these individual End-time Flowers. A dictionary (Oxford Concise™) has sometimes been used to comprehend fully, the words of The Divine voice used in expressing His intent. Because these Flowers have been received via dictation spoken by The Divine voice directly into the mind, the punctuation is subject to human interpretation. Occasionally however, when required for clarity or emphasis, the capitalisation of words, together with the paragraphing, have also been indicated by The Divine. Minor spelling 'typos' are scribal and, if any from a disobedient finger, then an apology is also included. The punctuation usually is the scribe's. The content follows the leading in the floral titles.

Great care has been taken to ensure scribal accuracy in hearing and transcribing what are now these printed pages of Divinely originated End-time Flowers of God. Every word is as received without later omissions, additions, substitutions or edits.

May The Holy Spirit so testify as such to every enquiring soul.

Please also accept my apology for not having also brought this page on the three earlier books, 10, 11, and 12, closer to your attention with the updating each deserved, for each was coming forth with a fresh discovery of directional content which may have been partially overlooked.

The Scribe, Hamilton, New Zealand.

Curtain Call

And I hear The Lord Jesus saying,
"The curtain call,
      as coming,
           is the show-stopper par excellence,
           is the getter of attention,
           is the opener of eyes,
           is the call made to the ears,
           is the mouth left wide-open in amazement,
           is the silence created through intense attention.

The curtain call supervises readiness to proceed,
           clears the countdown to continue,
           validates the process of transition.

The curtain call hones in on the music master's baton,
           on the sequences of the dance,
           on the dressage of the staged,
           on the movements of the guests for where they stand or sit.

The curtain call recognizes the singers as the songsters,
           for both pitch and tone,
           for both the lyrics and the presentation,
           as practised and approved.

The curtain call introduces and welcomes,
           identifies the obvious,
           chaperones the nervous yet grateful for the opportunity.

The curtain call honours the principals of The Hosts of Heaven,
           activates the motion as the sound stage comes alive,
           ensures all are present and correct as the curtain rises,
           at the signal of The Father to The Holy Spirit.

The curtain call sees the stage,
           of sufficient size and magnitude,
           is set in a natural setting of Jerusalem The Golden.

The curtain call of God has practised The Anthem of Divinity,
           The Song of The Lamb,
           the assembly of the tongues of angels,
      with those already appearing in their gowns of both Life and Martyrdom,
           together with The White reserved for The Multitudes:
           as arising from the survival of The Tribulation.

.

The curtain call initiates My Return to The Earth,
   initiates the fulfilment of the promises as foretold,
   initiates the coming reality of My Kingdom on The Earth,
   initiates the changes as My People are fitted out with updates for eternity:
      as it now beckons in encouragement of acceptance.

The curtain call approaches in keeping Faith with My End-time Books,
    in promoting access to My Grace while it is today,
    in preparation of all who are aware of the coming happenings:
      now seen as ones of closing proximity.

The curtain call of centuries is now becoming the curtain call ushering in:
     the transitioning of those surviving the accountability,
      inherent within The Coming Wrath of God.

The curtain call recognizes the foolishness of those who pay no attention to—
       the counselling of God,
       the warning of God,
       the offered hand of God,
    all those who would stay in unpreparedness,
    who would live in denial of their God,
    who would stay with the blasphemers and the wicked:
    both by nature and by the evidence as displayed,
    from within their own Freewill activities and actions,
       to those to whom—
       God is uninvited,
      yet knows all which there occurs,
       with the mayhem so created:
     resulting in admissions to the hospitals.

The curtain call lances the evil boils with their pus-filled centres of iniquity,
       of pornography,
       of violence,
       of fraud,
       of theft,
       of killings,
     of drugs to impact on the mind,
     of activities thought to be in private,
      which reject the morality of God,
       within the lies of man.

The curtain call is not hesitant in its approach,
   is not delayed because of unpreparedness,
   is not equipped with a blind eye which does not see,
   is not equipped with a deafened ear which does not hear,
   is not advancing where evil is discerned,
    without the imprinting of the onward role of The Justice of God,
     in an accounting for all which is uncovered:

as The Earth is cleansed for purity,
as being made fit to be included in The Kingdom,
of The Living Loving God,
as The Earth becomes a living colony of Heaven and The Heavens.

The curtain call has no fear of non-appearance,
has no fear of a failed use-by date,
has no fear of awakening in the past.

The curtain call of God does not leave out the turkeys as they gobble,
does not leave out the incapacitated
where senses are no longer sensible,
does not leave out the dying nor the recent dead,
unless there is no entry in The Lamb's Book of Life.

The curtain call of God removes the shadows from the shadowed,
removes the echoes from the echoing,
removes the shouts from the shouters,
removes the beggars from the begging.

The curtain call of God stimulates in growth,
stimulates in Faith,
stimulates in righteousness,
stimulates in expression,
stimulates in quests,
stimulates in being friendly and inviting.

The curtain call of God affirms the value of being under The Faith Field of Mortality,
affirms the confirmation of The Righteous Field of Morality,
affirms the requested availability of The Cleansing Field
of Grace,
affirms the necessity of Seeking The Field of Preparation,
affirms The gifts of My Spirit as on The Day of Pentecost,
affirms the benefit of attaining fluency in The Heavenly Gift
of Tongues,
affirms access to the given opportunity to select:
the destiny of choice as the goal of life,
to be so set in Faith for Freewill Activities—
with righteousness prevailing as the destiny is assured.

The curtain call of God closes out the time of Grace,
opens up the time of Mercy at The Bema Seat."

My Content Study Aid

Face of Prosperity

And I hear The Lord Jesus saying,
"The face of prosperity carries the signals of success,
　　　　　carries the emphasis of security,
　　　　　carries the features in their fulness,
　　　　　carries the outlines without the shadows linking lines.

The face of prosperity does not reflect the frowns of disappointment,
　　　　　does not reflect the leanness of a diet inflicted by a purse,
　　　　　does not chatter shake or vibrate in extremities,
　　　　　　　where nerves do not upset that which is at peace.

The face of prosperity has eyes which sparkle,
　　　　　has teeth which smile,
　　　　　has hair upon the head,
　　　　　has neither trace of long-term addiction,
　　　　　　nor of the need for tableting.

The face of prosperity beckons to encourage a close approach,
　　　　　creates a sense of confidence and wisdom,
　　　　　exudes a sense of truth untouched by a lie,
　　　　　has fingers which play in the field of righteousness,
　　　　　　　where all can be seen to be at ease.

The face of prosperity does not carry signs of concern unless in the presence of a lie,
　　　　　does not reach for a wallet unless benevolence
　　　　　　　　　arises for consideration,
　　　　　does not give what is not the ownership to give,
　　　　　does not bring recriminations to the table or the meal,
　　　　　does not linger where uncomfortableness is evident and in play.

The face of prosperity is one of reasonableness and of consideration for another.

The face of prosperity is accompanied by truth and honesty,
　　　　　is the holder of a character steadied by integrity
　　　　　　　　　of purpose and resolve.

The face of prosperity can be an answer to a prayer,
　　　　　can be the seeker of the peace,
　　　　　can be the extender of the hand of friendship.

The face of prosperity can open up the pathway to a better way of life,
　　　　　can circumvent the cesspools of iniquity and hate,
　　　　　can enliven a conversation with stories from the past,
　　　　　　which can bring a likely impact to and on the future.

The face of prosperity does not frighten little children,
        encourages them to come,
        has another story which they can understand,
        which they will want retold again and again,
          whenever a story time flowers forth into a waiting opportunity.

The face of prosperity can be a loving person in disguise,
          a welcome friend who remembers well a childhood,
              and wants to share the fun,
          a grownup child who does not succumb to the wasting of
                the time,
            where a memory cannot recall,
           or fails to put a sparkle in the eyes of a child:
           who catches very clearly what is being shared.

The face of prosperity takes pleasure in fulfilling the desires of others,
             in meeting,
             in surgery,
            someone who needs a surgeon's time and skills,
            who is then enabled and empowered to run and jump,
            as they play with others who are now seen as friends.

The face of prosperity does not misuse in selfishness the time elapsed upon The Earth,
          does not waste on solo sports that which could be placed in
                the hands of children,
          does not overlook the passing needs residing in a mobile chair,
            in a bed of sickness awaiting an organ for replacement,
            in a room of loneliness where visiting is unpopular,
              where the door is mainly closed.

The face of prosperity works hand in glove with those who answer needs,
        with those who have or can access funding,
          as an answer to a prayer,
        with those who still see the lighting of a face,
          as hope and life combine in the securing of good health,
        with those who really want to see the hugs go right around the room,
          to then result in venturing beyond the walls of man:
          into the life now possible outside among the beauty,
              of the ways of God.

The face of prosperity shares a shelter from the storm,
        shares a shelter as constructed,
        shares a shelter with the unprotected,
             who,
              with commitment,
              are called The Friends of God.

The face of prosperity laughs and smiles with joy upon a face,
      thrills and is excited by the achievements of the day,
            by the measuring of the rod of righteousness,
            by the cleaning of the schooling rooms,
                  where falsehoods often linger to so taint,
                      in being sinfully designed,
                    to mislead or to deny away from,
                        what God has put in place.

The face of prosperity is not a child of retribution,
      is not a child of faults and nerves,
      is not a child of hiding and dismissing.

The face of prosperity gleams in both the sunlight and the moonlight,
      knows the source of each,
      knows the fulness with the strength as wielded,
      knows the capabilities of each when found within the work-throw:
            of the moon-rays and the sun-beams as both interact,
            when God requires the strengthening of The Earth,
                with nourishment and growth,
                through the sharing of the rain.

The face of prosperity is welcomed by the knowledgeable and the kind,
            by the considerate and the thoughtful,
            by the nursing and the caring,
         for those still dependent on the help they long for to eventuate,
         so to succeed in vanquishing the inadequacies as inherited.

The face of prosperity is not often in the spotlight,
      is not often calling for attention,
      is not often vying with the rights and wrongs,
         when encountering the night needs and the day needs,
        of all who are forced to lie in wait for the dawning of a new day,
              where miracles have gone before,
              are in attendance,
          as they await the arrival of The Servants of The Lord,
                with all power,
                with all authority,
           under His proxy ministry of His Love,
         prior to His coming presence on The Earth."

My Content Study Aid

The Ways of Man

And I hear The Lord Jesus saying,
"The ways of man are coming to a head,
      are coming to a fixation on control,
      are coming to a struggle for the power of governance.

The ways of man are becoming used to their own greed,
      are becoming the destroyers of the light,
      are becoming the signallers of disaster:
                where responsibility folds its arms and waits.

The ways of man fail to read the signposts to salvation,
      fail to acknowledge the breeding pairs without morality,
      fail to recover that which has been squandered in the past.

The ways of man know roosters chasing one another to a mounting;
      know and observe the dogs,
            as filled with the same urges,
            in doing just the same;
      know partners now infected with behavioural attitude as seen
                in roosters,
                in dogs,
                in the bulls within a paddock,
            where morality is shattered,
            where ethics are contrived for acceptability.

The ways of man carry both genders,
            with all the in-between,
            to a coming time of demonic accountability,
   where the churches are not immune,
   where the clergy and the pastorates have the commonality of touch and friendship:
            which has walked its crooked mile into the courts of
                mistresses and masters of anything,
           except the presence of divinity with the honouring of God.

The ways of man have retreated from righteousness and truth,
      have adopted the lies and the deceit,
      have polished up their techniques of depravity with children,
              with the cameras:
      as pornography is spawned into a world of horrors and of deviants
                at large.

The ways of man are becoming short on integrity,
  on an ability to sort the truth to stand alone,
  on common sense which now kneels to preferences and methods:
   which decry the good and holy,
   which decry the marriage vows now
    with an 'if' or 'but',
 where a rewrite has now overwritten the sacrosanctity of The Edifices of God,
  those which now decry any form of righteous birthright or expectation,
   of an upbringing due a child,
  where God does have the final word and His guidance is the norm.

The ways of man breed supervision interned in unity of purpose,
   interned in the slave labour of the past refreshed and
    polished up,
   to be passed off as a new way forward where
    everything is free,
   interned in the stupidity of those who do not work,
   who are still embroiled in the failures of the left,
   who regurgitate what has already sickened
    the nations,
   who were forced to experiment—
   ultimately,
    when the free funds run out,
   to be under stress and fearful of collapse,
 with no way forward except more of the same which withers and infects.

The ways of man are driven by self-aggrandisement,
  are driven at the expense of others,
   who suffer deprivation and hardships in the cold,
  are driven by the thoughtless and the selfish,
   with unconcern for those all left in need,
    as seen waiting in the queue,
   where bread is at a premium,
   where worthless bank notes are printed for delivery,
    in a 'wheel barrow',
   where its contents require enlarging every day.

The ways of man see the revellers not working,
  see the revellers with their millions,
  see the revellers with their care free lives of luxury and cars,
   with dual homes set aside for rest and recreation,
   where cronies attend to play.

The ways of man see the revellers feeding at the apex of the triangle—
  for they are the issuers of instructions;
  are the lice upon the sheep;
  are the blood suckers which wound and weaken:

the victims on whom they feed,
the victims in their efforts to survive,
just to gather in the necessities of life.

The ways of man cannot be allowed to prevail in ♣the works of the flesh,
must be stopped by the ballot box,
by unrest in the cities,
by an insurrection of the people,
those enslaved and crippled by the removal of their hopes and expectations:
until notice is taken of injustice,
as the governance is changed,
where all can be taken into fairness of due consideration,
of how the cake is to be divided,
of how all may share,
in honest participation,
under ❖The Fruit of The Spirit.

The ways of man in wisdom await the coming Kingdom,
await the coronation of The King,
await the dawning of the new day with the promises in effect,
as evil is finally sequestered in its waiting camp.

Scribal Note:
♣"For now the works of the flesh are evident, which are: adultery, fornication, uncleanness, lewdness, idolatry, sorcery, hatred, contentions, jealousies, outbursts of wrath, selfish ambitions, dissensions, heresies, envy, murders, drunkenness, revelries, and the like; of which I tell you beforehand, just as I also told [you] in time past, that those who practice such things will not inherit the kingdom of God.

(The Bible, Galatians 5:19-21)
❖But The Fruit of The Spirit is love, joy, peace, longsuffering, kindness, goodness, faithfulness, gentleness, self-control. Against such there is no law."

(The Bible, Galatians 5:22-23)

Scripture taken from the New King James Version®.
Copyright © 1982 by Thomas Nelson.
Used by permission. All rights reserved.

My Content Study Aid

_____
_____
_____
_____
_____

The Family of God

And I hear The Lord Jesus saying,
"The family of God has many untold stories of existence,
   has many stories bound by companionship,
   has many stories reaching out to relatives,
   has many stories of rejoicing,
   has many stories of mourning,
   has many stories where credibility is tested to extremes.

The family of God is united in its approach to learning and discovery,
   in its regard for truth and fellowship,
   in its appreciation of the integrity,
      with the honouring,
    of the empowered and the empowering:
    as each stands within The Family of God.

The family of God varies in its intrusiveness into investigations,
   varies in its scholastic achievements leading to understanding,
   varies in its seeking of the unknown and the intriguing,
     in the venturing of the day,
   varies in its quests for the memories of the past,
     where gentleness ensued within the family home,
      as all was kept in orderliness.

The family of God has mastered the power of communication;
   has mastered the power of self-examination;
   has mastered the ability to speak unto the pets,
    with their selections of where and with whom they chose to live;
   has mastered the ability to count very quickly with correctness;
   has mastered the distinctions encountered,
     between the 'yes' and 'no' of all the languages;
   has mastered the new way of living with the simplicity of functioning.

The family of God leans upon The Teachings of The Lord Jesus,
   leans upon The Wisdom of The Father,
   leans upon The Activities of My Spirit.

The family of God teaches their children well,
   supervises their children well,
   instructs their children well,
   leads their children well,
   affirms their children well.

The family of God is cognizant of the gifts of the Spirit,
   is seeking preparedness and acquisition,
   is seeking the experience of Grace,

of Wisdom,
of Freewill,
of The Gifts of Prophecy,
of Interpretation,
of Exhortation,
of Encouragement,
and of the need for attaining full fluency,
in the Gift of The Heavenly Tongues.

The family of God lives their lives under the rainbows of Truth,
of Faith,
of Righteousness,
where Forgiveness also has an important part to play in the lives of all believers,
with commitment to the path of His Discipleship:
as spread with honouring in respectful fear.

The family of God has a composure like none other,
has a consensus of the truth,
has a compilation of a doctrine for the just and the righteous,
for the committed and the worshipping,
for the Apostolic teachings in the earliest of days,
for The Word of God as brought by an immaculate teacher of The Father's Will:
all of which Lucifer attempts to interrupt,
to distort,
to introduce the lies,
to strengthen the misconceptions,
to exaggerate or minimize the truth,
to spread across both the ignorant and the informed,
the cavalcade of nonsense associated with the theory of evolution—
without a start to life,
of the absenting of God,
of the ignoring all the evidence that the theory should be thrown,
upon the stockpile of the monkeys,
with all who are seen and heard to be promoting their agendas of disaster,
of stupidity,
of amateurish incomplete observations,
of the falsehoods in denials,
all of which do not arise from The God of Love,
surrounded by the whole of His creation.

The family of God has heard both the truth and the lies,
has long since discarded the latter,
has long since been recognizers of the former.

The family of God is extensive and compounding,
is shepherded and cared for,
is learning and growing both in faith and in practise.

The family of God is all that God wants it to be,
　　　　　is conforming and accepting,
　　　　　is understanding and frequenting,
　　　　　is building and admiring of the handiworks,
　　　　　　　　　of the edifices,
　　　　　　　　　of the beauty of The Glory as attached to God.

The family of God still suffers persecution from the ignoble and the ignorant,
　　　　　　　　　from the prejudiced and the hate-filled,
　　　　　　　　　from the spiteful and the unforgiving—
　　　　　across almost a thousand years of ingrained plotting and deceit,
　　　　　implicit in the dishonouring of their god of idolatry:
　　　　　　　　　who knows not love,
　　　　　　　　　who knows not grace,
　　　　　　　　　who knows not the abilities,
　　　　　　　　　with the doings of speaking and of action,
　　　　　　　　　which surely make a God a God.

Beware of false presentations of a god in a so-called holy book:
　　　　　which carries revenge with unforgiveness,
　　　　　to ungodly extremes of either punishment or death from its followers.

For these beliefs embedded,
　　　　　in those who should know better,
　　　　　carry the threat of enforcement,
　　　　　carry the posture of compulsion,
　　　　　carry the fixture of position which speaks of a falseness,
　　　　　　　inherent in the presentation as stemming from a prophet:
　　　　　　　easily seen to be false in his seeking after power and conquest;
　　　　　　　　　without caring for the reality of life,
　　　　　　　　　as bordered by obscene control.

The family of God has the wisdom to perceive,
　　　　　has the strength to ignore,
　　　　　has the presentations which will overcome,
　　　　　　　　　when in the righteousness of law,
　　　　　　　　　or the enslavement to a doctrine,
　　　　　　　　　　　from the horrors of the past,
　　　　　where Lucifer still has his on-going fling with enforcement,
　　　　　　　　　to the doctrine which breeds:
　　　　　either estrangement on disobedience by any of the family members,
　　　　　　　or the fear of death;
　　　　　which still promotes belief in a lie concerning the after-life,
　　　　　　　　　with the rewarding of encouraged sin:
　　　　　　　　　which The Loving God with Family refutes."

The Sabotaged and Incomplete

And I hear The Lord Jesus saying,
"Protect friends from the already sabotaged and incomplete,
                    who know and share the games of Lucifer,
    protect the children while in the ages of meddling and inquiring,
    protect the youths of both genders as investigators and the experimenters,
                    from receiving encouragement to continue,
                        with the nightlife of the deviants.

The sabotaged and incomplete know where like friends do gather in a tryst,
                know where they will not be refused,
                know where they can go and be assured of a bed.

The sabotaged and incomplete are dangerous and deadly with all they bring to bed,
                are opinionated and proud of what they have achieved,
                of how they may be infected at the expense of others,
                of when and where the unsavoury way of life
                                impedes and destroys:
                the future of the open and intended way of life,
                where the morality of God is alive and welcomed,
                for the future generations where inheritance is practical,
                to not be fraught with danger from infections.

The sabotaged and incomplete have lost their characters to Lucifer,
                have chosen to become one who greets the half-light,
                        who has grown into the mannerisms,
                which match the presentation of the new existence,
                        in both voice and appearance.

The sabotaged cannot recover what they have committed to Satan,
        are forever tainted with the sexual connotations.

The incomplete have now sacrificed some organs,
                in an attempt to pretend what they are not,
                in order to assume a different form of femininity,
                                or of masculinity,
                according to the dressage and the application of cosmetics,
                which is neither female nor male in outlook,
                                belief,
                                or experience:
                and from which they are unable to return,
                        in the sense of being whole.

The sabotaged and incomplete accompany the twilight,
                with the pulsing of the music,
                with others of a similar outlook on their lives.

So children are lost without accountability.

So children are mislead into the lifestyle of another.

So children may regret when they find there is probably no way back:
to from where they've come.

The sabotaged and incomplete seek out the tattooists in the night,
give no real thought as to what they are having added,
do not consider of how it will be received by others,
of how rejection may insinuate a pause
for reflection,
in affecting acceptance for a job.

The sabotaged and incomplete have inserted a struggle into their lives,
which is not easily overcome,
may have a sounding of regret,
which is unable to be voiced,
to an unsympathetic audience,
will have to live with what they have created,
will have to try to become assimilated,
within the grouping of the like for like.

The sabotaged and incomplete have shattered and/or separated lives,
from families with unforeseen results,
have changed the aspects of consideration,
from which their lives are viewed,
have hoisted up,
as if on a gantry,
what the darling of the family has now become
as a scarecrow in high places,
where viewing is quite easy,
but the suffering is difficult to express,
without the flowing of some tears.

The sabotaged and incomplete oft whistle and pretend,
oft laugh at a joke as it passes by,
oft pauses at a joke of humiliation,
which is as if spiked by a jagged sawtooth,
on the sensing point of pain.

The sabotaged and incomplete deserve sympathy for the lack of consolation,
for their journeys as the inexperienced,
seen heading into the unknown.

The sabotaged and incomplete must suffer the jeers and name calling,
from those once counted as their friends,
from those who now stand back and laugh,
at what a friend has become,
despite the care to details and what cannot be hidden.

The sabotaged and incomplete cannot be easily repaired,
cannot be reconstituted for what was there before,
cannot be compared without a smirk or shallow smile,
leading up to an inspection where consideration for another being,
never hatches an ending which is desirable,
in meeting with full appreciation for the skills involved.

The sabotaged and incomplete with neither repentance nor a change of heart,
are left struggling in the wilderness,
to whom God is not attending,
where there is a sneering Lucifer satisfied with all he has procured:
in leaving a captured body destroyed of faith,
forsaken of grace,
with the blasphemy of the lost leading far away,
from the spirituality of companionship with God.

The sabotaged and incomplete no longer are aware of righteousness and truth,
have sunk down into the mire
from which it is difficult to scrabble out,
to so reach the rim of containment,
where a call may bring a hand to reach out to grasp,
to pull a body back onto solid ground.

The sabotaged and incomplete should search the prayer fields of God,
should seek a new beginning,
should seek advice and comfort,
should repent of all which led unto the current situation,
should seek the handclasp of God amid a complete
and utter change of heart.

The sabotaged and incomplete are in need of the forgiveness of God,
to so turn from the past into the present,
so into the future with redemption borne of God."

My Content Study Aid

_____

_____

_____

_____

_____

_____

_____

The Guardianship of Friends

And I hear The Lord Jesus saying,
"The guardianship of friends should be a lasting tryst,
should be a promise unreleased,
should be within the markers of eternity.

The guardianship of friends signals to the others of a close relationship overseen by God.

The guardianship of friends signals the proximity of trust,
the proximity of truth,
the proximity where confidentiality is honoured
without an eye upon a time limit.

The guardianship of friends is not tainted by a lingering smell from the past,
is not tainted by carelessness when the tongue escapes the boundaries as deemed,
is not tainted by a huddle in a gossip where confidences may well be overrun,
where regrets come far too late,
where damage cannot be repaired.

The guardianship of friends is confirmed by objectives,
is confirmed by a way of life accepted in fraternal
brotherhood and sisterhood combined,
is confirmed by the knowledge base protected from intrusion.

The guardianship of friends does not shout the secrets of embarrassment,
does not whisper the secrets shared,
does not fracture at the slip of a tongue:
starting to broach what is to be held,
within the security of friendship.

The guardianship of friends does not violate the protected and the secure,
behind a wall of custom friends of many years survival.

The guardianship of friends must learn the territories and the bounds:
associated with what is gathered in for keeping,
of what is gathered in for sharing,
where the jokes are rampant,
where birthdays are naturally occurring,
where the weather fails to give offence.

The guardianship of friends is a subject aligned to an area of very special endeavour,
of extremely high valuation,
knows well the danger of infringement,
senses the potential for a loss of trust and confidence,
when sharing will again need to be reinstated.

The guardianship of friends is not an occurrence of sitting on a seesaw,
with its ups and downs.

The guardianship of friends is an occurrence which happens:
> when kindred spirits unite in understanding the basis of belonging,
> a life time of a membership as if of one another's family,
> a life time of remembrance of visits and picnics,
> > besides the rivers and the streams,
> a life time of seasides in the summertime,
> > with the sandcastles of youth.

The guardianship of friends is sometimes interrupted by moves
> > to meet the needs of employers,
> > to meet the necessities arising:
> from not being the master of one's fate,
> from being within a 'Yes' or 'No',
> from either compliance or denial,
> from being a transfer of the times,
> from being under the ultimate command of another:
> one who is seeking the benefit from a skill set of experience.

The guardianship of friends is easier when positions are secured,
> > by ownership and control,
> when business is soundly based by family management:
> with an united front expressing unison of purpose.

The guardianship of friends is not an echo from the present:
> > of what has come into existence,
> is a summation of the present satisfied by love,
> > by companionship:
> as covered by the existence of fellowship,
> with wellbeing of understanding.

The guardianship of friends has waves at all the windows,
> as leave is taken where friendship is both displayed and exercised,
> with the sincerity of meaning appreciated by both sides of a coin.

The guardianship of friends knows the scent of friends,
> knows the matching of good taste,
> knows the selection of a house distributing what is proud to
> > be their label:
> both in the physical and in The Godly Spiritual—
> both of which prove to be quite rare.

The guardianship of friends should have no need to settle on second best,
        to settle on their wardrobes based on need,
        to settle on the families being hungry and eating with much vigour,
        to settle on a day where hope is quite rare,
    where the purse is nearly empty,
    where both sickness and illness are sometimes forced to frequent attendance,
    where their existence is found to be within the fields of the lame,
                the pained,
                the restless.

The guardianship of friends keeps the quota down,
        stops the stupid exercise of gathering 'friends' in name only;
        to whom one never writes nor says, "Hello";
        of whom the names are never fully known;
        for whom the lands present their different spellings,
            for the testing of pronunciation;
        by whom the thousands ticked are supposed to
            affirm friendship with the count incurred:
                as a sign of being liked,
                as a flagstaff of convenience,
            where common sense is missing,
            not even being realized that such is so
            as the waster of the time and space:
        wherein stupidity is grasped without a reason,
      as meaning is distorted to that even when faced
            with neither understanding,
            nor of purposeful intention.

The guardianship of friends knows the walk of consistency,
      knows the greetings of acceptance,
      knows the familiarity implicit in the recognition from a distance,
          with the hugs or kisses;
          as the handshake becomes a barrier,
          no longer needing to be put to use.

The guardianship of friends is the supervisor of one another's children,
        holds eyes flicking from and to the welfare and the safety
           of each child at play,
           of each child at sport,
           of each child in a rough and tumble,
      or a hide and seek,
      or a chase and catch,
      or a rider of the rides as presented without any
        formal supervision:
           on the roundabouts,
           the swings,

the seesaws,
the jungle gyms,
the rope climbers,
and the slides:
where stray puddles in the hollows underneath,
can demand a downward glance,
at a new sensation which is usually ignored.

The guardianship of friends should not create an awareness from among the young;
unless a case arises from the hurt,
the injured,
or the cast aside,
where scores are to be evened out,
with a blow,
a push,
a shove which brings the tears;
or the snatching of a toy;
followed by a run for the parent in the fold.

The guardianship of friends,
rarely hears a call for help,
rarely hears other than the happiness of the settings of the day,
rarely hears the scraps and sometimes turmoil:
in the mixture of shouts and screams,
among the rampant and the strangers of intrusion.

The guardianship of friends builds upon the status quo,
maintains the caring and the loving as within The Will of God,
has eyes open as watchful and secure within the groundswells,
of opinion in arguments,
and some times violence,
where discord is sponsored by the evil and the ill-informed:
of both nature and of intellect,
still to be stuck with the destiny of default,
still to know not the opportunities arising from the knowledge tree,
as found within The Destiny of Choice.

The guardianship of friends spells out the end-time update,
to not be a part of betrayal:
when it matters most,
when all is falling down,
when being blown away,
when being swirled away,
when being burnt,
when being shattered,
when being raided,
when being stolen.

The guardianship of friends spells out the ravaging for food,
        for cooking what is obtained,
        for sharing what is even available with the friends,
        for as the food is shared when under His guidance and direction,
        with the sincerity of gratitude of thankfulness as established,
                so will the pot or pan not be emptied of its contents,
                is to be found as if stationed again upon a hillside.

The guardianship of friends follows in the footsteps of who has gone before,
        of the righteousness of protection from harm at the hands and
                    will of Lucifer,
                as curses are reversed,
                as scarcity is surmounted,
                as loosing and binding
                    limits in control,
        when Lucifer thought he had such all in hand,
        when The Wrath of God is finally seen in play,
        when God is seen to be endorsing all His promises,
                all His prophetic words,
        upon those receiving of His grace in truth,
                in integrity of purpose,
                while in prayer:
                which is being answered,
                as it is being spoken,
                in urgency yet maintaining,
        within the open presenting of The Fear of God.

The guardianship of friends is not heard for the plaintive cries of children,
        is heard for the calls in Faith of their Elders who know better.

The guardianship of friends will have its time of trial,
        deserves consideration as to how and what kind of behaviour,
                will be offered to The Lord,
        at a time when darkness would beset and grow upon The Earth:
                if mayhem can be orchestrated to destroy,
        the efforts and the prayers of the righteous fields of outposts,
                as prepared and sent in readiness for
                the greeting of The Coming King.

The guardianship of friends must not be at cross purposes in their coming time of trial,
        must not be choosing different paths,
        must not be running free and losing touch with one another,
        must not be surrendering to the force displayed,
                whether of the limited reserves of man,
        or the backup strengths of God now unfurled and fully active,
        in destroying evil wherever it is found
                as nurtured by idolatry;

into the reality of evil intent as seen to be free,
at its peak of power,
which only now can be seen subsiding,
as the battle looses its intensity in confirmation,
of The Righteous and The Faith-filled with The Hosts of Heaven:
all those who are The Sustained of God.

The guardianship of friends does not pick the rotten apples from among the grass,
resulting from initially being dropped in ripeness from an apple tree;
is expected to know the time when the fruit is ripe,
is fully ready for the table.

The guardianship of friends should not be looking out of season,
should be leaders of selection knowing the time:
of pumpkins,
of potatoes,
of soup,
of vegetables,
or with the fruit as ripened,
or with the eggs as laid,
or with the wine as pressed.

The guardianship of friends should be prepared with canned foods,
not in need of refrigeration when the lights go out,
should have laid a camping stove in for cooking,
with the methylated spirits fuel to start the burning of the kerosene;
or an alternative gas stove;
with matches also shelved;
where the gas is carefully held in appropriate
containers in reserve;
should have a supply of water when the mains do fail,
as the taps no longer answer calls either,
as hot water quickly fades away;
or to supply the needs of a sink or a toilet:
when a spade may well be required.

The guardianship of friends is at risk of interlopers,
when there is no fuel to be used within a car,
or other road-wary vehicle:
where enforced stopping and the siphoning of the tank of fuel,
brings such to a halt from which the vehicle is unable to continue,
from which there is no transport available to get home,
other than by walking across country,
by cycling,
or by animals,
all when absent from a queue,
where alternatives are easily stolen by force,
to commandeer for use on the roads and paths,
or through the gates and fields.
Until normalcy returns order from the lack of services,
from theft,
from robbery,
from battering in doors:
as all start to become unpleasant memories of the past;
as they make room for The Godly King with His Kingdom—
soon to be installed."

My Content Study Aid

_____
_____
_____
_____
_____
_____
_____
_____
_____
_____
_____
_____
_____
_____
_____
_____
_____

The Furnace of Freedom

And I hear The Lord Jesus saying,
"The furnace of freedom is the refining fire of God.

The furnace of freedom is the furnace of deep control,
    the furnace of the melting pot,
    the furnace which brings the dross unto the surface,
    the furnace well acquainted with the gleam of Gold.

The furnace of freedom is active in a time of preparation,
    in a time of cleansing,
    in a time of determining purity within a heart of commitment.

The furnace of freedom melts to separate the floating from the sinking,
    melts to restore the original from the contaminated,
    melts to declare the purity attained in the furnace known to God.

The furnace of freedom knows the end from the beginning,
    the starting from the finishing,
    the input from the output,
    the achieving of the polishing of purity,
      of the innate eternal property of The Gold of God.

The furnace of freedom witnesses to the fire of God within the fire of man,
    witnesses the impact of peace as purity approaches,
    witnesses acceptance of the options available for application,
      within the modified Freewill of man,
    as understanding dawns on a new day,
    as The Freewill of man attempts to align itself,
      within The Will of God.

The furnace of freedom does not go out halfway through,
    sees what is once started right unto completion with
      the attainment of success.

The furnace of freedom liberates man from the bonds of Satan,
    looses man from the satanic impulses,
    leads man to consider the future available in choosing
      to become a child of God:
     as an adoptee into The Family of God.

The furnace of freedom cannot be quelled by man,
    is not quelled by God.

The furnace of freedom raises up purity from what has been trampled into The Earth,
  raises up the righteous to stand tall as the foxgloves
      as they bloom in steps and stairs,
  rises with the break of dawn,
    which opens the beauty of the heavens and The Earth,
    in cascades of colour in readiness,
     for the short reiteration of the pageantry of dawn,
   where the birds do join in their chorus with their songsters
       and their singers.

The furnace of freedom is not a smokestack running wild,
  is carefully governed under the oversight of God,
   in the presentation of the fire as it cleanses and fulfills:
  The Will of God in determining the righteous presentations of the mindful,
     as governed from within their own Freewill.

The furnace of freedom neither vibrates nor shudders,
  is very smooth in operation,
  is very careful there are no infringements of the standards:
      as sought for remedy,
      as sought for refining under grace,
    as sought for seeking the outflow of the revised approach,
     to Holiness and The Fear of God.

The furnace of freedom is not a flash fire running out of control,
  is a carefully governed fire burning up the last residues of sin
      within a temple,
  having a blaze up as any and all lies are consumed in
      their entirety,
    as they reach their flash-points,
     leaving no scorch marks on the clothing,
  where a body of commitment offered up the stains,
  which had accrued over time as Grace was set to handle the invigoration:
   of a newly assembled cleansing of the body soul and spirit,
   as seen to be built upon the framework of accountability,
     within the groundwork of Freewill,
  readied to accept responsibility for the state of housekeeping so required.

The furnace of freedom does not require repeated lighting,
  can repair and renew all which it encounters,
  can discharge and separate all still posed as hangers on,
  who refuse to budge until they hear the declarations:
    of the involvement of 'The Blood of The Lamb',
      of 'The Name above all Names',
  being called for a complete wash-down of
    all which is encountered,
    all which is sticky and wants to stay,

all which is hiding in denial of authority,
all which hears the tongues of heaven,
to then so decide it is the time to move,
to vacate,
to leave no residues behind,
in a body now filled with
rejection slips galore,
as the body becomes a temple,
as a new guest has come to settle in,
to stay.

The furnace of freedom brings a change in lifestyle,
brings an acknowledgment of an emptying of the sin fields of man,
brings a heartfelt change in policy to the new perceptions:
affecting both Righteousness and Truth,
under the twin searchlights of Faith and Trust.

The furnace of freedom does not flare up in drafts,
burns evenly until the dross is all destroyed,
and the glowing embers are finally all consumed.

The furnace of freedom knows sin for what it is,
does not need help in selection,
can handle blasphemy and God denials from the past,
has crunched up the lies as they were dried out for the torching,
as if charcoal from the past.

The furnace of freedom sets the calendar date to this day of new beginnings,
in opening up a new destiny of choice,
in removing all doubt that there is a new counsellor now in
place to guide,
to direct,
to advise on the pathway to The Stars,
to so locate with insights into the gifts of God,
where the future awaits within the fields of God."

My Content Study Aid

_____

_____

_____

_____

_____

_____

Meeting of The Ways

And I hear The Lord Jesus saying,
"The meeting of the ways is when circumstances complete,
      with divine appointments in the offering.

The meeting of the ways can be varied and prolonged,
    can be turbulent and disrupting,
    can be exaggerated and disappointing.

The meeting of the ways can result in the lending of a hand in difficulties,
    in the lending of the tools to make objectives easier,
    in the lending of a site with potential promise for
      an off-road bike trail:
    in testing skills with fast reaction times.

The meeting of the ways can be intuitive in daylight,
    can be inviting in the night light,
    can be retrospective when carefully considered with all
      the implications.

The meeting of the ways does not lead to collisions,
    can be a fork in choices,
    can be an offshoot into a different way where investigation calls.

The meeting of the ways can lead to a dead-end,
    can lead to a perfect picnic spot beside a waterfall careering
      down a mountainside.

The meeting of the ways can be the intersecting at a country store:
      one stocked with the necessities—
  complete with popular thirst and appetite quenchers available for selection.

The meeting of the ways can be a bike ride to a resting place,
    can be the summiting on a mountain top,
    can be assisted or obstructed by the wind,
    can be surprised by the rain from a sky which appeared to
      be benign.

The meeting of the ways does not bring clashes to the fore,
    does not count spills or trips as necessary,
    does not expect to be subjected to a change in clothing.

The meeting of the ways can be circular or rural,
    can be straight and true until a turn around is required.

The meeting of the ways can be cut according to the time so allocated,
    according to the time of rest and relaxation,
    according to the time for chatting

and of introductions,
where polite questions need to also carry answers.

The meeting of the ways can be held up by the traffic lights,
can be held up by the stock transfers,
can be held up by the density of traffic in a hurry.

The meeting of the ways can intersect at many differing locations,
at many different blockages,
of tourists with their self-contained vans,
which are likely to do something very silly,
when the driver is gazing out the window,
of farming tractors pulling implements,
of flooding from a rainstorm,
of a high tide round an inlet,
building on the sea wash from the wind power.

The meeting of the ways is sometimes very trivial—
just a wave to a passing tractor moving to another field,
just someone at a corner crossing with the buzzer pressed
but waiting,
just waiting for a space upon a roundabout,
when the traffic is at its densest
at the early morning,
and the latish afternoon,
just a caution at a school crossing,
as the children gather under the guidance
of a teacher,
waiting to be released to cross.

The meeting of the ways can be appointments at a church,
can be appointments settling for attendance to a car,
can be the intersecting of the scope of life itself:
where the very trivial,
such as a cup of tea or coffee,
can become a matter of some concern:
of the likely quality of the food or drink.

The meeting of the ways is difficult with pets:
especially cats and dogs with their own likes and dislikes,
especially when inclusive of their hunting instincts,
which want to bring the trophies inside the home,
to show proudly all what they have achieved,
and brought home for inspection;
for a significant bit of praise.

The meeting of the ways can be an area of concern,
when a driver suddenly thinks he can put two items,
both in the same place and time.

The meeting of the ways knows the noise will not be unduly pleasant,
while money is the call,
while inconvenience is sorted by some insurance
for the incident.

The meeting of the ways can have very happy endings,
when families unite with families,
as memories are shared,
and new ones quickly develop:
with a cautious smile or blush.

The meeting of the ways can bring occasion for a wedding,
can progress to a family,
can seek and solve the mysteries of life in growing to maturity.

The meeting of the ways can still be in place with an unbroken tie of marriage:
good for sixty plus years and memories galore,
with grandchildren quite numerous and highly valued,
as they drop-in,
call or visit,
when the seas are not called in to separate or dislodge,
the basis for a nest on foreign shores.

The meeting of the ways should have happy recollections,
can be the joining of a couple,
can be the matching of two spirits,
where interests overflow as conversation leads,
into the grander possibilities,
arising from the original meeting of the ways.

The meeting of the ways should not infringe on the morality of God,
should always keep the lives in tune with Truth and Honesty,
in the presence of Righteousness and Faith,
in the seeking of Wisdom with The Companionship of God."

My Content Study Aid

_____

_____

_____

_____

_____

_____

_____

Watering of Friends

And I hear The Lord Jesus saying,
"The watering of friends is not fed upon the wastelands,
            is not limited to oases,
            is not appraised from a distance.

The watering of friends is deserving of a closeup inspection,
           is deserving of water in abundance,
           is deserving of water without limitation,
           is deserving of water in surplus of the needs of thirst.

The watering of friends is oft-times to do with the portage of the water,
                the bringing from a distance,
                the laying of a pipe with a constant gentle slope.

The watering of friends can be achieved by water under pressure
              as issuing under greater pressure
              as it progresses through the self-pumping of a ram.

The watering of friends may need to account for their wider needs for animals,
               for their requirements on a farm,
               for their handling of the milk flow
                 in both the morning and the early evening.

The watering of friends can be as the captured outflow from a stream or brook,
              as it has been treated to both cleanse and purify.

The watering of friends needs a source of running water,
           the ability to heat sufficient for the needs,
        the assuredness that the source of water will not progressively dwindle,
                 to so fade and pass away.

The watering of friends is sometimes dependent on the security of ownership,
           of stress in a dry season,
           of moisture needing to be pumped in cloudless times,
               when the rain has gone elsewhere,
               as the clouds have given up.

The watering of friends can speak of searching animals where their tongues are dry,
                where their troughs are empty,
              as the lowing and the bleating continues,
         until the tanker arrives with short term satisfaction
                with the water as delivered,
                 to ensure thirsts are met,
             are known with the sounds of slurping,
        as their troughs are also filled with equal urgency.

The watering of friends has a surplus better than a scarcity,
>> has cleanliness better than dirtiness,
>> has a storage capability better than a shortage running low,
>>> with emptiness approaching.

The watering of friends sees technology improving,
>> sees drains becoming clearer,
>> sees waterways losing their cloudiness,
>>> as stream beds achieve viewing of their bottoms,
>>> even so as muddiness has been relegated,
>>> from being a frequent sight in the not-so-distant past,
>>>> prior to stream fencing of the stock.

The watering of friends is much more than just sprinkling them with water,
>>> from a hose on a hot summer's day;
>>> with the shrieks of children as they scramble to run inside,
>>> only then to turn to go hunting,
>>> for the water pistols of their brothers:
>>> then brave enough to return as the armed and dangerous;
>>> with the equipment which can squirt fifty to sixty paces,
>>>> or more,
>>> in sending half-a-cup of water on its way.

The watering of friends hears the screams of wet dismay
>>> become the shouts of wetting satisfaction,
>>> as the hose is quietly turned off,
>>> so wetness can be averted,
>>> while acquisition of a water pistol increases in demand,
>>> prior to running dry.

The watering of friends is much fun,
>>> when all is warm and perspiring,
>>> when the sun rolls out its heat,
>>> when swimming costumes are highly favoured,
>>>> where a swimming pool is close at hand,
>>>> is open with the watchers;
>>>> or a full trough of water is remembered,
>>>> where the animals often quench their thirsts.

The watering of friends has its time within a garden,
>>> where two hoses are employed,
>>> where sabotage is useful,
>>> but squirting is more fun,
>>> from a nozzle with a jet or spray,
>>> depending on the inclination or intent,
>>> of the velocity and the reach,
>>> of the quantity and targeting ability;

to have one want to stop
with the shout of 'pax',
which immediately redirects the hose,
to a peaceful call acknowledged;
as mayhem is wound down.

The watering of friends must not feel they are being picked on,
must have the opportunity to give as good as they receive,
to not feel ganged up on,
to not feel too many on to one,
to not be allowed to continue,
past the stage where tears may appear,
where all the fun is lost for a moment of stupidity,
where the young received the brunt,
when no one called, 'Enough'.

The watering of friends has its days of fun with its day of seriousness,
has its days of outwardness with its days of inwardness,
has its days of merriment with its days of wonder;
with education to the fore,
amid the playgrounds of play and laughter.

The watering of friends sometimes need careful piloting,
should not be taken to extremes,
where someone feels left out,
or not welcome to take part,
in the way they would like to do.

The watering of friends includes the teaching of how to swim,
of how to float,
of how to splash and dive,
so drowning is not an option among the lively and the brave,
where knowledge and practice can bring all safely home,
from the playgrounds of the sandy sea shores,
or the shivering lake edges resulting from the wind,
or from the river just asking to be dammed:
so ensuring where it flows is a measure of control;
to end a fun-filled day where all are satisfied,
all are fed on the food of the day:
a mixture for the body soul and spirit,
and indeed,
for everyone invited with surety of their footing,
in the watering of friends."

Stepping in The Mire

And I hear The Lord Jesus saying,
"Stepping in the mire is a case of not looking where one's treading,
of not looking where one's going,
of not looking at the path ahead with its conflicts,
with its mess.

Stepping in the mire is not good for shoes,
is even worse for sandals,
is terrible for bare feet in the slime.

Stepping in the mire is entering a microcosm of life,
which cannot be seen to be moving,
which cannot jump upon a piggy back,
which cannot be usurped by the presence of an animal.

Stepping in the mire is difficult to reverse,
is difficult to revert to the time just prior,
is difficult to avoid a further misstep,
in the hurry for release.

Stepping in the mire is far from satisfactory,
is far from a focussed outcome to a step.

Stepping in the mire can be not very bright,
brings anguish to the face,
starts the scraping of the footwear,
calls the offending animals some unusual names.

Stepping in the mire introduces the swamp land with the bogs,
the wetlands with the peat,
the mud which wants no release,
is embedding all to which it clings.

Stepping in the mire sends a signal to beware,
of where the other foot is placed,
of whether the other foot can take the weight,
of whether both will sink together,
as floundering messes with the need for balance.

Stepping in the mire can speak of being surrounded by unattractive options,
by superfluous regulations,
by the possibility of being stuck with immobility,
as assistance is not available in the situation,
where depth is busy sucking and nothing wants to yield.

Stepping in the mire should find feet fitted out with gumboots just in case,

should find the presence of an exterior rubberised boot wash,
with changing a much easier solution.

Stepping in the mire can rapidly get worse,
as the bog gets deeper,
as the water overflows the gumboots in reaching knee height,
as the socks get wet with mud and swamp life,
as the gumboots start to squelch,
may even have to be taken off and drained,
by turning upside down,
for rinsing out the swamp residues still clinging to the inside of
the gumboots,
which are purposed as if for wellingtons in the keeping dry,
are chartered with protection from immersion in the mire.

Stepping in the mire is not as a result of the non-wearing of a hat,
of the non-wearing of a raincoat,
when the clouds arise as a darkening occurs,
with a threat materialising in both space and time,
with the initial sprinkling of the grass as the
animals seek tree shelter:
where they can stand and wait,
for the clouds to decide what they intend to do.

Stepping in the mire often results in a lookup at the sky,
often results in an assessment of a change,
often results in a hurried walk back home.

Stepping in the mire is not the dressage for going shopping,
is not the dressage for going visiting,
is not the dressage for travelling in a vehicle,
which is all spruce and clean.

Stepping in the mire does not rate within the heart's desire,
does not rate where there is an impediment at foot,
does not rate if such is imposing an accompanying stench,
which cannot be misunderstood as to its origin.

Stepping in the mire brings a vacuum to the conversation,
brings exclamations of dismay,
brings staring to the eyes which signal disbelief.

Stepping in the mire is far from a common occurrence,
is a rarity not known for its frequency of acquiring footprints,
is a miss-evaluation of what was casually positioned in the way,
of what was lying-in-wait of careless stepping,
as such results were unexpected,
as an undesirable target was neither discovered nor foreseen,
in time for an avoidance call.

Stepping in the mire should not become a repeatable offence,
>should not represent a chance to instal a nick-name bearing relevance,
>>to the disjointed happenings of the day.

Stepping in the mire can bring an untimely end,
>to what was until then a very pleasant day.

Stepping in the mire is best not done deliberately,
>leaves a lot of questions to be answered if it were the case,
>>and not just an accidental slip into a liquid mess;
in raising such as 'why' and 'when' and 'how' such could be thought desirable:
>>as the stink created is smelt to permeate surroundings,
>with inclusion of the clothes and surface smears as well.

Stepping in the mire is best not done as a sign evidenced in celebration of Halloween,
>is best not done when out and then returning home,
>>with an unwelcome surprise for all who have active noses,
>>>for those who therein dwell:
>>especially on an occasion when there was no early assistance
>>>with the cleaning,
>>prior to the drying and the forming of a crust."

Scribal Comment*: Thought for remembering:*
>*'If a little bird flies by,*
>*and drops a drop in Anthony's eye,*
>*cheer up Anthony, don't you cry,*
>*it's a darned good job that cows don't fly.'*

Thanks to my mother -
>*wherein my Christian name is used twice with some delight and enthusiasm!*

My Content Study Aid

_____

_____

_____

_____

_____

_____

_____

_____

_____

_____

Riding on An Elephant

And I hear The Lord Jesus saying,
"Riding on an elephant is something most people will think they will never do.

Riding on an elephant has its ups and downs.

Riding on an elephant can be identified and agreed as to the basis of the ride.

Riding on an elephant can be a very frequent mode of transport,
    where the elephant is wearing a disguise in the physical restrained,
        but performs with the same intent in the spiritual set free.

Riding on an elephant in the natural first requires a country,
    where elephants are found,
    where elephants are not startled by the activities of man,
    where elephants are experienced with what is expected from them,
        as they trudge back and forth.

Riding on an elephant with its mahout is likely to be an experience remembered,
        although achieving very little in a practical sense.

Riding on an elephant is a measure served up to a visitor,
    is something not likely to be repeated,
    is entirely unproductive,
        except for payment of the return fare,
        as requested for the circular length of ride.

Riding on an elephant can be a new experience,
    can be a stale experience where boredom reigns through repetition,
        as time appears to drag through both the day and the night.

Riding on an elephant can be exciting once or twice,
    where freshness of intent is applicable throughout,
    where the time frame is extensive and cannot be hurried any more,
    where the bounds are set before commencing,
        so are known throughout the journey.

Riding on an elephant sometimes has a quest for food,
    sometimes has a quest for sleep,
    sometimes has a quest for entertainment on the way.

Riding on an elephant can open up the doorway to the stars,
    can open up the needs and wants,
        the desires and longings,
        the service and anticipation.

Riding on an elephant can be a jet plane in the sky reaching out to distant lands,
with the takeoffs and the landings,
with the loadings and off-loadings:
between which the arrival names do change
in a reflection of the time;
can be a commuter train in tunnels through a city on an hourly run;
can be a busload taking hopefuls on an outing for a day,
or on a trip to where relationships do dwell,
as they,
both the traveller and the resident
eagerly await arrival with the greetings born of circumstance;
can be a sea cruise on a ship
with an itinerary of distant ports and customs;
can be a train trip stretching across the countryside,
viewing the new and what was previously the distant,
now inbound for other cities in their homelands,
after days of travelling into the climate changes
as encountered;
can be a huge trailered and laden trucker's home,
willing to share on a cross-country trip,
with the wares as ordered for delivery,
where timetables are rigid as they await fulfilment under contract.

Riding on an elephant can be exciting and rewarding,
when considered in perspective of the spiritual embellished,
with the freedom as relevant and deserved,
when the prophetic is encountered and leads into adventures:
of The Body Soul and Spirit
when accompanying a walk with God,
in freedom and with understanding in a two way conversation,
where not a word is spoken yet communication proceeds
without a hitch,
as wisdom is transferred into the soul and the spirit on request,
as the tongues of heaven are active fluent and adopted,
for the pathway to the stars.

Riding on an elephant cannot be ascribed to anything any bigger than
The Personage of God,
The Entity of God,
The Being of God,
where His authority with Truth and Righteousness,
always leads into His fields of Faith and Grace,
for all so bound within the boundaries of mortality,
where miracles are waiting:
for the ready and prepared,
for the committed and the faithful,

for the poor and needy,
for the grateful and the welcoming.

Riding on an elephant bends the boughs of promises,
into reach of eager hands;
bends the concepts of a circle,
into the frontier of a globe;
bends the bus stops in a city,
into where they are most favoured;
bends the shops with merchandise,
into the specials with the outcries;
bends the use of the footpaths,
closest to the carparks born in freedom,
closest to the walkways leading to the interests of many,
closest to the shop fronts which offer shelter from the rain.

Riding on an elephant can be difficult to dismount when it is most needed,
can be difficult to account for the needs:
of those who climb upon an elephant,
of those who get giddy just by looking down upon the land,
as they tense to strengthen their grip upon their seat,
of those who may infringe the basis of good health:
as the elderly and the tired,
who would like the comfort of a sleep
in the midst of movement.

Riding on an elephant is an open question:
as to where and when,
as to why and how,
as to selection of the elephant with a choice of its
projected destination,
where speed and capacity can sometimes trump the views,
with appealing aspects,
when travelling through the jungles of The Earth:
seen as both the creators and reporters of the daily news."

My Content Study Aid

_____
_____
_____
_____
_____
_____

Faith in Time

And I hear The Lord Jesus saying,
"Faith in time speaks of life within mortality,
              speaks of life in the presence of the devil,
              speaks of life where nothing is assured except
                            The Love of God The Father,
                                of God The Son,
                                of God The Holy Spirit:
                      The Triumvirate of God as explained and witnessed,
                              as committed to in companionship,
                              as leading into Truth and Righteousness,
                  with an opening into Eternity,
                  with The Destiny resulting from a very significant choice.

Faith in time greets the inexplicable,
              harnesses an objective way of living in a rusty world,
              awaits with eager anticipation the fulfilment of the end-time promises
                                      of God.

Faith in time points the way to the measuring of reality,
              points the way to living to maturity,
              points the way to a life of Righteousness with Truth,
                  where lies and deceit are discarded to keep the devil company,
                  with all his cohorts in his coming internment arising from The Garden,
                            when Godly censorship is manifested in judgment,
                                of the devil's application of his own Freewill.

Faith in time is only a temporary phenomenon found within mortality,
              has no requirement to exist elsewhere on any other synopsis of existence.

Faith in time came into existence,
              to cover the period between The Cross of Christ,
              and the permanent return of The Lord Jesus to The Earth:
             where Faith with Truth is,
                      and has been,
                  the prime requirement in the building of Christianity,
                      within the hearts of man in their sojourn,
                      within the time as allocated to each and every life,
             to be found within the setting for preparation,
                        for the transfer to the final destiny of eternity,
                    as prepared in readiness by the gardening of God.

Faith in time is not a clockwork function,
              is not a pre-emptive strike,
              is not the end summation of the potential to be found,

in each life commitment made to become a follower of Jesus,
where The Eternal shelters and protects the destiny of choice,
as such becomes closer by each day,
in the effectiveness of Grace in clearing the slate of man,
who knows with understanding the potential of the offer,
in including the deep significance inherent in the definitive invitation.

Faith in time does not spin man round and round,
does not lead man in the circling of a mountain,
does not attempt to hold man back from all he wishes to achieve
in climbing,
in summiting,
that which stands before him with the honour of the testing of its height.

Faith in time keeps count with Grace,
keeps count with the ageing of man,
keeps count with the expectations of The End-time Wrath of God.

Faith in time has a reckoning with The Freewill pursuit of man,
with The Freewill fitted out for either honouring or
respecting with nothing in-between.

Faith in time allocates a time of preparation,
a time of becoming fluent in the tongues of heaven,
a time of matching prophecy with the interpretation,
a time for a strengthening walk with God
where Faith can build in Truth;
where satanic matters can be excised from The Temple with its invited guest;
can be discarded from any position of influencing a life,
to be built on the attaining of the destiny of default;
can be vanquished from consideration by The Freewill of lies,
concerning the promises of God with a mindset based:
on chasing after ill-gotten wealth.

Faith in time holds the key to The Proxy Ministry of God:
holds the key to open doors to His supply,
in meeting the desires of the heart;
to His love and care in tending,
to all within His flock;
to His grace of forgiveness and the refiner's fire,
in the ridding of the sin;
to His healing power of illness or disease with
bone disfiguration,
to His working of miracles for bodies in need of repair;
to His signs and wonders in targeting idolatry,
as stumbles are prevented,
as the path is cleared.

Faith in time has been an extended call for man,
        covering all that man has done and achieved,
    for Lucifer or for Jesus,
    in these two thousand years odd,
    where teaching has been widespread,
    where progression has been remarkable,
    where progression would install the names of miracles on many:
      in the realm of flight,
      in the realms of hearing and seeing from afar,
      in the realm of medicines,
      in the realm of travelling to the moon and return,
      in the realm of telescopes and all being discovered in the days
               above the clouds,
    yet also with the power of light,
       of radio,
       of telephones,
       of vehicles with equipment of construction:
     when shown unto those who could visit from the past.

Faith in time is truly a marvel to review,
    is truly a time of significance within the measured growth of man,
    is truly quite remarkable for what is now seen as possible,
     when within the innate abilities of man as he chooses to make war,
     in order to seize what he cannot obtain by any other means.

Faith in time knows that war is the last weapon in diplomacy,
     is the highpoint of dictatorship,
   sees Truth as the first catastrophe that falls wounded to The Earth."

My Content Study Aid

_____

_____

_____

_____

_____

_____

_____

_____

_____

_____

Faith Truly Perceived

And I hear The Lord Jesus saying,
"Faith truly perceived as the originator of the call of God separates,
>> by the nature of its declaration,
>> the falsehood from the truth.

Faith truly perceived uplifts the spirit and the soul,
> uplifts the sanctified within the realm of the spirit,
> uplifts in the transferring of wisdom if so sought,
> uplifts in opening up the conversation channels previously unknown,
>> where thought empowers the will,
>> where concepts are exchanged,
>> where knowledge is confirmed,
>> where Freewill is loosed into the guidance of God,
>> where the foundation of Faith is firmly attached to truth:
>>> which no longer vibrates randomly within its stall.

Faith truly perceived is not separated from God by even a whisker,
> is not separated from God by anything at all,
> is nor separated by any evil jurisdiction,
> is not separated by the righteous will found in commitment,
>> by the righteous will found in the binding of a vow,
>> by the righteous will found in the ongoing eternal
>>> love of God.

Faith truly perceived does not echo round an auditorium,
> does not carry shame in a confession,
> does not put doubt upon a testimony.

Faith truly perceived is not based on controversy from the past,
> is not a carry over of arguments within a home,
> is not a seclusion of withdrawal.

Faith truly perceived is vibrant and alive,
> is confident and real,
> is secured and forthright.

Faith truly perceived carries the patterns of emotion in control,
> carries the principles of righteousness in obedience,
> carries the seeds as set to sprout within eternity,
>> as wisdom is implanted,
>> as capability is evidenced by experience,
>>> all founded within the strength,
>>> within the capacity of Freewill.

Faith truly perceived assists the growth of man,
        assists the knowledge base and the inclinations,
        assists the release of effort with attainment,
            of thoughtful supervision,
            of thoroughness in action:
                from where stupidity is the first deletion,
                from the storehouse of the soul.

Faith truly perceived inherits a future based on growth,
        inherits a future based on the experience of others,
        inherits a future of fulfilment where promises are redeemed,
            as miracles occur within the full tableau of Faith,
                then seen in action.

Faith truly perceived is the backbone of support,
        is the backbone strengthening resolve,
        is the backbone supplementing the proceeding of the will
              of My people,
            when entered in commitment.

Faith truly perceived is as a nut within its shell,
        needs protection from where it falls,
            from what it is set to do;
        needs to decide how a task is to be accomplished in light of
            the preparation,
            which has gone before,
        with the most effective means of fulfilment,
        in confirming within The Opened Will of God.

Faith truly perceived is the guardian of the gatehouse of each Temple,
        is the guardian of who may pass therethrough,
        is the guardian of the workers and the achievers,
          who can complete either the spiritual or the physical task as set,
            to be so carried out to completion,
      with full and wholesome satisfaction,
      with the finished objective of The Temple now operational,
      with admiration for the craftsmanship employed,
          for the results of prayer with declarations of The Word,
            of perseverance as completion is assured.

Faith truly perceived extends and does not weaken,
        modifies in correction,
        supports the weak and timid,
        assists the strong and restless,
        holds fast to the mature and the windswept by the hurricanes of life.

Faith truly perceived ensures the preparation of The Bride in full readiness for inclusion,
throws out the seeds of doubt wherever,
and by whomever,
they were attempted to be sown.

Faith truly perceived is a governing factor when applied to the vital side of life,
not in what is being achieved,
but in what is being avoided:
with the ultimate farewelling of the destiny of default while within mortality,
so the destiny of eternity can eventually open in its fullness,
with all which it empowers,
as a dwelling space with a promise of a place prepared,
all within the gardening infrastructure of The Lord Jesus,
where surprises and amazement is installed as the studies of the day,
as both change and location require new means of establishment,
for The Temples now seen in the beauty of inheritance,
with the jewels,
as befitting,
to be placed on The Temple Gowns of Life.

Faith truly perceived fulfils in its entirety its arising from The Cross,
its benevolence as birthed on Christmas Day
with the fulfilment of The law,
the covering of grace and the reconciliation of God with man
and of man with God,
as seen and received by man through The Cross at Calvary,
where man was positioned to receive a fresh vista of all that God intends,
accompanied by the means He employed for this to be so brought about,
when records could be kept with memories sustained,
across the coming generations of the centuries,
until The Father set the scene for The End-time of His Wrath,
as intertwined within the end-time prophecies:
in preparation for The Second Advent of His Son—
The Lord Jesus with His Kingdom's reign upon The Earth."

My Content Study Aid

_____

_____

_____

_____

_____

_____

Faith Well Rewarded

And I hear The Lord Jesus saying,
"Faith well rewarded is remembered throughout eternity as promises are honoured,
as companionship with God prevails
at the ultimate level of existence.

Faith well rewarded will have no grounds for dissatisfaction,
no grounds for dismay,
no grounds for the devil to say,
'I told you so'.

Faith well rewarded has no evidence of favours awarded,
has no evidence which would destroy The Faith,
has no evidence necessary to contradict a lie.

Faith well rewarded is the ongoing confirmation of a Faith while it is current,
alive and vibrant as in the surviving memories,
of My people of commitment who both love and honour,
the reality of their Faith,
as miracles signs and wonders blossom from The Faith:
as both tendered and fulfilled from the first few tentative steps,
to an an everlasting confidence as heaped upon:
an expanding eternal pathway to the stars.

Faith well rewarded does not drop hints to the devil or his feedstock,
to the devil's train of copycats,
to the fissures of disease,
to the crevices where illness breeds its strains of
sickness and collapse,
to just across the table near an altar of make-believe,
where idolatry is rampant and the curses of the past four
and ten generations are all alive,
inherited and active in the gloating fields of systemic pains,
of fractures,
of displaced and distorted bones,
as the flesh attempts to cover in the pitiful,
where suffering is the greatest and appearance is tainted,
by the attention of the demons,
as the pitiful all go careering down a chute to placement,
in the bin as captives of weird and demonic slavery,
as it springs the traps on drugs,
on witchcraft,
on astrology,
on tattooing,
and on all the associated black arts of man,

that follow with his loss of righteousness,
                                    of conscience,
                                    of Freewill,
            as addiction rules both the day and the night,
                    with the body in peril of collapse.

Faith well rewarded knows the call to testify of Jesus,
            knows the inhibiting result of an absence of the testimonies,
            from those who would be the ones as to be numbered in The Bride.

Faith well rewarded raises up and yields,
            raises up and is fluent in the gifts of God,
            raises up with understanding the interpretations:
        in the hearing of the many,
        in the presence of the few,
        in the fellowship of similar gifts as bestowed within the walk with God,
            where both baptism and pentecost are the marked days within a life,
                of discipleship and acquisition of The Proxy Ministry:
                with The Authority to hear,
            to speak the words in declaration of The Healing Will of God,
                            as a sign-off of The Trust of God,
            where a transitioning is called for from The Spiritual into The Natural,
            as The Natural receives that which was first visioned by God,
                            unto The Prophets,
                            and His dreamer servants:
                those who know and use the sixth sense of man,
                in conversing with The Living Loving God,
                with a fully functioning fully secure relay station,
                which cannot be usurped within the connection links,
                enabling thought transference as installed and used.

Faith well rewarded is to be experienced on all aspects of inheritance,
            as heavenly tongue fluency is achieved:
            The Rhythm of The Saints;
            The Inside of The Eyelids as digital projection screens,
                            which can be watched and read;
            The Absence of Entity as the means of extremely fast response,
                            across distances within mortality;
            The installing of multiple tongues upon request,
                    which are able to bring Heavenly Wisdom with them;

The Gaining of Fluency in speaking the selected heavenly tongue,
as chosen with interpretation or instilling meaning,
when a tongue is chosen as the means of communication,
which is much faster than the speed of light,
as mass is not involved and only information is sent to
destination co-ordinates,
across both time and space where White Holes exist,
and blackness cannot enter;
so obviously data describing mass with its material as
information only,
can also be re-inverted to the particular mass,
from which it was first derived at a location,
of exceptional distance when the co-ordinates are known,
to be live and operational.

Faith well rewarded hinges on achieving the fluency of heavenly tongues,
where perseverance is required,
until correcting pronunciation is sought and attained,
so practice with the syllables can move on to an
approved completion.

Faith well rewarded here is but a synopsis of the concepts,
as mentioned just above;
they all can be experienced in the twelve books already written,
with the first nine book indexed in Book Eight.

Faith well rewarded is within The Works of God,
is within The End-time Psalms of God,
is within these thirteen End-time Dictated Books of God,
wherein lies the righteousness,
the truth,
the honesty,
the integrity,
the end-time revelations of The Prophetic Will of God."

My Content Study Aid

_____

_____

_____

_____

_____

_____

Faith Delivered

And I hear The Lord Jesus saying,
"Faith delivered is for the patient and the adamant,
                the quickened and the foresightful,
                the earnest and the believing,
                the persevering and the triumphant.

Faith delivered speaks of hopes and dreams being met,
                of healing of the pain and abscesses,
                    as health partitioned times of prayer have both come and gone,
                                with attention as required,
                  as God has seen and sourced,
                    with righteousness and wisdom restored and justified by God.

Faith delivered moves with the seasons and the temperatures,
                          as found within a dwelling;
            moves with the clothing deemed as necessary,
                          within the building as on offer;
            moves within the transport in conveyancing,
                        with the comfort as encountered.

Faith delivered notifies the completion of a prayer,
            notifies the fulfilment of a need.

Faith delivered greets in reception of a wave of gratitude,
                  of an expression of thankfulness,
                      for the freedom from the pain,
                          as was carried and suffered,
                          until the release occurred.

Faith delivered is recognized for its end result,
                for its release from the satanic vortexes,
            as they twisted and revolved the spasms of the pain,
                      which swept over in undulations of intensity,
            with each passing wave rolling in to bear down upon the bones.

Faith delivered brought Glory in Release,
            brought Glory in newly found freedom,
            brought Glory in the absenting of interlocking muscles,
                  of the freeing from cramping onsets specific to an area,
                  of headaches invading with intensity to make thinking
                            nigh impossible.

Faith delivered turns adversity into a joyous rebound:
            gives new life and meaning to A Blessing,
            stretches out a hand which no longer has the shakes.

Faith delivered witnesses the moving of the mountains,
            witnesses the raising of the sick from their beds of pain and illness,
            witnesses the healing of The Lepers from their leprosy,
            witnesses the recovery of The Victims of poliomyelitis.

Faith delivered witnesses the removal of the demonic influencing,
            witnesses the effectiveness of The Gifts of God,
            witnesses the results of The Blessings,
                        as received from God,
                        upon the temples in His care.

Faith delivered removes the influential works of Lucifer:
            removes the curses left in place across the generations,
                        which bring harm and interruptions to the intended peace of God;
            removes the influencing of the drugs in drinks and cigarettes,
                        as introduced to attack the brain,
                        wherein lies the resting place of wisdom,
                        and of how such will be used;
            removes the demonic triggers in the setting up of a chain of dependency,
                        designed to shorten dramatically the time frame
                        available in mortality,
                        for establishing an eternal relationship with God.

Faith delivered impacts on the lives of My people as committed and accepted,
            impacts on the lives of The Multitudes still seeking recognition,
            impacts on the presenting and understanding,
                        on the perceived practicality,
                        within the invested reality of God.

Faith delivered is always:
                        a welcome component of existence,
                                    within the construct of the temples;
            a welcome surprise within the existence of the witnesses;
            a welcome addition in the amending of,
                        the bearing of the pain and the inflictions,
                                    as brought by the demonic entities,
                                    who would thereby stay in comfort,
                                    until dismayed to be thrown out.

Faith delivered sees the beauty of surroundings,
            appreciates The Master's touch in bringing enjoyment to each day,
                        with the weather and the growth patterns:
                                    so easily observed,
                                    so often just ignored,
                                    so rarely admired for what they really are—
                        as wonders in the making for their sojourn in the sun.

Faith delivered is evidenced throughout the whole of creation,
>   where even the blind and the deaf can appreciate the change in their surroundings—
>>   as the flowers present their perfumed centres to the bees,
>>   as spring survives the winter;
>>   as the birdlife join in the harmony of their morning ritual choruses,
>>>   while the demands of nesting keeps them busy,
>>>>>>   in feeding throughout the day,
>>>   with consistent journeying back and forth to and from the families,
>>>>   as brought into existence just a short time ago,
>>>   which are now fast growing up in preparation.

Faith delivered sees yet seldom praises,
>>   hears yet seldom turns the head,
>>   witnesses yet seldom stoops the nose.

Faith delivered,
>   unless tied into reception,
>   remains unknown to most who in business and daily activities overlook:
>>>   the decorations of The Florist and The Gardener at large;
>>>   the stream life with its own submerged abundance of life;
>>>   the sea with its rolling feeding capability,
>>>>   permeating right throughout its depths,
>>>>   where hunger is continually satisfied,
>>>>   where life is constantly imperilled.

Faith delivered is a marvel to behold,
>>   is the substantiation of life within a chain of progression,
>>>   yet in the organised overall care of The Loving Living God,
>>>   for all He has created and where they have been placed,
>>>>   for their species to survive.

Faith delivered witnesses the interruptions to the species,
>>>   as wrought by man upon the creative presentations,
>>>   in evidencing the complexity as placed upon The Earth:
>>>   The Display Case of The Glory of God."

My Content Study Aid

_____

_____

_____

_____

_____

_____

Victory in Review

And I hear Jesus saying,
"Victory in review brings innovation into cascading falls,
        brings insight into a better way of attending to the needs,
        brings inspection into the checks and balances
                    on all that has gone before.

Victory in review settles in being seated on a stump in the sunshine of the day.

Victory in review lists the present with impact on the future,
        lists the currencies which have shrunken in the shrivelling,
            as they no longer carry their initial responsibilities,
        lists the changing boundaries where nations suffer dislocations,
                which do do not fare them well.

Victory in review sees mistakes within the past,
        where greed and avarice were the watchdogs of success,
        where emphasis on land accumulation,
            was the be-all and the end-all
            of the measure of success,
        where stability and growth were not the prime directives,
            in the governance of nations.

Victory in review changes with the input of the season,
        changes with the snow upon the ground,
        changes with the ice within a river;
        changes as the attitudes are overcome,
           as they fought unto a standstill,
           as resources were consumed and could not be replaced,
           as manpower was seen to be diminishing in the shortage
                in the factories,
           as reserves succumbed to being drawn down by,
              the most urgent orders,
           as destruction and fracturing brought production to a halt,
           as transportation hindered the transferring of what was left of
                bulk deliveries,
            to the positioning where sought and awaited:
          for the bringing of relief,
          for the continuing in the achieving the objectives,
         as detailed but failing to be attained with what was held
                in-hand,
         as fuel became more critical in importance by the day.

Victory in review was not helped by a late review,
        was not helped by the turning of the tide,
         was not possible where advances became quite rare,

as retreats soon became the orders of the day,
as the likelihood of defeats began staring in the face,
as victory started freezing or melting,
as it walked away on the long way trudge to home.

Victory in review can be be seated on a smile surrounded by much comfort,
surrounded by much history,
surrounded by much mayhem with the
bloodshed which has gone before.

Victory in review congratulates the decision-making,
lingers on the seesaws of control,
recalls the corridors of power as laid down for trampling,
remembers the telescoping of the distances as proximities approached,
as the fairgrounds were not heard,
as the strain was evidenced on faces wearied by experience,
on the road to achievement.

Victory in review is not always the receptacle of what is right and just,
is not always the bringer of satisfaction
for what has been seen and done,
is not always the best melting pot for righteousness and truth,
which are only too soon seen to fall,
to be left struggling upon
the roadside of despair,
as they are deserted,
are left unto themselves.

Victory in review is as a two-sided coin:
where only one side counts the gains as they accrue,
where only one side counts the cost as lost in the totalling run amok.

Victory in review is overseen by God,
receives prayers from both sides of the coin,
receives the calls on hunger;
as the distraught and homeless now wander,
in the streets of rubble with the signs of fire;
receives the prayers of gratitude and victory,
where no tears appear upon the face,
for what has been inflicted upon the innocent and the grieving,
for what can be seen from a given distance,
neither repaired nor replaced as embedded in
the seeds of destruction:
now fully grown and without compensation,
for all which has been wrought upon their fellow beings,
with the harvesting of death and enmity,
as the crop of war.

Victory in review sees God sorting out the specific prayers qualifying for attention,
from the pain and agony,
for the losses of family support,
for the children which were taken,
for the destruction of the shelters now viewed
as rubble in the streets.

Victory in review can be both kind and cruel,
can be both sought and shed,
can be both the source of relief and of dismay:
as the future is considered,
as wherein each surviving soul must find a place to fit.

Victory in review does not carry any credits in the sight of God,
does not carry either approval or the blessings for the decision-makers,
who created havoc in the onset of a war:
those who sat in leathered chairs and scarcely flinched when the bombs did burst,
those who had the cheek to send their families to places deemed as safe,
while the war that they started raged and swept across the lands,
where the tolls could not be counted,
where the birthrights were forever lost.

Victory in review recognizes the crimes of the centuries which result in the loss:
of Faith,
of Truth,
of Righteousness,
in the loss of a time of preparation,
in the abrupt shortfall,
in the suddenness of interrupting time loss,
for the option of a commitment to eternity;
as the gates of Hell are opened ever wider to receive the qualifiers,
as the liars and the infractors of the morality as instated by God,
within the years of extensive madness of man as if reduced to animals,
as seen and known by God:
with all the damage and the losses which have followed in the dust."

My Content Study Aid

_____

_____

_____

_____

_____

_____

Blending of The Sacred Interests

And I hear Jesus saying,
"Blending of the sacred interests see the blending filled with marvelling at a cold attack,
see the blending in a micro furnace close up and far from restraint,
see the blending seeking postures which will lead unto an altar.

Blending of the sacred interests see the seizing of the circular,
see the hands now fingering the gold,
see the feet involved in the wearing of the gold,
see the golden band surrounding the circumference of piety and love,
see the golden scroll in readiness to be unrolled so to be read.

Blending of the sacred interests hear the whistle of the practise swing,
of the two-edged golden sword as released from its scabbard,
as calling for attention,
as sought and trained in style,
as awaiting the formidable and the overbearing
presence of the lion,
replete in the wild with a roar in announcing,
in the roaming beyond the smoke,
in the prowling with the flames;
as the sword does point in readiness of being armed,
to separate the head from the neck if posturing is evident,
if action is required in resting on the call of the guardian angels,
seen massing for defence or for attack,
depending on the trumpet blast,
as it sounds throughout the heavens within the signature range of God.

Blending of the sacred interests can reach out far and wide,
can stretch out deep and high,
can attend the interests of God wherever they may be found.

Blending of the sacred interests can hear a twang with the release,
can sense the amazing speed of the arrows,
as collected for the bow of record,
for The Rider of the white horse.

Blending of the sacred interests see many readied for release,
see many profiled with a message,
see many bringing fire to the start of the refining.

Blending of the sacred interests see many held in readiness,
to scatter the seven bowls the seven angels hold
within His Throne Room,
on the seasons of release.

Blending of the sacred interests reach out to the straight and narrow,
      put to instil that which is respectful or imposing,
        that which is graceful or reflective,
        that which is circular or elliptical,
      as each structure breeds its points of well-being,
        in the years bred of consideration.

Blending of the sacred interests must not become sources of idolatry,
        of idols kept on altars,
      of many kept to remain before My people
        with their images as created,
      so to put on show for all to see and witness,
        when among the narrow-minded,
    or the collectors who would rather gather in and not discard.

Blending of the sacred interests are difficult for some of God to accept and grow,
      for some of God to acknowledge and
        not withhold,
    to use and not to break,
    to appreciate and neither chip nor dent,
    to prepare and present within The Light and The Will of God.

Blending of the sacred interests amassed in the repository
      are the items valued by My Church,
        the items inherent with their memories,
    as gathered or crafted or painted in times of need
      or of celebration,
      or of indignant separation,
      or is based upon remembrance
        of the welcomed miracles,
        arising from the prayers of My people,
        in their times of conflicting desperation.

Blending of the sacred interests reach across divides,
      reach across the splits and ill feelings,
      call across for the onset of unity,
    where doctrine has been at the root of that which has grown,
        flourished for its season,
      to break the ties which held to create the boundaries,
        which brought dissent,
        dismay,
        and dissatisfaction even unto war.

Blending of the sacred interests
      speak of My two commandments with the rescinding of the law;
      speak of My baptism by example of immersion;
      speak of My communion when My people gather;

speak each individual commitment to follow Me and only Me,
with neither idolatry nor worship gone astray,
in declaring their triune destiny of choice within Eternity
with God;
speak My gifts at Pentecost for the tongue of man,
in his attaining fluency of expression;
speak the inheritance of Freewill from The Cross of reconciliation,
under redemptive sacrifice;
speak going unto The World with The Word and My teachings,
to both The Gentiles and The Jews.

Blending of the sacred interests are to bring unity of purpose,
unity of belief,
unity of teaching,
unity of assimilation,
unity of the understanding of doctrinal release
which qualify,
in those seven items,
the release of Christianity from the bondage of the edifices
with their leadership inherited—
all those among the sects,
the faiths,
the diversity of My people in their denominations,
as guided by their founders of construction,
to be in unity before the altars of The Trinity of God.

Blending of the sacred interests are not separated by the will of priests,
of pastors,
of clergy,
of ministers,
of brothers,
of sisters—
all those who would stand before a gathering,
to have failed in preaching The Gospel in its fulness;
so Hell has its existence doubted,
so Sin is scarcely mentioned,
so The Morality of God is stolen,
to be substituted for the adjustable ethics of man,
as they are adopted by the waylaid ministry of My church,
in all their pagan nonsense,
as no longer witnessed by My church astray,
as not called to account by leadership,
now found to have lost their vision in the presence of our God."

Selecting The Worth Visiting

And I hear Jesus saying,
"Selecting the worth visiting requires a word of knowledge,
                              requires certainty of conviction,
                              requires certainty in the absence of the lies.

Selecting the worth visiting is a measure of support,
                              is a measure that the truth may be waiting to be told,
                              is a measure that evidence is still awaiting an outlet of integrity.

Selecting the worth visiting can require a lot of travelling,
                              can require a strange timetable of arrivals and departures,
                              can sometimes best be served by the presence of a second witness,
                                        in case liars are presented in the court room,
                                        where the justice of man is served to all concerned.

Selecting the worth visiting can require a lot of searching,
                              can require a lot of evaluation of past evidence,
                              can require a lot of effort in assessing current situations.

Selecting the worth visiting requires diplomacy and accuracy,
                              requires the possibility of wrongful imprisonment,
                              requires the likelihood that others will be lying.

Selecting the worth visiting means careful approaches initially,
                              means an understanding of the situation as it developed,
                              means the possibility that access will not be granted.

Selecting the worth visiting means verification of what can be seen for evaluation,
                              means checking on the tokens of wealth displayed,
                              means background checks of relatives,
                    of how and where the crime occurred with the timeframe to arrest,
                                        and how the case was closed;
                    whether a close relative was likely to know more that was admitted.

Selecting the worth visiting can be often found within the church life,
                              is easiest when the suspect is on bail or is yet to be arrested,
                              is at its most difficult when counsel is not helpful,
                                        where proceedings cannot be shared,
                                        where doubt on trustworthiness is thrown,
                                                  from every corner of the pitch,
                                        where witnesses are scarce or unavailable,
                                        where testimony is difficult to have sustained,
                                        where evidence may be secreted and not shared
                                                  from the office of the prosecution.

Selecting the worth visiting entails checking and rechecking,
of reading and re-reading,
of interviewing and re-interviewing of all relatives and friends.

Selecting the worth visiting requires spotless records of enquiry,
of matters leading to a resolution,
of the signalling of suspicion,
of the checking of alternatives,
of the verifying all which has been at the scene
when all first came tumbling down.

Selecting the worth visiting needs to know of enemies,
of jealousies,
of envy,
of the devious and deceitful,
of spouses who may have secret lovers
who want to remove the victim,
square and centre within the frame as plotted,
as set-up to destroy.

Selecting the worth visiting can be harrowing and fraught with danger,
can be unequal and biased,
can be penurious and frightened,
can be suicidal and distraught.

Selecting the worth visiting may not have any visitors,
may not have anyone willing to take a bet on innocence,
may still be a teenager now cycling in despair,
may not be able to find any reserves of strength,
any shoring up of reserves which can be used,
are at a loss to know where any friend exists,
where any trust is placed,
where any outcome,
other than the gaol,
are not on the scales of hope or maybe,
or the vocabulary where money may be mentioned,
and no-one runs away except for sceptic smiles,
quickly put in place with cold hands which twitch,
as if searching for a solution with sufficient plausibility,
to be examined and tested for viability,
as a likely reasoned outcome.

Selecting the worth visiting should be a message to the innocent,
should be a message to the trusting,
should be a message testing for entrapment,
where fraud may be suspected with online banking backing up suspicions.

Selecting the worth visiting can be quick and fast,
                    can be sure and certain,
                    can be watched and proved.

Selecting the worth visiting requires a close relationship with God,
                    requires experience based on trust,
                    requires the helpless seeking support,
                    requires the quiet wondering what their future holds,
                            and is there anyone who knows where help is found,
                                    to be welcomed with arms held wide.

Selecting the worth visiting can be a dragged out affair,
                    can be very quick and simple,
                    can be active and obvious,
                    can be hidden and mysterious.

Selecting the worth visiting needs studying of any siblings,
                    needs discussions with the parents if appropriate and accessible,
                    needs security of conversations extended to protection,
                where any potential effect would carry an outcome of a suitable explanation.

Selecting the worth visiting is best done with the opening,
                            of a defining word of knowledge:
                    can set all to rights with very simple questions;
                    can justify the time and the results in lifting,
                            the dependant from the fire and smoke;
                    to assembling a practical and honest solution to the
                                    current situation;
                    which maybe blocked by obstructionism:
                            where guilt is sought to be kept,
                            where it currently reposes."

My Content Study Aid

_____

_____

_____

_____

_____

_____

_____

_____

_____

Harnessing The Energy

And I hear Jesus saying,
"Harnessing the energy demonstrates the triumph of the trial,
      the success of theories put into practice with ability to be checked and verified,
      the concepts of scale and access able to be spread across The Earth,
                  of both man and God.

Harnessing the energy is an imperative for man from God,
           applies throughout the universe,
           is easily transferred,
           is easily manifested in duplication once discoveries are stationed,
                  and yields begin to rise.

Harnessing the energy is free to all to use,
                once the homes are built,
                once the networks are complete,
                once the protection is in place,
                      from the jealousy,
                      the envying,
                      the battle lines of man.

Harnessing the energy arises from the potential of the fireball of The Earth,
                the fireball which comes and goes,
                the fireball which unleashes as it irradiates,
                      in all its pristine glory,
            upon The Earth at large as equipped and ready,
                  as qualified and exposed,
                  as prepared and waiting,
            in a working mandate to overcome and so be put to work.

Harnessing the energy is from a welcome source,
                which all can understand with deep appreciation.

Harnessing the energy results from confirming the know-how of adoption,
                the know-how of the size and scope,
                the know-how of operation within
            an endless accountability for safety and perusal.

Harnessing the energy can be seen in action,
           can be affirmed as a working model,
           can be supervised,
           can be admired for the ingenuity of man,
                in assessment of the planning,
                which leads unto a conclusion of success.

Harnessing the energy is a turning point in the history,
of the development of man;
opens up the pathways as tried and tested to unlimited capability;
seconds the high and low places of desertification into the
servanthood of man;
turns and proposes fresh prospects on the job fronts,
where locations for communities may now be seen:
to be both viable and based,
to be able to develop and to grow,
to be so enhanced by the free contribution,
within the welcome supply chain for collection,
the fire ball of The Earth from where heat and life do emanate.

Harnessing the energy opens up new applications for building and construction,
where fuel costs are not relevant,
where productivity can increase the welfare prospects,
of the involved and the supportive,
of the investing and the builders,
of the new concepts to be applied to the cooling and the heating;
as electricity moves from incurring an ongoing feeding luxury,
into being a true tool of man where running costs are lonely,
are no longer the dominant part set for consideration:
in equations of production and dispensing,
across the broad parameters of life styles and dependencies,
with the attendant servicing costs of life.

Harnessing the energy opens up the way,
for the electrified freight vans and trucks of convenience fitted:
with road-tracking capabilities;
with submission of addresses;
with batteries on standby;
for recharging on demand;
for when costs are not as sensitive,
for when freight is more consolidated.

Harnessing the energy is available to nations,
is available to update the cities of the past;
to supply the expectations of the cities of the future,
to be at the concentrated,
to be at the isolated,
where the fireball is held in readiness to supply:
the necessary component for pickup on The Earth.

Harnessing the energy is about thermal coefficients,
with heat transfer and storage,
is about the holding and release to meet specific needs,
is about the efficiency associated with manipulation,

on both the long and the short hauls,
as well as the static in consumption.

Harnessing the energy is concerned with the conversion efficiencies,
in the supply trains of proposals:
with the measuring and holding to account;
with the gauging and the setting of the delivery pricing;
with the return on capital;
with longterm investment in support.

Harnessing the energy should not see streetlights shining in the daylight,
should not see air conditioning being wasted,
should not see cars being unduly held-up for re-charging.

Harnessing the energy requires thought put into the infrastructure,
required for the smoothing of operational considerations,
bearing on delivery and the sustaining,
on an on-going basis of reliability.

Harnessing the energy will change the face of The Earth,
will change the demand for:
oil with its tankered shipments with the infrastructure,
in harbours at wharves and in the use of canals;
turbine generated capacity from rivered waters;
windswept areas;
tidal flows in seas,
nuclear fuelled power stations with the disposal needs of
avoiding future environmental contamination.

Harnessing the energy is about to change the wealth of nations,
is about to save and not to cost,
is about to eliminate the disposal problems with using nuclear fuel,
is about to summon up the strength to become adoptees,
of what has been verified and seen to work,
within the fields of practicality,
of long term cost of servicing,
of producing where the scope is no longer limited,
by the resources to be found originating upon The Earth:
while The Sun does shine,
does not vacate its responsibilities,
continues as the major and the dominant,
cost free heat source of The Earth."

My Content Study Aid

Managing The Curiosity

And I hear Jesus saying,
"Managing the curiosity applies only to the inexperienced,
               only to the first-time arrivals,
               only to the scene as set for welcoming,
                   with the bedding-in where all is unfamiliar,
                   in leaving much to be acquired.

Managing the curiosity is not painful to the intellect,
          is not painful to assimilation,
          is not painful for what the morrow will require.

Managing the curiosity is not subject to being harmed,
          is not subject to surprises filled with dread,
          is not subject to the absence of wisdom from the understanding.

Managing the curiosity thrills the chartered to show and to describe,
             the operational aspects within the time frame
                   being experienced,
             the time frame never seen before in presence,
         may have been within the dreamscape of the night or day,
         may be able to jog the memory when emerging into the reality
                   of existence.

Managing the curiosity brings peace of mind to the investigator,
          brings a lifestyle with surprises,
          brings new customs with the needs to comply with new ways,
             involved to satisfy the uptakes of the spirit soul and body.

Managing the curiosity is not designed to frighten,
        is not designed to magnify the outlooks of the nervous and the timid,
        is not designed to hold the unfamiliar in a scene of close relationship.

Managing the curiosity has many aspects to arousal,
         has many levels of encouragement with incremental increases,
         has many thought processes requiring activity for acceptance.

Managing the curiosity will not strain common sense,
         may bring some surprises in the applications,
         may lead to questioning as to the best way forward.

Managing the curiosity leads in twos or threes,
             where each can be attended to with queries,
        is not there to be either rushed or ignored,
               into a mode of misunderstanding.

Managing the curiosity is sampling by request,
                is sampling by selection,
                is sampling by experience.

Managing the curiosity is sampling as a whole,
                in the build-up of all three to a completion point,
                where security and certainty are the back stops to experience;
                where nightmares have no standing,
                        are not generated within the fields of God,
                which handle newborn temporary curiosity for the benefit of all.

Managing the curiosity has still images available for inspection,
                has recordings made from an ongoing existence,
                has comments from a combination of the informed,
                        the assured,
                        and of those at home.

Managing the curiosity leaves no one terror-stricken or upset,
                leaves no one with their curiosity sated and not wishing to continue,
                leaves no one wanting to avoid the introductions,
                        to the newly acquainted and sustained,
                        to the historical and the present:
                        to the interesting and the serving,
                    where familiarity breaks down the protective barriers,
                        as bred from ignorance or from fear.

Managing the curiosity is seen as a custodial duty,
                        for bringing knowledge to all involved,
              is seen as explaining the differences not expected,
             is seen as explaining those with different structures and appearances,
                    as they dwell within the strands of life.

Managing the curiosity is not a matter of getting wet,
                is not a matter of strange voices,
                is not the strains of songs or music.

Managing the curiosity is mainly carrying the modes of introductions,
                        from the species requesting contacts,
                with those desiring to attend the introductory phases,
                    of assimilation from the kind and loving.

Managing the curiosity is as if a two way street,
                  where footpaths exist on both sides with their walkways,
                to view across the gap where no traffic moves,
                nor blocks the views of one side or the other.

Managing the curiosity can see the perambulations of the time period,
as set for visitations,
of how progression is achieved,
of the going to and fro,
of what may interrupt or bring cycles to an end,
with the gestures both of welcome and of farewell.

Managing the curiosity addresses questions of clothing or of skin,
of sensing and of registering,
of voice concerned with hearing,
of thought processing for transmission,
with relay stations to the fore.

Managing the curiosity generates many questions,
some of which should neither be posed nor answered,
when non-uniformity of publicity surrounds,
in terms of dictated fashion and whether clothing should or must be worn,
when temperatures within the areas are as they seem to be and felt.

Managing the curiosity can sometimes require diplomacy,
in handling with great care,
where the bounds of protocol may have been inadvertently overstepped,
are thought to have left a snub in place.

Managing the curiosity can occasion much interest,
can use many approaches designed to be free of offence,
is wary of the gesturing which is so easily misunderstood.

Managing the curiosity can end like a bath plug with a gurgle,
accompanied by a swirling draining vortex in the water of support,
in the water there for play,
in the water nursed for warmth,
where startling is assured,
where emptying is somewhat chaotic,
in being both rushed and a little providential."

My Content Study Aid

_____

_____

_____

_____

_____

_____

Tempering The Steel

And I hear Jesus saying,
"Tempering the steel takes skill and expertise,
        takes patience and thoroughness,
        takes effort with concentration for reward.

Tempering the steel can be a noisy affair in the practical,
        can be a silent affair in the spiritual.

Tempering the steel is best done after due consideration,
        after a request for strength,
        after an assessment of the might and power as sought.

Tempering the steel seeks empowerment for a battle,
        knows the building blocks of tongues,
        knows the wisdom contained within the gift of knowledge.

Tempering the steel speaks of forward expectations,
        speaks of an assessment of the stormy weather seen approaching,
        speaks of envelopment within the thunderbolts of God.

Tempering the steel requested has an input to the sizing of the hailstones,
        has an input to their density of falling,
        has an input into their velocity achieved.

Tempering the steel can be softened by non-usage,
        can be threatened by weak tempering,
        can be stored in accordance with The Will of God.

Tempering the steel does neither float nor eddy,
        does neither circle nor capture,
        does neither crow nor cry.

Tempering the steel is in a time of preparation,
        is in a time of need foreseen,
        is in a time where armies are called to march,
                to assemble,
                to impose the fear of man,
                    into the prospect of defeat.

Tempering the steel sharpens up the point,
        sharpens up the cutting edges,
        sharpens up the deadliness of that which is wielded in the hand of
                    one running,
        or from the back of a charging horse:
        whether made of flesh or of the metal of the day.

Tempering the steel has a clang and ring,
        gives way to the guiding of the hammer blows,
            on the anvil of the heated and the fired,
        draws its strength from the enfolding and the stressing,
            of the fineness of the blade.

Tempering the steel is applied to differing sizes,
        is applied to differing strengths,
        is applied to differing reasons for the contour of the carrying.

Tempering the steel determines how it is to be handled,
            when under stress and strain;
        how it is to be weaponized to the satisfaction of the bearer;
        how it is to instil the fear in advancing;
            with a call to the other to turn and to retreat.

Tempering the steel hears the clash of anger,
            witnesses the thrust of victory;
        sees the pall of defeat staring in the face,
            with the hope knocked aside and fallen to the ground.

Tempering the steel can be trustworthy and vanquishing,
        can be seen to stand and not to yield or break,
        can be seen to advance and not to miss,
            with the stab of certainty and accuracy.

Tempering the steel has its day in history,
        has its day of memories,
        has its day of time upon a wall.

Tempering the steel is ready for a flare-up,
        is ready for the back-stabbers,
        is ready for the chase after those who choose to run.

Tempering the steel overcomes the iron and the bronze,
        overcomes the pike and the arrow with the shield,
            of glancing blows and bouncing arrows.

Tempering the steel is not hesitant to charge,
        is not hesitant to swing or to impale,
        is not hesitant to throw or to spear.

Tempering the steel speaks wariness into a fortress,
        speaks wisdom into conflict,
        speaks soundness into strategy,
        speaks to the common sense with the best way to attack:
            which may well be with a pen.

Tempering the steel feeds the ink onto the nib with its steel tip,
with the power to write under the authority of instruction,
with the concepts which overshadow any call to violence,
with the power to write in fulfilment of the end-time drafting
of the peace.

Tempering the steel is not a signifier of the approach of violence,
is not an accurate indicator of what the future holds,
is not an implant of what others may be thinking,
is not a hint for reliance as to the outcome of the end result.

Tempering the steel can see it transformed into ploughshares,
can see it demonstrating its prowess with the fields of peace,
can see its followups with assistance in the harvesting:
with assistance in the gathering,
with assistance in the sorting,
with assistance in the bagging,
with assistance of the pen nib in extending the
contract bearing food,
with the delivery of the same.

Tempering the steel can power the means of movement,
can power the engines of might and majesty,
can power the engines of speed with access to a racetrack.

Tempering the steel has nearly lost the right to tinker,
has nearly lost the clout to hammer,
has nearly lost the skill to handcraft,
where emphasis is on the finery of detail,
as rust is banished from the stainless,
as pots and saucepans carry no contamination to what is
placed therein,
for onward preparation of the beautiful and the tasty.

Tempering the steel succumbs to automation,
succumbs to speed and pressing,
succumbs to price and quantity,
succumbs to value and longevity.

Tempering the steel has journeys through the mill,
has journeys of discovery,
has journeys of exuberance when comparisons are made,
when selections establish preferences,
when the well made and valued stand
tall before their critics,
to let the wares so speak:
in performing the functioning as both expected and approved."

Minding The Baby

And I hear Jesus saying,
"Minding the baby is a heavy responsibility,
    is not easily avoided once imposed,
    is not easily substituted once selected.

Minding the baby is a short term tasking where eyes are actively required,
    for ongoing observation.

Minding the baby can be a human consideration under care;
    where most have had their turn,
    or can be the vision of bringing a concept,
    also under care,
    into the reality of existence before both man and God,
    where supervision is quite critical with its planning going forward,
    where preparation is best when closing with a confidante,
    where success is more assured as progression advances to fulfilment,
    where details are examined and re-examined for operational perfection,
    with respect to bearings and to axles,
    as they transmit the power in transit to the endtime firing
    of compression,
    as the charge explodes.

Minding the baby within the bounds of mechanics,
    sees a lot of smoothing and polishing of the strategic connectors,
    used to link the force fields to the slaves,
    used to make the turbines spin within control,
    used to ensure the governors can limit with demand,
    used to verify the power train is secure in transmitting,
    turning momentum into the feeding of the generators:
    with the output being able to process the requirements,
    of the streaming lighting of a city,
    included within the energy needs in totality of all which is required.

Minding the baby sees the attacking of the water flow,
    cushioned by the substance of the dam,
    cushioned for the peak demand,
    cushioned for the meal times and the air conditioners,
    cushioned in the future for the charging of the transport,
    in all its shapes and sizes,
    with the batteries aligned as set up for the recharge done at speed.

Minding the baby is to ensure its growth and capability,
    can service future needs,
    can convert the sunlight into an electrical power train
    of significance,

will not be the scene of delay and dissatisfaction,
will not suffer criticism for what others did not foresee,
will not be the limiter of success in expansion right throughout
the nation,
where the concept is available and fully understood.

Minding the baby requires diligence and commitment,
requires integrity of purpose,
calls for certain capabilities.

Minding the baby does not generate the echo of a cry,
does not involve the transfer to another room,
does not select a younger person to a watching brief.

Minding the baby is helping with the timetable,
is an extra pair of hands,
is there until release into the care of a closer relative.

Minding the baby is one of familiarity,
is one of recognition and support,
is one where the clock is seen to click away,
the measure of accepted responsibility.

Minding the baby has a period of consent,
has a time frame for return,
has a time limit to when an accurate release is expected,
by the return of the guardian of the baby,
when the watch does change.

Minding the baby sets no cake upon the table,
lights no candles with a count,
holds no reserves in need of examination,
changes the clothing according to the need.

Minding the baby does not visit or invite,
does not supply a toy when not required,
does not furnish the baby's access area with items,
which are not already there and counted.

Minding the baby can investigate and explore,
can pick up and suck,
can fiddle and grab.

Minding the baby is an activity occurring in the flesh,
is accompanied by a voice developing,
is sharing a perception of the world in which the baby has existence,
can seek random satisfaction,
can have the needs all met and fully satisfied,
can expose any weakness in the system as designed to care and comfort.

Minding the baby hears voice put to an urgent demand,
        hears voice put to an unfamiliar face,
        hears voice put to non-satisfaction with the surroundings,
            as being encountered on the day.

Minding the baby leads and is obvious,
        takes and transposes,
        shakes and makes a noise designed to carry interest to distract.

Minding the baby sees reaction to a sudden noise which cannot be identified,
           which is too loud and intrusive,
           which surprises and upsets the balance
             of the world existing all around.

Minding the baby may decide to go on a crawling spree,
           or roll from back to front,
        as space is gained with attention focussed on something,
        considered worth the study under a close up examination,
           which requires placement in the mouth.

Minding the baby sees attention falling on a bottle,
          warmed and ready to be offered,
          sees a hand arise in an attempt at non-acceptance,
             with the arrival of the tears,
         both plentiful and prolonged upon the cheeks.

Minding the baby is tried with varying pacifiers as distractors,
          which suddenly will not work,
         sees reversion to the crying with intensity,
        with but a moment's fixation on the offered,
        sees the door opened with a rescue imminent,
         as a familiar face arrives upon the scene,
         with a voice which can be recognized,
         and has the arms outspread.

Minding the baby sees a huge sigh of relief,
         from one no longer in command,
      with smiles wreathed on all the faces,
       as recognition satisfies the youngest present,
        who just moments ago was seriously dissatisfied,
         was demanding change,
        with a voice now silenced in contentment,
         with what has been achieved."

My Content Study Aid

Missing Out On Fun

And I hear Jesus saying,
"Missing out on fun is not difficult to achieve,
             is not difficult to regret,
             is not difficult to wish otherwise.

Missing out on fun can be matched by alternatives,
           can be superseded by alternatives with greater attraction,
           can be the result of a memory which failed to keep an appointment,
                        at due time and date.

Missing out on fun is annoying in retrospect,
           is annoying if it resulted in a lonely stay at home,
           is annoying if the appointment was welcomed,
                and the experiencing of missing it is a disappointment,
                     which could have been avoided.

Missing out on fun depends on a definition of what fun is all about,
              may have had the style and pace,
      where attendance was not attractive,
      where the fun proscribed may have been specific,
         yet spectacular,
         in involving:
              skydiving,
              rock climbing,
              cave snorkelling with roped descents and retrieves,
              rivers rated as three or more for white-water rafting,
              cross-country motor bikes prepped for the occasion,
              trail bikes on their tracks as pedalled to completion,
              moving treasure hunts where rain suggests umbrellas,
              gliding along the length of mountain ranges,
              twenty kilometre marathons after due practice,
              swimming distances as set within the sea,
              cycling to exhaustion,
              running cross-country over mountain passes.

Missing out on fun lists twelve instances in the outdoors,
           where the participants sometimes queue,
              in thinking they are about to be having fun,
           overlooking the blisters and the scrapes mixed in among the scares,
        as boldness is mixed with pleasure in the gatherings arranged.

Missing out on fun could well be the fun of static reclining while seated in a chair,
                  where the views are quite extraordinary,
                  where the sun may be striving soon to be too hot,
                  which leads into a hunt for compensating shade.

Missing out on fun could be a picnic on the seashore,
a picnic in a playground,
a picnic on a river bank where trees are quite profuse,
with grass for the spreading of the rugs,
with the picnic utensils and the array of food prepared in advance,
while the river with its stony bed,
scarcely knee deep in even the deepest holes,
flows clear and slow with tranquility for the setting of the scene,
in its journey across the plains,
as it move towards its home within a not too distant lake,
where its life force is shared with artesian water serving homes,
with the bubbling up of springs around the edge of the marshy swamp,
which introduces first-hand the fresh but sluggish streams into the lake,
as destined by the expanse now with their waters,
in flowing in a bull-dozed opening past the thrown up boulders,
from the workings of the sea.

Missing out on fun can be a sweet-making time,
of preparing the setting of coconut ice or toffee,
for the sweet-tooths at the card games,
or Monopoly of the evening,
or cooking up a steamed pudding as an evening dessert,
with golden syrup at the bottom,
and later equipped with a good book to read.

Missing out on fun can be the camping out in a tent,
on the back lawn at home,
with items deemed as necessary for a sleep-out,
with a little comfort.

Missing out on fun can be the call of homework,
can be the call of dishes,
whether up for washing or for drying,
or of the call to bed with 'lights-out',
following closely on its heels.

Missing out on fun is not so bad,
when there is a lot of fun to miss out on,
when ideas flow without much effort,
as the board games are uncovered and displayed,
as the Chessboard mounts its kings and queens,
as Snakes and Ladders end up with the snakes,
as letters form the words in Scrabble in the capturing of points,
as Darts are not so popular with the misses on the wall,
while Draughts and Checkers start a jumping race,
right across and round the boards,
and Fighting Patience for two with two packs,

adds speed and slickness to establish the cards in sequential piles,
                                  with one's cards established on the Aces,
                                          and to be the first one 'home'.

Missing out on fun does not include TV,
                          which is but an ongoing complete distraction,
                          which serves no living purpose,
                as it demands the ears and eyes with serials or advertisements,
                as it attempts a nightly effort to create a want from the violent or obscene,
                as it kills the conversation and the evenings' games,
                          as well as the turnout of the sweets,
                                          the desserts,
                                  or the supper of buttered toast and jam,
                          because the nonsense might be missed,
                and hence there to form a conversation piece for tomorrow—
                                          whether at work,
                                          or at school,
                                          or encountering when shopping.

Missing out on fun needs an update to the definition,
                          one with relevance and applicability,
                          one with a tendency to establish numeracy and vocabulary,
                                  in keeping pace with the progression of each life.

Missing out on fun is somehow part of life,
                          is somehow not often really serious,
                          is somehow a timeout from undue relaxation,
                                  where a TV dominates all to whom it is displayed,
                                  as learning is not equated with the images as seen,
                                  as price and quality are very rarely linked,
                                  as 'want' and 'get' is the TV sustenance programme,
                                          called up throughout the day and night,
                                                  with only small bits of nourishment,
                                                  or the quenching of the thirst;
                                          except when selection is particular,
                                                  as morality is honoured,
                                  while ethics do neither play nor present,
                what should be the expected core behaviour of both man and woman."

My Content Study Aid

_____

_____

_____

Seeking Forgiveness

And I hear Jesus saying,
"Seeking forgiveness should be embedded in the spirit and the soul,
    should be a prime directive for achieving the health of the body,
    should be set in motion as soon as the need arises.

Seeking forgiveness should not wait for the closing of the fair,
    should not wait for incubation to continue,
    should not wait for the building up of an explosion which does
        no-one any good.

Seeking forgiveness requires a cap in hand,
    requires glistening within the eyes,
    requires confirmation of a restoration with the evidence of hugs,
        as transformers of an apology into language,
        that a body can fully understand.

Seeking forgiveness should not become a habit,
    should not become set upon a throne seen to be lacking wisdom,
    should not relax and smile when matters remain in trouble and still
        to be resolved.

Seeking forgiveness should not strike an echo in a workshop,
    should not hum and hah in commitment to a decision,
        in need of being exercised,
    should not burn and run with a problem twisted into double,
        with a scowl set upon a face in trouble.

Seeking forgiveness does not need to break the ties of friendship,
    does not need to be allowed to catapult a relationship,
        onto disposal on a smelling rubbish heap,
    does not need to become a beggar of release,
        when an apology in sincerity can return
        a situation,
        to where it was growing and prospering,
        prior to an error of approach,
        or the words as issuing from the mouth.

Seeking forgiveness does not need to be dramatic,
    does not need stretching until further stress is evident,
    does not need undue repetition in the removal of the new stain from
        the shopfront.

Seeking forgiveness rolls up the tide and witnesses it soon to ebb away,
    goes for a walk alone and realizes the answer,
    so necessary to soon be put in place,

is wary in approach to not strengthen further,
the groundswell of offence where such has been chaperoned,
to now wither on the branch of opportunity,
to be splayed upon The Earth,
to now disintegrate leaving nothing requiring servicing,
into what previously had no existence nor reason for despair.

Seeking forgiveness can potentially raise the anchors of a ship so it can beat a fast retreat,
so the vacant lifeboat can be given new life with a fresh coat of paint,
in readiness for a voyage into a rescue well deserved,
among the strong and the decisive.

Seeking forgiveness can be wet or dry,
can be happy or disturbed,
can be concentrated or quite flippant,
where sincerity may be questioned.

Seeking forgiveness may be prolonged and far from trivial,
may be the bringing of some dirt onto a brand new carpet,
where heels and toes are best not set to grind it in.

Seeking forgiveness can take one to a well,
can take one sprinkling water on a face,
can take one into a place of silence,
where counsel may be best not sought.

Seeking forgiveness can be an approach to God,
can be an approach to those as deemed to be friends,
to those whose counsel should be relevant,
to those with an interest in settling to resolve the conflict,
arising from the shadows of a conversation.

Seeking forgiveness should be asked and given,
should be sought and received,
should be forsaken and forgotten.

Seeking forgiveness is not worthy of a record in a diary,
is not worthy of the maintaining of an active memory,
is not worthy in appealing to a biased adviser,
who is wanting to be paid.

Seeking forgiveness is not a long drawn out affair,
should be short and to the point,
should be accurate and truthful,
should be forthcoming and resolved.

Seeking forgiveness has no skill attached,
has no justification involved,
has no cry for mercy established nor deserved.

Seeking forgiveness should not be treated as an heirloom of a victory,
as a history for an archive,
as an example of selfishness personified.

Seeking forgiveness is not based upon the 'I' and 'me',
is not placed before a judge,
is not concerned with the righteous or aggrieved.

Seeking forgiveness is about the humble and mistaken,
is about the grieving and apologetic,
is an awareness of relationships potentially destroyed,
is the compound fracture of what is sticking out and awaiting
a repair,
is the resolution of the pride and prejudice attempting to be masked,
by the dark side timing of the moon seeking to stay hidden,
in denying each and every bit of responsibility.

Seeking forgiveness opens the doorway of approaching,
temporarily mislaid friendship on a quest for restoration,
in an all encompassing recognition of that,
which has been lost.

Seeking forgiveness deserves to make possible the bonding of the past,
the reinstatement of what has been put at risk,
if allowed to fester in the presence,
of a newly created sore within a heart.

Seeking forgiveness should be enabled to accept,
and to receive a welcome back into the fold,
without any reservations,
where no one feels humiliated,
where love is to the fore,
in an acknowledgment of the need for redemption to take place,
upon the tableau known as life;
and the auspices of The Smiling God of Nations and Eternity.

My Content Study Aid

_____

_____

_____

_____

_____

_____

Trusting as The Truth

And I hear Jesus saying,
"Trusting as the truth is a precarious road to follow,
                     can be a means of misleading,
                     can be an error in assumption,
                     can be a disaster in the making.

Trusting as the truth needs to be on insight and discovery,
                             if spread upon a table for acceptance,
                             if written in a letter of disclosure,
                             if circumspect yet waiting for acceptance.

Trusting as the truth has charlatans aplenty,
                has liars presenting falsehoods with an eye upon the money,
                has the gifted creating sympathetic proposals,
                     which put tears into the eyes,
                     which are more careful when remaining dry and speculative.

Trusting as the truth has a history of success,
                   by people wanting to believe:
                                 that which they are told as fact,
                  not the possibility of fancy leading to the raiding of the pot,
                  by a beggar quickly changing into a fraudster and a thief.

    Wisdom after the event is too late for recovery,
                          after the funds have flown and gone,
                                 on their journey to foreign climes,
                     is too late to be called the use of wisdom,
                          but rather to be added to the fields of experience,
              when dealing with the world-wide greed and dishonesty of self,
             when masked by difference with the difficulty of using any means,
                                 of valid identification,
                     as to what is and isn't in the sight of others,
                     who do not declare their ulterior motives,
                     to be associated with their future actions,
                     to the victims of their lies still awaiting discovery,
                     in arising from their wilful spreading of deceit.

Trusting as the truth is far from a good idea,
          can beggar the sympathetic and considerate,
          can bring poverty upon the believing and the gullible,
          can resort to searching and locating as to where and why and how,
          the wealth of one is transitioned into the unearned wealth of another,
                    in the lands of make believe where nothing is,
                              as assumption would bespoke,
              where honesty with integrity is nowhere to be found,
              where mischief and falsehood is expected,
                  from every knave at large,
                  and no-one is disappointed or concerned,
                  with the outcomes of joint collusion,
                  when orchestrated from the distance of an
                              unknown destination,
                  where the murderous prevail with cheap prices on an
                              auctioned life,
                  on any such which attempts to bring trouble,
                          with accountability,
                        into the nests of rogues.

Trusting as the truth is not generous with its payback,
          is not generous in its treatment,
          is not generous with its form of reward.

Trusting as the truth sees the scapegoat fall upon his reward of penury,
              in exchange for uninvited generosity,
          where scoundrels fed themselves upon the savings born of others:
                  still living under the concepts of trust and honesty,
                    which no longer serve the mobs at large,
                  with their misshapen ideas of integrity,
                      as to what they are entitled.

Trusting as the truth is a dangerous variable in life,
              by which some would attempt to live,
              by which some are almost certain to become disenchanted,
              by which the ill-gotten gains are transferred to the rogues,
                      the liars and the cheats—
                      the architects of fraud,
           in this withered time of honesty and integrity of purpose,
          as the weeping morality of God switches into,
                      the cheering ethics of man:
                  where the rats and mice,
                  the rodents of the rubbish heaps,
                  sift and access for a meal.

Trusting as the truth cannot rely on devious examples,
              cannot rely on what has been and happened,
              cannot rely on what is taken and unrecoverable,
              cannot rely on what was accepted as the truth,
                      yet was wandering in the graveyard of iniquity and loss.

Trusting as the truth when encountering deception believed and actioned,
                  has no way of recovery in seeking recompense or amends,
                  has no way of repairing the fragility of trust,
            when trust has not been verified,
            when trust is being so weakened until such is sheared in half,
                until trust is no longer usable as a basis,
                      or within a decision making process,
                leading to the poaching of the rainbows of the streams
                          and foreshores,
              where limits are imposed and broken,
              by the would-be seen as upright,
              as they are judged to be among the greedy and the stealers,
              wherein harvesting rights are exceeded by the catchers
                        and distributers,
                  who become the forbidden sellers,
                  in the hotel bars and grounds,
                  of all they fish and catch without a licence,
                  or a right to sell,
                  or fitted with a conscience,
                      wherein they may stop to think,
                      of what happened to the extinct;
                      to those now on the way as the calls of birdlife,
                      deemed fit for the table,
                      gradually fall by the wayside,
                as falsely pleaded rights and ignorance with poaching,
                    overwrite the protection with the efforts,
                    to protect that which can kill the golden goose,
              which cannot lay eggs fast enough for replenishment,
              to bring about the enabling of survival in the native
                          forest setting.

Trusting as the truth negates the positive,
                upon reflection on the negative,
          negates the past experience for the new in hand,
          negates the policy of rationing so all can have a taste,
          negates the ignoring of the future needs,
             for the potential of self-help exposing greed in the here and now,
                where cars should meet with confiscation,
                    so excess is avoided in the future taking,
                    by those ignoring the upholding of the law."

Investing In Shared Facilities

And I hear Jesus saying,
"Investing in shared facilities opens the gate of entry to the possibilities,
  opens the emphasis on holidaying with the crowds in the
    summer season,
  where relaxation mixes with the fun and sunshine,
  or within the spring or late summer or autumn or the winter,
  when the fish are more plentiful and the catches are seen to increase.

Investing in shared facilities spreads the cost of holidays,
  spreads increases in the asset value,
  reduces the costs of a mortgage as resolved with apportioning,
    as the splitting of the services,
  of the rates and insurance as equated to the allocation of the
    shared rights of use.

Investing in shared facilities is often talked about but rarely done,
  is often considered for advantages,
    yet rejected for lack of control,
    in the decision-making process,
  with the pressure of practical time-driven controls and affirmations.

Investing in shared facilities can entertain a boat,
  can entertain a yacht,
  can entertain a barbecue,
  can entertain a fishing pod for its powered underwater travelling,
    to the offshore catching grounds,
    where retrieval can be quite simple,
    where the catch is likely to be plentiful,
      for a meal or two or three.

Investing in shared facilities can be occupied by one family at a time,
  can be rented for sole use by an external family,
    who booked with certainty and responsibility,
  can be shared by both or more families at a time,
    where everyone is satisfied and there are no complaints.

Investing in shared facilities can see the phone lines twitching,
  can see the thoughts progressing,
  can see the perusal of the calendar,
  can see the satisfaction when red ink defines,
    both the starting and ending,
    of a single families' coming occupation.

Investing in shared facilities requires leaving as you would like to find,
  where cupboard shelf-space has food restored,

as it was first encountered,
has bills for services for water,
electricity,
gas and landline paid automatically with procedures,
with their switches,
all left in place and operational for micro waves,
deep freezers,
refrigerators and TV's with variance in use.

Investing in shared facilities can be a complex pastime if someone is prone to forget,
is prone to leave the switches incorrectly set,
is prone to upset the smooth running of control.

Investing in shared facilities opens doorways to retreats,
opens doorways for a single person to be alone and write,
opens doorways so someone can stop and think,
so someone can concentrate and plan,
so someone can rest and be at peace,
or drive and witness the beauty of the world to quietly read,
in a lay-by or an overview,
books both of knowledge and of wisdom.

Investing in shared facilities has its time of usefulness,
with enjoyment as set within each family,
has the age group ready to receive and to have fun,
ready to care and to look after one another,
ready to shop or swim or paddle,
to play upon the beach,
to fish from the shore,
when nothing is biting,
when boredom calls for change,
to exploring among the rocks,
when the waves do not present a challenge,
when harm is not considered threatening,
for the cautious and the curious.

Investing in shared facilities can express the love of parents for their children,
can keep everyone active and walking on trips
of exploration,
into the torchlight of the darkness to expose the lack
of depth,
in old mining tunnel shafts which were stopped,
to be left as a note to history,
when colour was not found.

Investing in shared facilities should be enquired about,
    as to the effectiveness of drainage,
    whether there is surface flooding from the rain,
    or tidal surges from a storm at sea,
    imposing flood perimeters,
    on the creeks and streams as they fill to overflowing,
    to inundate the roads and access points,
    to properties not seen in normal times.

Investing in shared facilities may need understanding of the sea levels,
    may need caution with pricing as asked upon a settlement,
    may need some reserves to attend to differing forms of maintenance,
    both inside and outside the dwelling place,
    in being marketed on the land whereon it is placed,
    and how water depth in seasonal variations,
    can influence a decision by the wise.

Investing in shared facilities requires extreme caution:
    where the threat of fire may also raise its ugly head.

Investing in shared facilities needs the appropriate escape clauses,
    where one family can shed its interests,
    when the ageing family has interests seen to change.

Investing in shared facilities may well be unwise,
    if facets of control leave a lot of 'what ifs' with unsatisfactory answers,
    with likely difficulties foreseen.

Investing in shared facilities can be difficult,
    when the glow has settled in the west,
    as excitement has declined,
    with the familiarity of the time as spent,
    with the practical aspects of keeping all amused,
    with interest waning on a wet and rainy day,
    as tempers start to flare with a lack of things to do,
    when cars come under pressure to simply head for home."

My Content Study Aid

_____

_____

_____

_____

_____

_____

Going Down A Rabbit Stop

And I hear Jesus saying,
"Going down a rabbit stop is limited to an arm with reach,
> to an arm which has been there before,
> to an arm which knows what it will find.

Going down a rabbit stop ends in a short straight followed by a widening bend wherein
> the nest is formed,
> has clues as to what is happening,
> has clues as to what can be expected,
> by those who would like to have one or more pet rabbits in their home.

Going down a rabbit stop when the stop is open,
> is really not advisable,
> as the doe is inside at home busy feeding her family,
> with no other means of escape except though the open stop,
> from which she can exit very fast.

Going down a rabbit stop is easier when the stop is back-filled with some earth,
> is camouflaged with leaves or twigs or grass—
> the detritus on the scene,
> this signs the doe is out in feeding for herself,
> while her sealing of the stop is mostly uncompacted
> and easy to remove.

Going down a rabbit stop should have a basket or a shopping bag at the ready,
> for transporting the small and the blind until their fourteenth day,
> when their eyes are opened to a world,
> where sight can recognize a mother,
> with the supplying of the milk.

Going down a rabbit stop with an arm in readiness can seize and remove,
> one kit at a time into the transporting hold-all,
> wherein the kit will cuddle and not attempt escape.

Going down a rabbit stop has a kit in the hand for the return to home,
> do not hold the kit by the tail,
> for an unexpected leap forward will create,
> a tailless future pet with a tail still being held tightly,
> between the thumb and finger,
> but now also in the presence of the surprised,
> and upset tears of innocence.

Going down a rabbit stop on a task of pet procurement,
> will bring joy and happiness unto a family,
> as the pet thumps on the floor with its back feet,
> as a warning of visitors approaching to a door.

Going down a rabbit stop brings the need to feeding to that,
which has been captured,
which can easily be supplied with milk,
as an eyedropper becomes the perfect tool for milk slightly warmed,
while liquid honey on a teaspoon is received with much licking and approval,
until the day when a piece of bread is shared and dragged away to privacy,
and there is a slight nibbling at the sowthistles with their milky sap,
which quickly become the flavour of the month,
where the younger the plant the less bitter it will be.

Going down a rabbit stop can lead into a feast of fun,
until the pet matures and goes looking for a mate,
whereupon it will wander further and further from home,
until one day it fails to return,
yet long distance eyesight in a paddock,
may one day focus on two rabbits frisking in and out of fence lines,
and happy in their play.

Going down a rabbit stop creates memories for a life time,
will have a guest who goes in and out of doors,
who has earned the freedom of the run of the home,
who know where the warmest places are found for basking in the sun,
who knows where the food is laid and for whom it is intended,
who recognizes all the others at home within the rooms,
who shares the spaces of the warmth,
the warm ashes in the grated hearth after the fire has gone out;
and a trail of ashy footprints on the board floor as the pet trails off,
to the cardboard carton lined and comfy,
in which the little rabbit does both sleep and rest.

Going down a rabbit stop will result in a pet which romps and plays within the garden,
which both senses and warns of intrusion,
which will follow and accompany,
which will be friends with an unrestrained pet magpie,
or a pet lamb on a chain;
to prevent an attack upon the vegetable garden,
without a second thought.

Going down a rabbit stop is not without reward,
creates many opportunities for delightful photographs,
in the process of families growing up;
creates many jokes where pets are observed and doing funny things,
creates surroundings where the wild is able to adapt to a friendly life with man,
is able to recognize a mother's image,
which was bespoke and adopted,
without a break in trust.

Going down a rabbit stop does not create a companion who likes swimming in a pool,
                                        who likes any sort of water other than
                                                        the lick-able,
                            where the water lingers on the blades of grass,
                                        from dew within the morning.

Going down a rabbit stop can apply pressure to the sowthistles as demand increases,
                        can apply pressure to the preferred and liked—
                                    to a carrot in the raw,
                                    to a lettuce nice and crisp,
                                    to a cabbage on the side,
                                    to a small piece of cheese,
                                    which is held between both paws,
                                    while standing up and looking quite quaint.

Going down a rabbit stop or visiting a pet shop,
                        can be the means for children,
                        to reduce the punch and yell,
                        to seek the sheltered and protected,
                        to establish a relationship with the small and cared for,
                            with the hungry and in need of feeding,
            with the relating and the fearless as based on trust and understanding,
            where a pet can learn and follow,
                            can sense and feel a part,
                            can be protected and secure,
                                    while remaining as a rabbit,
                                    with a spring within its step,
                                                to help it on its way.

Going down a rabbit stop can witness the scared and the predated,
                            with a life quite rare as some become adopted,
                                        into a family which cares,
                        where kindness is assured,
                        where attention is provided,
                        where love is seen to carry its very own reward."

My Content Study Aid

_____

_____

_____

_____

_____

_____

Growing In Wisdom

And I hear Jesus saying,
"Growing in wisdom should be one of the objectives of man,
        should be an outreach he can conquer,
        should make a difference to his speech.

Growing in wisdom witnesses improvements appearing in the placement of the tongue.

Growing in wisdom puts a staff upon the lips,
        puts a buckle on the teeth,
        puts a silencer within the throat:
            which can come and go when authority is released,
                so nonsense will not flow.

Growing in wisdom initiates upon request,
        initiates as the tongues of heaven infiltrate the tongues of man.

Growing in wisdom downloads and expands,
        constructs and reforms,
        impresses and confirms.

Growing in wisdom is as honey in a jar,
        is best when spread quite thinly,
        is sweetest when in a liquid state:
            when not left to solidify,
        is most appreciated when not mixed up with jam,
                but retained in purity.

Growing in wisdom shares wisdom at a table,
        shares wisdom in a time of relaxation,
        shares wisdom when difficulties abound and time is very precious.

Growing in wisdom recalls common sense,
        recalls past experiences,
        recalls what is necessary and what is not.

Growing in wisdom separates the needs from the wants,
        separates the ability to evaluate and relate,
        impresses with the brevity of the tongue.

Growing in wisdom mixes and removes the contaminants of thought,
        holds and retains the impressions with the avenues
                where the shade is spread.

Growing in wisdom reserves the status of the honouring,
        reserves the perspicacity suited to an application,
        inserts the perspicuity into a thought patterning readied for release.

Growing in wisdom sees a thrusting of the light,
           a brightening of the way,
           an effectiveness in both the sorting and the moving forward.

Growing in wisdom awakens to a steadfastness in design,
               which satisfies and amplifies both the intent and the attitude,
                        inherent in approach.

Growing in wisdom isolates the trip wires before they can be put in place,
            isolates the weaknesses which hide the fractures and
                      excessive strains,
            isolates the unverified for their strength and staying power.

Growing in wisdom reduces the assumptions,
           does not play with randomness,
           appreciates the true and the tried.

Growing in wisdom is too late after an event,
           instead then speaks of experience,
                    with the cost of the delays.

Growing in wisdom is well worth the seeking with the ongoing fulfilment,
           is well worth the magnification of examination,
           is well worth the backstop of unfermented knowledge:
               before it becomes clouded by the difficulty to evaluate effect.

Growing in wisdom seeks the deposited and the safe,
           seeks the true and the trustworthy without a sign of making-do,
           seeks the finished and the perfect with the glow of engineering:
               where breakages are avoided,
               where plastic can carry the load within performance,
                    and without disgrace.

Growing in wisdom is desirable when witnessed within the life of man,
           is desirable as desires are strengthened,
           is desirable as knowledge is installed,
               with confirmation of the means of application.

Growing in wisdom is not a short course in semantics,
           is rather an experience of linguistics and logic,
               where learning has no limit among the scope of investigations,
                    based within eternity.

Growing in wisdom sees wisdom unashamed,
           sees wisdom in the infinite,
           sees wisdom altering the entity of man.

Growing in wisdom comes from the sharing of the intellect of God,
         comes from the willingness to acquire all which God would share,
         comes from the procedures of advancement as found within the gifts of God.

Growing in wisdom circulates the sustainable,
>maintains the interest in attainment,
>visits the wisdom of the outpouring and how it is applied.

Growing in wisdom does not encounter sheets of disappointment,
>does not encounter vortices of pain,
>does not encounter promises which surprise,
>>by being still unfulfilled and waiting,
>>upon The Will of God.

Growing in wisdom is an activity which starts within mortality,
>when the request is made of God.

Growing in wisdom is an activity which continues,
>within eternity of the everlasting:
>of the onward voyaging of both man and God,
>>in each other's presence.

Growing in wisdom empowers the knowledge within mortality,
>of understanding The Power of Faith with Truth,
>of understanding the expanding end-time knowledge;
>as complete within My nine End-time Psalms of God,
>and My four End-time Update Companion Books of Grace;
>as complete with My Commentaries on The Book of Daniel,
>and on The Book of Revelation in Book 2 'GOD Speaks to
>>Man on The Internet',
>and also on The Book of Ezekiel in Book 3 'GOD Speaks as
>>His Spirit Empowers'.

Growing in wisdom cannot be reversed once started by request;
>is immediately under the delivering system of God:
>>for both now within the balance of Mortality,
>>and the onward life within The Active Kingdom of God."

My Content Study Aid

_____

_____

_____

_____

_____

_____

_____

Games Upon A Hill

And I hear Jesus saying,
"Games upon a hill are variable and fun-filled,
        are high and lifted up,
                when free from trees and snares,
                        from bushes according to their height,
                when they want to halt a game or make it difficult to play,
                when recovery is involved and the object can't be found.

Games upon a hill,
        where the wind is at its best,
        are best played where grass abounds,
                and horizons are not hidden,
        where the wind can blow in freedom,
                with its run unimpaired,
                as it rises with the hill.

Games upon a hill can use a ball of string,
              to which a kite is tethered as an anchor for control;
              from which a kite is flown,
              when the wind is more or less consistent,
                and the string is either wound in or to be let out.

Games upon a hill can involve the kites of skill and imagination,
                  as they hesitate and soar,
                  as they demand release of more string,
                  as they plummet to the ground,
                      in a nosedive of a gust.

Games upon a hill need the infantry to be able to play and run for home,
           to not be blindsided by the vegetation with its height and thickness,
        which impose a practical inability to push through and out,
                        to the other side.

Games upon a hill can include the games of tag,
        can include the games of hide and seek,
            with the 'he' firmly stationed with eyes shut,
            while a count of 50 or of 100 is completed to start the game,
                as hiding is attempted,
                and the 'free run' attempt to pat the home base,
                with a quick cry of '1,2,3, home',
           before the 'he' can do the same with '1,2,3, caught',
        can signify success on those who ran to hide,
                who attempted to come home,
                or were caught in the process;

can include the games of sneaking up,
     when a back is turned,
     while others have the right to move,
     until the back is suddenly reversed,
     with any notice of a movement underway,
                    is promptly called as 'caught'.

Games upon a hill can be a slide on a sheet of cardboard,
                    where the grass is thick,
     can be a slide into and through some mud,
          to where prior consideration has been given,
          as to the likely state of clothes;
     can be a frolic in the snow,
          a high speed cardboard-on-the-snow trick,
          where all do call for more;
     or where a toboggan or a sledge can be mustered:
     for the sleigh ride of a lifetime,
     after which faces are aglow and repeats are in demand.

Games upon a hill can be vested on a ski field,
               where the ups and downs attempt to surpass one another,
     or investing in a downhill ride inside a large but bouncing ball,
               which runs until it stalls to end up looking round.

Games upon a hill can be a ride upon the ski lift seats,
     can be a ride inside a seated gondola with the viewing of the
                         mountain heights,
               with the ground a long way down,
          and settled in to a return down-trip to the snow.

Games upon a hill can be coasting or be powered,
     can be together or apart,
     can be nervous or thrilled with the cry for more,
               or a look that says 'I'm really not so sure'.

Games upon a hill can go on all day and even into the night,
          when driven by demand upon a recent fall of snow,
          when the lights are bright and everything is lit,
               in giving the impression of a fairyland at night.

Games upon a hill can be so wonderful an experience,
                    that no-one wants to go to bed,
     but to stay up late with a special enjoyment of the sights:
     as if of signs of wonder as spread upon the snow,
     when taken to the huts within the snowfields,
     where sleep and views are difficult to have linked together,
     in enjoyment as one is eventually seen to yield unto the other,
     as the lights go out and silence comes to starts its reign.

Games upon a hill can capture a feast of memories with the cameras,
  can capture a longing to return,
  can capture a craving to improve,
      on what and how each did do before.

Games upon a hill include the tireless and concerned,
    as they watch and guard the errors with the mischief,
    with the first-aid dressings ready with availability,
        if or when deemed necessary,
          to control concern.

Games upon a hill can be a hit with all those who participated,
      with all those who enjoyed the fun and food.

Games upon a hill can fill cars with chatterers on the way home,
        unless overtaken by a sleep and the fall of night.

Games upon a hill can install stories told in class,
    can respond with stories written down,
    can maintain the stories with photo images galore.

Games upon a hill result in stories with a life,
          still kept in older years within an exercise book,
          where such was written as remembered and retold.

Games upon a hill can serve up and remember:
          excitement at the time,
          of how and when what happened,
          and who caught whom and why.

Games upon a hill can go marked down in history of the youth time,
        in the running and the carefree,
        in the mayhem and the laughter,
        in the whispering of secrets,
        in the spying of the hidden,
        in the retelling of who did what.

Games upon a hill cannot be exaggerated,
        for all that happened is already at the top,
            is already in excited hands,
      where voices were raised in laughter and contentment,
              with all that was seen and done on a hill top,
                that was visited and generated,
                a lifetime of the memories as created,
                to so linger long and far with God,
                and the children waiting for maturity."

Planes and Gliders

And I hear Jesus saying,
"Planes and gliders witness the updrafts and the downdrafts,
    witness the concerns and the scares,
    witness the frightened and the terrified.

Planes and gliders set the pace or compensate,
    set the onset of a gasp or the satisfaction of a shrug,
    set the consolation of unstable air or the handling of concern,
        with the pitches and the dives,
        or the flat falls starting in a float,
        in ending with a thud.

Planes and gliders both have secrets of endeavour:
    have secrets in their rates of climb,
    have secrets in their glide paths with the distance they can reach,
        for a wheels down on a runway,
        with people looking on.

Planes and gliders are both subject to the rate of climb and lift,
    are both subject to common sense and the price of peril,
    are both subject to being trapped within an air current,
        where the uplift violently tosses and turns without regard for life,
        in turning the cabin upside down within a cloud,
        where horizons may be lost.

Planes and gliders although both are quite small among the mountains,
    propellor power is advisable over wind,
    when landing on the high pitched snow fields,
    for the presence of much exclaiming and admiration,
    for all which is seen to be on show,
    for that which poses threats when seeking
        to once again be airborne and looking down.

Planes and gliders have their own properties,
    which are best if carefully kept within their corners,
        where they play.

Planes and gliders can veer and crumple when attacked,
    can even call for help,
    can even need assistance to see the mindful wanting,
        to be homeward bound in safety and in time.

Planes and gliders should not venture up alone,
    where patterns are unclear,
    where wind gusts can be strong,

where mistakes are unforgiving,
where lives can be placed at risk.

Planes and gliders are not light-hearted in their attitudes,
are not light-hearted in their altitudes,
as they always play for keeps,
when locked within the valleys of the ice and snow at a height,
where airlift is insufficient to clear the lips and rims,
of the high points of the valleys,
where landings were attempted,
while distance likely killed the calls for help.

Planes and gliders are not necessarily the play things of amusement,
are often the architects of suffering and of death,
are often with the result of having put those in the cabin
out of reach by radio,
where temperatures are dropping,
where night is blanketing all with another fall of snow,
where survival is imperilled as searching has no clues,
nor directions likely to assist in the bringing of success.

Planes and gliders await for the storm to subside,
await for searchers who can spot,
await for winds to abate,
so valleys can be searched,
before the night returns.

Planes and gliders know well the chances of search and rescue,
know well the possibility of the unheard cry for help,
know well the loss of direction and of navigation,
as the storm did vent its fury,
until it finally gave up to let,
the desperate and the urgent as summoned,
to take to the skies again.

Planes and gliders are the archetypes of freedom,
are the archetypes of the unforgiving,
are the archetypes of the plotted and secure,
when intermingled with an urgent cry for help,
which wakes all bands up as records are bound in their creation,
within a transmission to where help may be found,
and would be readily available.

Planes and gliders with their passengers may be rescued,
when assumptions are seen as valid,
when time is on the side of those now gone astray.

Planes and gliders gone astray rarely return as an entity of wholeness,
rarely can be found in time if co-ordinates are unknown,
with localities uncertain.

Planes and gliders can sometimes pay a very heavy price,
for venturing into the central valleys,
or along the rims of mountain edges,
where the valleys or the wind gusts,
have their own means of entrapment.

Planes and gliders can be played with in the form of models,
in the presence of a flat paddock with short grass,
for a takeoff or a landing;
where a powered run and flight is very satisfying,
where flying on the wire is ideal for the newly birthed to freedom,
for all who watch in appreciation of the effort from those,
who have built and sized so all is best suited,
to a controlled flight where wind will not distort,
but power is not wanting,
as climbs with zooms or inverted flight,
are easily accommodated,
when practice is assured,
when confidence proclaims,
an experienced hand is now being seen at the controls;
so it follows on the capability of a hillside,
with its updrafts and remote control,
which determines where the glider is best suited so to glide,
as it travels back and forth in maintaining of its height,
as it hopefully avoids the low bushes which may entrap,
or entangle that which flies above them,
at the mercy of the wind.

Planes and gliders can be readied for the thrill seekers as they come of age,
where building is possible,
where basic plans are quite simple to follow,
with hand-me-down advice or calling on an advisor,
who knows which way is up,
on how to fly inverted for everyone's enjoyment,
of what is both possible and practical,
on a day well spent."

My Content Study Aid

Ice and Icicles

And I hear Jesus saying,
"Ice and icicles are not very strong adventurers,

like to stay within their fold,
like to know wherein their mainstay lies.

Ice and icicles sometimes are not recognized,

can cause a slippery slip,
can bring to pass a lack of braking on the sealed roads of man.

Ice and icicles are the cold products of The Earth,

recognize their neighbours of the frost,
try to avoid their transients of the snow and hail.

Ice and icicles settle where the sun has gone to rest,

where the heat has all transferred to a larger void,

when the blankets have been mislaid,

where warmth is at a premium but cannot be sustained.

Ice and icicles have a relationship as to a parent and a child,

as to a home base charged with the supporting of the dripping,

with the freezing as expected,
with length being extended by

the outreach of the related growth.

Ice and icicles have a limited life within the sunlight,

a limited life born of the wonders of refraction and reflection,

with the killer of absorption;

a limited life as The Earth wakes up to greet that,

which was busy in the night,
which is destined for a melt-down,

as the icicles again begin to drip,
in their signing of farewell to this time and day—
where once they earned a greeting for their beauty

and their charm—

but now are assigned to a role of retreat and shrinkage,

before the sovereignty of God.

Ice and icicles are without the strength of fire,

do have a strength all of their own,

with the expansion of their size from their starting point,

within their liquid phase,

as they get down to work to insinuate themselves,

into the cracks and crevices,
into the pipes and tunnels,

where insulation cannot obstruct as tunnelling continues,

in the forcing of the path—
not to be discovered until the sound of dripping,
arouses the suspicions,
of the happenings of the night.

Ice and icicles know they have inherited their lands of dominance,
where the landscapes are all white,
where opportunities to freeze are granted willingly and often,
where it is easy to get lost and life is perilous at best,
where curiosity and investigation rule the lives of
the foolhardy and the brave,
where the sun is keen to take a well-earned rest,
from the watching of a child going round in circles,
to so leave the hidden for discovery,
by the searchers and the uncoverers of history,
as preserved and protected,
from any and all interference,
from the trampers of the surface.

Ice and icicles are aware that it is not always necessary to ascend the heights,
to encounter them at work,
that they know the mountain tops whereon they are both
welcomed in attendance,
where burrowing can afford protection from the gales and storms:
intent on visiting the heights of creation with the beauty,
with the caution necessary in the shadowing,
in the matching up to the fitness for the challenge,
where success is measured by the placing of the footsteps.

Ice and icicles do not bother with their age,
are content to come and go as variance controls,
as measurements are made,
as information is garnered by the frostbitten
and the drillers,
wherein the air is tested for its composition,
in the very distant past,
as examples of acceptance of the reality of the practice,
found to be inherent in the periods,
of the eras,
of the aeons,
prior to time being posted for working as directed—
as a slave of one's fellow man,
as effective unto this very day,
where money,
with its obtaining,
is the chief concern of man.

Ice and icicles are the history paths preserved for man to know,
are now having their doors of access,
being opened wide and inviting,
as comparisons are made,
as evaluations are assessed,
as duplication is required in the testing of integrity.

Ice and icicles have served man well in the chests of knowledge,
as saved and retained,
as uncovered and protected,
as assessed and compared,
as recorded with the written and described,
as determined and made public,
as future strategies are considered for the setting
of carbon dioxide levels,
in the atmosphere with reference to those attained in the growth cycles,
for the feeding of the dinosaurs,
for the storing of the plant life for the oil fields,
which have so influenced the progression of man with that discovery,
which stopped the extinction of the whales for their oil.

Ice and icicles are a lot more important than just for placing in a drink,
than for throwing in a tray of fish just caught,
where all else is forgotten,
where just heat absorption is the primary focus of the mind,
with the results it brings with the fall in temperature,
as the sensitive are preserved,
as marketing is improved,
as demand is strengthened,
as man survives with what he cannot now do without.

Ice and icicles have been busy in the past in acts of preservation,
are still busy in the present in indicating cross-assessments,
requires an unbiased examination,
to determine the steps to the best way forward,
in this time and age;
in learning from the records of the past extremities,
with their tolerability for guidelines to the present,
with the future voyaging of man upon The Earth:
under the oversight of The Loving Living God."

My Content Study Aid

Wild Horses on The Run

And I hear Jesus saying,
"Wild horses on the run have a goal they are desiring to achieve,
　　　　　they are expecting to encounter,
　　　　　they are seeking so to be on time.

Wild horses on the run still have miles to travel,
　　　　　still have footprints to leave within the mud,
　　　　　still have the freedom to back up the shortcut,
　　　　　　　　　via the river with a swim.

Wild horses on the run know where they are going,
　　　　　know where the desert has a flush of grass,
　　　　　know the run will be rewarding and worth the effort,
　　　　　　　　　as the herd is gathered,
　　　　　　　　　as the horses all decamp.

Wild horses on the run know the high desert well,
　　　　　know where the army has manoeuvres with their tanks,
　　　　　know where the annual round up is held;
　　　　　　　　for the breaking in with the auctioning of the horses,
　　　　　　　　with their transfer onto the farms for riding,
　　　　　　　　　　by the late teens and early twenties,
　　　　　　　　with the foals at foot,
　　　　　　　　with an eye upon the local show
　　　　　　　　　　where dressage with the riding,
　　　　　　　　　　is the judgement of the end result.

Wild horses on the run are not captured in their entirety,
　　　　　always leave the majority of the heard running free for another season,
　　　　　take just sufficient to meet the known requests where sizing is important,
　　　　　　　　where nature may carve a path to greatness.

Wild horses on the run can both bite and kick,
　　　　　can both buck and stomp,
　　　　　can scrape to remove whatever is attempting to cling
　　　　　　　　　on to the back.

Wild horses on the run know the catch points of the past,
　　　　　know how to slow down the chasers with the traitors,
　　　　　　　the ropers and the leaders on the way to entrapment,
　　　　　　　as the corralled and the waiting,
　　　　　　　　　for what the new day brings.

Wild horses on the run know the escape routes very well;
　　　　　know the rivers with the crossing points,

at times within a season;
know an active swimming session will be likely,
to reach the far shore of a river,
when a fresh is flowing with the loss of clarity,
as depth cannot be plumbed at speed;
yet where safety may abide.

Wild horses on the run are best captured via encirclement,
with the objective of gradually slowing all down to a standstill in a yard,
where a lassoed neck will not start the herd to shy,
in bursting out from such restraint,
with the herd again prone to pick up speed.

Wild horses on the run can be lassoed and tethered,
can be removed from the herd into singletons in
unaccustomed situations.

Wild horses on the run still have their favourite drinking holes,
still have their favourite sleeping areas,
still have familiarity with that into which they have been chased.

Wild horses on the run will jump and canter off into the distance,
will career with rolling eyes and trembling,
for what is being a forced experience.

Wild horses on the run may decide to stop and stare,
may stand and be ready to take off,
at the signal from the head movement of the mare.

Wild horses on the run are considerate of the foals,
do not leave the exhausted and the small to be left behind,
will ensure they will be able to head,
for the hideouts in the brush,
that reaches to the neck and mixes up pursuit.

Wild horses on the run are wild but may have seen it all before;
may know well the chase and catch;
may know well the lassoing and the felling;
may know well the rope strain on a pommel;
may know well the attraction of a foal as roped
and tied;
yet within the sound calls of the neighing,
with the snuffles of its mother;
may know well the fear of desperation,
as issuing from the foal in need,
in calling for assistance,
or confirmation of a nearness,
when the mare is out of sight.

Wild horses on the run do not result in becoming lost,
on their own home patch of desert,
do not result in confusion as to the right way back,
do not suddenly become ignorant of the herd's signal postings,
of the markings for re-assembling in familiar territory,
after the sudden need for dispersal.

Wild horses on the run are tested for the survival of the fittest,
the survival on the surroundings,
wherefrom a meal can be gathered,
wherefrom the bounty may be such as can be shared,
before the need arises to move on to the water,
with the security of position.

Wild horses on the run know how to kick up their heels,
when unthreatened and among the herd,
when nature calls without alarm,
when the birdsongs confirm the lack of predators,
or the hunters with the ropes.

Wild horses on the run always think they know where they are going,
yet sometimes some do run astray,
to lose directional sense,
to run into an entanglement,
from which there is no immediate escape.

Wild horses on the run are truly majestic animals with a sense of well-being,
with a sense of the mothering of a child,
with a sense of responsibility so the child is not left to suffer,
is not left to be lost and not be found.

Wild horses on the run have minds to tell the stories:
of their lives within the wild;
have appointed days when such stories will be heard,
for all who want to listen;
have story sessions of remembrance,
where all may be welcomed to join in,
to so recount what was not able to be heard,
with understanding at the time;
until the day of entry:
into The Life Fall of Eternity with God."

My Content Study Aid

_____

_____

Firing of The Military

And I hear Jesus saying,
"Firing of the military can make a lot of noise,
               can make a lot of action,
               can blend the past into the future,
               can signal change of livelihood from within The Will of God.

Firing of the military does not speak of gun smoke,
               already has the targets waiting for the orders,
               is designed to separate the men from the boys,
                                  without complaint from either.

Firing of the military does not need a range,
               is not in need of uniforms,
               can safely ignore all the means of transport,
               together with the prepared meals on the tables.

Firing of the military requires a change of venue,
               requires a change in orders,
               requires a change of objectives as made known,
                              and to be carried out.

Firing of the military can be put out by a fire hose with the washing down,
               can be witnesses to the closing and the moving,
                       to the querying and the guessing,
                   to the turmoil within the finding of a new way to carry on.

Firing of the military floats on a groundswell of opinion,
               floats on instructions from on high,
               floats on the coming absenting of the force or arms.

Firing of the military is a very complex task,
               is a very short instruction with a long tail to follow,
               is a repositioning in different garb waiting for fulfilment,
                            with a roller-coaster ride.

Firing of the military adjusts well to the toothaches,
               adjusts well to the families,
               adjusts well to the inspections and the training.

Firing of the military adjusts well to the time at home,
                    to the time available for children,
                    to the time able to be allocated from the rearrangement
                                of the families,
                        the schooling with the learning,
                  with any second jobs which may appeal,
                  as they go past the window of consideration.

Firing of the military is like a bombshell in the base,
　　　　can leave people running here and there,
　　　　　　　　in the weakness of command;
　　　　can have instructions being verified,
　　　　　　　　but then not knowing what to do;
　　　　can have the command structure drifting with the wind—
　　　　　　　　in not being able to tell from which
　　　　　　　　　　direction it is blowing,
　　　　　　　　　　or the strength involved.

Firing of the military is like watching the fall of dominoes,
　　　　under the concentrated fire of a machine gun belching bullets.

Firing of the military sees the bases dismissed one after another;
　　　　sees the writing on the wall,
　　　　　　　　for the intentions in the weeks and months ahead;
　　　　sees the pack horses busy in the loading of the unwanted,
　　　　　　　　where destinations are undecided with capacity uncertain,
　　　　　　　　as they disappear into the enfolding night.

Firing of the military brings chaos where once was calm,
　　　　brings doubt where once was certainty,
　　　　brings mischief where once was order,
　　　　　　　　as possessions quickly start to go missing,
　　　　　　　　without the likelihood of retrievability.

Firing of the military has ramifications deemed as unimportant,
　　　　　　　　as they move into the past,
　　　　has sights now set on the higher goals,
　　　　　　　　as they come into fruition,
　　　　　　　　as people continue to live in the places they call home,
　　　　　　　　where family inheritance rights over contents,
　　　　　　　　　　now hold sway,
　　　　　　　　as homes are acquired and deemed to be owned,
　　　　　　　　　　by the occupants declared.

Firing of the military sees some buildings changing functions,
　　　　sees some buildings being redefined,
　　　　sees some buildings being scrapped or delisted—
　　　　　　　　whose time has come to die.

Firing of the military sees The Chaplains very busy,
　　　　　　　　as options for the establishment of The Churches,
　　　　　　　　　　within The Edifices of God,
　　　　　　　　from the choices as considered for approval or dismissal,
　　　　　　　　with the stocking of interiors from the inventories,
　　　　　　　　　　both available and satisfactory.

Firing of the military leaves vehicles available,
        leaves apportionment within the confines of a base,
                as titles may be transferred,
                for ongoing use and application.

Firing of the military sets a hearthrug before a chimney,
        sets consideration into the future,
            determines a structure as a gift,
      maintains the status quo where churches are involved,
           where functioning with life support needs,
           are sourced and maintained for the benefit of all.

Firing of the military is everywhere occurring,
        is everywhere applicable,
        is everywhere within The Power and The Authority of God,
                on My Second Advent on The Earth,
        as the days of Satan are numbered and dated for relinquishment,
           as his jail term also starts,
           for his followers and their hangers-on.

Firing of the military will not have quasi-troops playing at enforcing,
                a power struggle on a Nation State,
      will see such all annihilated,
           when disobedience is evidenced,
           when the ring of fire is called into existence,
              as warnings are assured for understanding,
              as to the intended penalty.

Firing of the military brings obedience to righteousness and truth,
        introduces peace at the foothills of the mountains,
           of up and down the peaks,
            of across the flatness of the plains,
               and of the rolling hills.

Firing of the military ends the time of war upon The Earth,
        scraps the weapons as they melt,
        scraps the swords within their heaps,
        scraps the caravans of death.

Firing of the military invokes the best in man with freedom,
        invokes the widespread quest for peace,
        invokes the superlatives of achievement before The Face of God,
           where Glory is released for The Father and The Son,
              as The Holy Spirit visits and affirms,
                that which is now released,
              into the keeping of My People."

Keys to Friendship

And I hear Jesus saying,
"Keys to friendship facilitate and ease,
        enlighten and counsel,
        absorb and expand the ways to friendship,
                with the closeness of adherence.

Keys to friendship solidify the grip of friendship,
        solidify the evenings together,
        solidify the knowledge bases of interest,
                of how they work together.

Keys to friendship centre on the commonality of purpose,
        the cycling of interests,
        the seasons of fruitfulness,
                the times within the sun.

Keys to friendship can be motivated by times upon the seashore,
            with a fishing rod in hand,
            with children running free on slides,
             on seesaws on roundabouts and swings,
            with games of putting golf,
            with arcade amusement scenes,
             where games are played to be enjoyed,
             where reflexes are tested,
             where manipulation scores,
        where reflexes are speeded up for the gaining of success,
               or where a hammer dings a bell,
               or skittles are supposed to fall.

Keys to friendship makes the most of friendship,
        builds upon both Trust and Faith,
        where both carry the seeds as planted,
             to see them growing by the day,
        while yielding memories a-plenty with fun entwined in laughter.

Keys to friendship do not break the curtains held in Trust,
        do not prolong the answering of the door,
             nor worry at the phone with delays.

Keys to friendship carry Trust as being met and answered,
        explore the necessity and the readiness,
             of the burners with their fittings,
         when electricity fails to answer its call to service,
             surveys the storage of the gas canisters,
             with ignition couplings as required.

Keys to friendship cover the harbouring of Faith,
        the integrity of honouring,
        the impressions of surroundings—
           those which indicate to and confound the unprepared,
       for what makes a house both into a home and a sanctuary,
        where safety is a warranted assumption,
        with the fence which protects all within,
        from the free fall happenings outside,
        explicit to the contributory funding from borrowings and debt,
           which should not exist,
      which cannot therefore invade foreclose influence or push aside,
           that so born of Faith,
        with all which is so gathered in,
        when security and probability jettison any attempted onset,
           of fear of what lies outside,
           where it is likely to be insignificant,
           as well as unknown.

Keys to friendship are not dependant on locks and bolts,
        are not declaring of any rights or wrongs,
        are not summarising of what will come and go,
        are not protective of what is already fully covered,
        are not choosing to exist in the outside world,
           where cameras may be seen to spy with lenses,
           while batteries are maintained on recharge,
           where alarmed attended security is a close adjunct,
              associated with the fear of intrusion,
              as both sold and labelled,
           until a power cut destroys the link to the needed action.

Keys to friendship have no passwords to remember,
        have no keywords to recall,
        have no long phrases to retype.

Keys to friendship exist only in the spiritual,
        offer no hindrance in the physical,
        have no keyholes needing keys that fit and enter.

Keys to friendship don't need polishing per se,
        as there is no physical entity of existence,
           they do,
           however,
           need polishing with current usage by the week.

Keys to friendship are carried very easily,
        have no need to be inserted or turned,
        are very light within a purse or wallet,
           do not weigh matters down.

Keys to friendship are everlasting,
    are listed in effectiveness within mortality,
    are forever valued highly when focussed in eternity,
      among the larger numbers of relatives with the friends of friends.

Keys to friendship can lift the spirit and the soul,
    can lift and remove the pain to outside the room,
      to harness and embolden as introductions multiply,
      to so enhance the prospects for discussions,
        on a lively scale.

Keys to friendship can bring calmness to a body,
    can release some excess stress,
    can motivate recovery,
    can turn the world around for a single person.

Keys to friendship can be raised and lowered as the seasons change,
    as the hours do darken or lighten according to the cutoff point,
    as the clock counts out the hours for when the sun can set or rise.

Keys to friendship are the little traits and whispers,
      which speak but not betray,
    where secrets are intense and held up to the light,
    where truth is ecstatic and spreads itself around,
      and up and down putting smiles on all the faces,
      as being guardians to the open secret just imparted,
        to the honest and the trustworthy.

Keys to friendship depend on manners to allay the ready and the hungry,
      as the evening meal awaits in readiness,
      for the prayerful to make voice in thankfulness,
    with unchallenged eagerness to partake and to appreciate,
      that which has been laid before them,
      for recharging all the effort of the day.

Keys to friendship include remembering one another,
      in the prayers throughout the day,
    so none may be hurt or injured,
    so non may need a dressing or a covering for a wound,
    so all may be rejoicing in each heart,
      as bodies souls and spirits go cascading into beds,
      with the closing of sincere thanks for the day—
    to The Loving God of All whom will dwell and govern,
    within His Truth and Mercy of His Coming Kingdom."

Beckoning of Eternity

And I hear Jesus saying,
"Beckoning of eternity opens up the steamboat of express upon a river,
knows where it is going,
with the passengers about to board.

Beckoning of eternity has much to say and know,
has much to share and learn,
has much to see and to acquire,
as an understanding of the edicts applying to Eternity
within the rule of love.

Beckoning of eternity speaks of encouragement to prepare,
speaks of encouragement to accept the invitation,
speaks of The Gifts of God as witnessed in Mortality,
yet ignored with very little attempt to obtain the fluency,
as strongly recommended,
so the tongue may be silent in Eternity,
yet the brain may still speak across the exceptionally large unlimited distances,
that Eternity can navigate,
still to report to home within an instant.

Beckoning of eternity does not bend a sapling reaching upward,
does not attempt to stretch that which is growing very quickly,
is yet to understand how matters can be interrelated,
at the start yet merged soon thereafter,
when wisdom becomes known,
among the growth spurts as encountered,
in the support of the need to achieve vitality,
for a long term ahead,
which is known to complete upon request,
without failure to confirm.

Beckoning of eternity sees a lot of waving at a distance,
sees a lot of gesticulations which are mostly not understood,
sees a lot of remonstrating
when messaging is leaving a lot to be desired,
sees the results of attempted communications,
when the end results saw fluency as ignored,
and interpretation as a whole new landscape
imposed upon the plains and hills,
where now silence mostly reigns,
as chattering has long time ceased,

as languages now suffer from the lack of transitioning,
among the tongues of both man and heaven,
where intellect was seen as challenging,
where practise was seen as having no advantage,
within the learning curves of man.

Beckoning of eternity witnesses the mistakes of man,
witnesses man's forsaking of the truth,
witnesses the lack of fluency accrual,
within the sixth sense of man,
where the tongue is not put to the interpreted encouraged,
while the tongue-tied watch yet can not speak,
across both voids and space,
until the basics become mastered,
as the recommendations start to install,
the movements of the tongue,
with the new mastery of vocal signalling,
being built upon the thought waves of the brain.

Beckoning of eternity indicates a solid response of being placed,
at the tail end of mortality,
at the tail end of understanding with the naivety involved.

Beckoning of eternity is calling to prepare,
to read again the fullness of the gift of tongues,
so such can be practised to meet the coming need,
where tongues can be shunted back and forth,
can be sung both up and down,
can be started by any letter of The English Alphabet,
where knowledge rests at home,
where the tongues can change at will,
can scale both up and down,
to at least some eighty to eighty-five different ones or so,
as heard landing on the tongue with speaking rights,
as fluency is achieved,
as more are requested,
as the speaking continues until the tongue does change,
as the brain is forced to follow:
when repetition is requested,
as pronunciation needs correction until it is correct.

Beckoning of eternity knows well The Rhythm of The Saints,
which has been heard and understood,
when getting into bed,
when listening with interest and timing,
to that which can be made audible or silenced when required,
as the beat is generated within the range,

of about twenty beats per minute plus or minus two or three,
as listed for attention with reports,
via the transmitters of the body,
directly to our God of action and repair,
of the rhythm monitoring the details as marked for recording,
somewhere within the landscape of eternity.

Beckoning of eternity invites the showing up of The Absence of Entity,
makes known its presence through existence,
which cannot be refuted by the medical profession,
when the entity decides to go,
and to return some time in the future,
with everything still left and running as it was,
with the entity in charge in the driving seat,
and clocking an average speed of seventy kms per hour,
for some fourteen kilometres,
through a country township,
when the happening was begun at just a few kilometres outside of the township,
eventually,
after only the clock or watch had moved,
in recording a later but current time by some twelve minutes,
with a great deal of puzzlement for man as to what had actually happened,
as there was still driving on the road at seventy kilometres,
with the recognition of the passing of a golf course.

Beckoning of eternity has some very interesting facets,
opening for closer examination by man,
opening for thoughtful evaluation,
opening for answering of the how the why and the when,
with a whole range of what-ifs.

Beckoning of eternity is opening some of the mysteries of God,
in the end-time of mortality;
where the unknown by man,
is but the common sense of God."

My Content Study Aid

_____

_____

_____

_____

_____

_____

Linking Arms

And I hear Jesus saying,
"Linking arms indicate a friendship based on trust,
        a relationship without deception,
        a future which is assured by the present.

Linking arms fulfil a feeling of contentment,
        a feeling of belonging,
        a feeling where consistency does reign.

Linking arms do not require a password,
        do not foresee a request,
        do not ever feel rejection.

Linking arms are signing to the day that all is well,
        are signing to the friendship that such is secure and able to continue,
        are signing to the world that overcoming trials and difficulties,
          do not surpass the love and the consideration,
            the power and the strength,
        of standing with and alongside The Saviour of The World,
                The Redeemer of Mankind,
                The Sacrificial Lamb,
            so man could have his own Freewill,
            so to be accountable in all he says and does.

Linking arms recognise relationships between the genders,
        recognise relationships of friendship and of implicit trust,
        recognize all which has been buried in the past,
            no longer to have a call upon a conscience,
            no longer to carry the feelings of guilt or grief.

Linking arms are not expressing solitude,
        are affirming togetherness,
          in stepping out together,
          in peering in the shop windows,
          in venturing inside,
          in laughing at the jokes,
          in what can be seen as an unusual setup,
                as to how it should be described,
            when the garb does clash both in colour and in style.

Linking arms are seen sauntering down the street,
        are not in a hurry,
        are not conscious of unfriendly stares,
          as sources tend to amuse,
          bringing waterfalls of giggles with all the joyous notes.

Linking arms take both into a coffee house for their morning tea or coffee,
with a piece of cake or two,
as conversation continues unabated,
while magazines and newspapers fail to catch the happy glistening eyes.

Linking arms stop to admire the stems of orchids,
for sale on the way in,
and even more so on the way out.

Linking arms love to browse and linger,
love to look and see the contents of Two-dollar shops,
with what could enhance the outlook of a niece or nephew,
as they grow and change in acquiring,
more confidence by the day.

Linking arms have a time and place when strolling round the town;
do not see them entering a liquor house,
or where the prices soar;
do not see them being self-conscious,
or waiting for a bus,
checking out the time or having no compunction,
when walking out without a purchase.

Linking arms speak of no concerns,
speak of confidence in their reasons for existence,
speak of a lack of interference in their objectives for the day.

Linking arms can sort out casual meetings of other friends,
can bring an invitation for further cups of tea,
can extend the conversation into areas not visited earlier,
as relatives are enquired after,
with a sincere interest in their health and well being.

Linking arms are just a casual hold,
are neither specific nor attention getting,
are not looking out of place:
where slight embarrassment may redden a face or cheeks.

Linking arms can help and assist with certainty,
when footpath edges need attention paid,
to the imbalances of the crossing,
while the lights just glow and chatter in the offering of permission,
to leave the safety of the footpath,
to venture into where the cars and trucks are busy,
in their rushing to and fro,
only seen to be stopping when under enforced duress.

Linking arms do not see many staring pairs of eyes,
        are not concerned with what the encountered may think,
                as thoughts are neither likely to be made known,
                    or able to be changed.

Linking arms are walking at their ease,
        are not tensed up in trying to beat their given time slot,
                for their crossing rights at the corner,
        are not concerned at their last few steps,
                when silence again reigns from the chatterer,
            as the lighting so again forbids a presence on the road,
            to insist the gathering be imprisoned on the footpath,
            to so build in readiness to again invade the road,
                when permission is so given,
              and the motivation is quite strong.

Linking arms do not last where uncertainty exists,
           where a stumble may occur,
           where a trip may cause a sudden lurch,
           where an arm may be grabbed more firmly,
              for steadying the uncertainty of age or sight,
              or of the unevenness of the paved way forward.

Linking arms are enjoying their time together,
        are considering their next stop,
        are looking at the menu as displayed outside a restaurant,
        are wondering what they all can mean:
        as to which are the salads and what the accompanying meat or fish may be,
           unless there is a tendency to be two vegetarians at large,
              which may not have been strictly supported,
                by the fare as selected,
              as a contribution to their morning tea.

Linking arms are not unduly concerned about the makeup of their lunch,
              are willing to discuss it with the staff inside.

Linking arms have their uncertainties resolved,
        have had served up the plates of interest with the cutlery required,
             are now settling down to the pleasantness of companionship,
              within the encountering of the midday timing,
              of the outing prior to the turn for home."

My Content Study Aid

Farewelling of Mortality

And I hear Jesus saying,
"Farewelling of mortality sees the people going,
                sees the people leaving,
                sees the people both negative and positive.

Farewelling of mortality is a seeking of a movement,
                is an end-time commitment to that with which they can agree,
                sees the people standing at the exit door and looking up a hill,
                or now standing at the entrance way,
                in order to attend to both the farewells of going,
                with the greetings of the coming.

Farewelling of mortality introduces the coming reign of friends;
                while evidencing the jackpots of the knaves,
                to be left to curl up in dismissal of their sleep.

Farewelling of mortality hears the footfalls in the halls,
                while all the feet do tramp within the absenting of Grace,
                in the timeframe of Faith.

Farewelling of mortality kicks the butchers out from the shopfront,
                with the closing of abortions;
                kicks the wayward and the genetically-disturbed,
                out from The Edifice of God,
                as the deniers of The Cross.

Farewelling of mortality allocates the atheists and the agnostics,
                to being grouped together,
                with those with chances which they blew,
                from which they cannot recover.

Farewelling of mortality changes the ship which carries passengers,
                with their negative levels of commitment;
                changes the approaches to a venue with the gardens,
                where the committed and the graceful,
                the loving and the caring,
                the members of the work gangs,
                are called up to attend their membership,
                within The Household of God.

Farewelling of mortality melds the families with unity of purpose,
                signs acceptance for the emigrants approved to attend,
                a new found era of existence,
                as immigrants within the knowledge base,
                of The Bride of The Christ—
                The Messiah who can sort and weave.

Farewelling of mortality leaves the scheduled under questioning,
        leaves those now dressed in white,
            as the unsubscribed survivors of the tribulation,
        leaves their destiny as plucked for survival
            among the innocent and the ignorant,
                where the chances of selection with withdrawal,
                    were not easy to discern.

Farewelling of mortality allocates to the destiny of default,
            as determined by Freewill of respect;
            or to the destiny of honouring of the committed,
            with the sharing as tasked unto completion.

Farewelling of mortality sees exits bounded by Freewill determinants,
                for the goats and for the sheep.

Farewelling of mortality has left it virtually too late,
        to change the tickets now,
            unless they can make an exit—
            as though through the flames.

Farewelling of mortality raises the question:
      of being a participant in partaking of the bread and wine;
     raises the question:
      of an entry in The Lamb's Book of Life;
     raises a question:
      of baptism by immersion;
     raises the question:
      of familiarity with both Faith and Grace;
     raises the question:
      of a life lived within The Freewill of righteousness and truth;
     raises the question:
      of the handling of sin;
     raises the question:
      of an acceptance of the pentecostal gifts of God.

Farewelling of mortality requires an exit clean and swept,
           if the grave is to be avoided,
           if the call is to be direct,
           if The Freewill activities can be assessed as being—
               in a relationship with God:
           arising from the sacrificing of The Son,
               where grace and faith prevailed,
           throughout the centuries ever since The Cross.

Farewelling of mortality is serious for those who know not God,
        is serious where ignorance is unlikely to be pleaded,
        is serious where whole families are affected,

with destinies still assessed as within that of default,
or denial,
at the forefront of a false belief.

Farewelling of mortality is a marker point of history,
is a marker point for satan and his rituals,
is a marker point denoting the onward success of Christianity,
with proof as to the afterlife worth establishing and living,
in the presence of God The Father,
God The Son,
and God The Holy Spirit,
in gathering together as The Three-in-one.

Farewelling of mortality is not a vacuous affair,
is not a chasing after shadows,
is not a lifting up of dreams,
is not a running round in circles,
is not a climbing of a mountain to escape.

Farewelling of mortality can be likened to:
the climbing of a staircase from the ground to a higher floor,
then the staircase is pulled up to prevent retreat,
or second thoughts from the multitudes as carried,
both forward and upward to a new way of life.

Farewelling of mortality can be likened to:
departing on a voyaging ship where the destiny is known,
is about to use its harbour,
where embarkation is not complex,
and all has been prepared.

Farewelling of mortality can be likened to:
an emigration as backed by an adjacent immigration,
of the body soul and spirit to a new land and scope,
of assimilation where much can and is,
to be seen and done.

Farewelling of mortality is a one-off concept,
which can be introduced by death,
which can now be introduced by transitioning to a higher plane,
where life continues to expand,
to qualify for advancement into an eternity,
where all the constructs and the concepts of man,
can be merged and interwoven:
with the prepared and waiting,
as to be introduced by God."

Preparation For The King

And I hear Jesus saying,
"Preparation for the king sees The King preparing for all He must say and do,
for all He may encounter,
for all He may need to circumvent,
in the coming trials of presentation.

Preparation for the king cannot be drawn from the past,
when belief structures are so different,
when time and grace and truth with faith are all fast disappearing,
from the strongholds of man.

Preparation for the king is in the fields of visions and of speech,
of both dress and presentation,
of both knowledge and description,
of both wisdom and communication for
the all inclusive:
from the babes in swaddling clothes to the elderly,
where both are seen to be at rest.

Preparation for the king speaks of opening the gateway,
to the reality of a Kingdom now close at hand in readiness,
for the introductions to the staffing mixed with governance.

Preparation for the king has no inclination for the facetiousness of a court jester,
for the space of courtyards for parades and showmanship,
for the commemorations of what have happened in the past,
for the significance of individual happenings,
which have occurred upon the way,
to a coronation with a wedding feast.

Preparation for the king has many stages on which He must stand,
has many stages for which He must successfully pass through,
has many stages where Truth and Righteousness must be seen
to overcome—
even to and for the stragglers,
who are always the last to both arrive and to comprehend,
the status of the day,
and the authority presented for assimilation.

Preparation for the king requires the higher echelons entitled with enablement,
to carry staff and staves.

Preparation for the king requires His bands with experience to be stationed,
throughout His kingdom with their music at the ready,
as wherein His Colours reign.

Preparation for the king sees the evidence of the planning for His kingdom,
of the detail and the ramifications,
of the peace threads with their niches,
of consent and admiration,
of the peace mills busy grinding up an outcome,
to be spread both far and wide throughout the tablelands,
whereon the tables can be set with the fare of God,
as held in readiness within a grand supply,
which can be multiplied very quickly and without delay.

Preparation for the king does not see an agenda where there are holidays for rest,
sees an agenda which copes into the future,
which is able to peer around the corners,
which can remove the dust with the broken
promises of others,
who speak in ignorance of their own capability,
and the degree of unearned trust.

Preparation for the king covers being ready for meeting disappointments head-on,
for encountering that which needs to be
dismissed as of no account,
with unworthiness sufficient to be not considered,
for a stake within The Earth,
as a future outpost of The Edifice of God,
upon an island in the sea.

Preparation for the king is in a state of readiness,
to deal with problems built on concepts,
where buildings as proposed,
are either too big or too small for all which must be met,
within the bounds of containment:
the sphere of qualifications of design,
for which there is much failure,
as ignorance does not call on the knowledge base of God.

Preparation for the king is not concerned with masterpieces,
is concerned with perfection in terms of solid
public presentations,
of the effort in the matching of rewards.

Preparation for the king is not a difficult phase through which to travel,
so the outcome is seen to be rewarding,
so all is seen to be in order,
so all is seen to qualify according to design,
with construction as arising therefrom.

Preparation for the king will not end up being stuck upon a glitch,
>will not end up being short of what is critical,
>will not end up with counting totals not verified,
>>when put under repetition.

Preparation for the king has summation sheets at length,
>has specifications galore,
>is a quantity surveyor's nightmare requiring to be resolved,
>>prior to the commencement on a site,
>>selected for a key positioning,
>within the interweaving of the finished articles,
>>as sitting on The Stones of God.

Preparation for the king has all the sheets complying with assessments,
>complying with the building plans,
>complying with the internal fittings,
>>together with the decorations.

Preparation for the king leaves no stone unturned on checking the foundations,
>leaves no boat untested by a seaworthy trial,
>leaves no aircraft to fly the skies,
>without pilots familiar with the routes,
>as measured by the placements of the ups and downs required.

Preparation for the king avoids disasters based upon longevity,
>avoids disasters based upon inexperience,
>avoids disaster based upon unfamiliarity,
>avoids disasters based on sabotage,
>where something can be seen as moveable and also incorrect.

Preparation for the king is in managing a takeover,
>is in managing a transition of accountability,
>is in managing the birthing of a kingdom,
>>where peace within eternity does reign,
>>without any further short-term satanic interference:
>>which will be a long time coming,
>just prior to an encounter of the finality of control."

My Content Study Aid

_____

_____

_____

_____

_____

Escalation of Surroundings

And I hear Jesus saying,
"Escalation of surroundings speak of time frames becoming tighter,
$\qquad\qquad$ becoming more frequent,
$\qquad\qquad$ becoming more intense,
$\qquad\qquad$ becoming less reliable,
$\qquad\qquad\qquad\qquad$ more open to attack.

Escalation of surroundings see weather growing fiercer,
$\qquad$ see the wind puffs becoming gales,
$\qquad$ see the hurricanes outlasting the residues of daylight,
$\qquad\qquad$ as the roofs are completely scattered by being blown apart,
$\qquad\qquad$ now being well on their way as kindling for a fire.

Escalation of surroundings see stress spots changing sides,
$\qquad\qquad$ experiences electricity being cut,
$\qquad$ with water mains being empty,
$\qquad$ with pressure failing in the building for a fire spray,
$\qquad\qquad$ or the pumping out of flooding.

Escalation of surroundings are fast attending to the loose ends,
$\qquad$ are shutting down the telephone wires with the networks,
$\qquad\qquad$ from being able to meet their responsibilities,
$\qquad$ are closing down the sewerage and how it can be treated,
$\qquad\qquad$ as the pumps are gradually fading to a stop.

Escalation of surroundings witness the rain clouds starting up a downpour,
$\qquad\qquad$ very quickly wetting everything,
$\qquad\qquad$ not precisely covered up.

Escalation of surroundings can hear the surging of the seas,
$\qquad$ as the breakwaters are topped,
$\qquad$ sending waves quickly getting deeper,
$\qquad$ moving faster down the streets as shunted by the gales,
$\qquad\qquad$ with hurricanes in tow,
$\qquad\qquad$ with the filling of the garages and houses,
$\qquad\qquad\qquad$ still not sandbagged,
$\qquad$ as the water still rises to become a moving overcomer.

Escalation of surroundings have the waves and winds increasing,
$\qquad$ see the surging of the sea,
$\qquad$ with the flooding of the city enclaves,
$\qquad\qquad$ now seen to be susceptible:
$\qquad$ of the shorelines' constructions and living spaces,

for as the water rises so the stay-behinders and the obstinate,
together with the elderly,
see their lives becoming more at risk,
becoming more stranded in their refuges,
as time restricts its hands for rescue,
from an ever increasing angry sea.

Escalation of surroundings are not easily stopped or reversed,
are not easily keeping the stop banks from preventing the flooding,
of the inbound tide as it breached in several places,
which are starting to join up.

Escalation of surroundings see the evening lights go out in many districts,
as they fail to come back on.

Escalation of surroundings hear the spluttering of the rescue boats,
with volunteers in place,
going up and down the streets looking for white flags,
at the upstairs windows,
now asking to be saved,
in the torchlight of the darkness of the night.

Escalation of surroundings start to make apparent the seriousness,
of requests for rescue,
which will mostly have to wait for daylight to return,
when water levels may possibly be stabilized,
with the threat levels being assessed made known and actionable.

Escalation of surroundings need a trigger to start things getting worse,
when there is no real reason as to cause.

Escalation of surroundings on a basis such as that,
are not of God.

Escalation of surroundings seen to be perverse have demonic overtones,
which can be traced and vilified,
as starting with Satanic impulses inserted in the weather system,
where no one benefits except to see fresh trails of destruction,
of that which had just been the homely prides of man.

Escalation of surroundings have numbers attached for significance,
from within the count of man,
so expectations can be fulfilled by each damage trail,
as it is likely to be left,
as it is prepared for its attack,
on the resources and the abilities of man.

Escalation of surroundings can be widespread and severe,
　　　　　　　can leave scattered waste yards of the debris,
　　　　　　　　　　　for neither rhyme nor reason except because he,
　　　　　　　　　　the dark lord can:
　　　　　　　　　　　　　as a means of declaring a status of revenge,
　　　　　　　　　　　　　　　　　arising from his,
　　　　　　　　　　　　　Lucifer's expulsion from the heavens.

Escalation of surroundings should not be a tiptoe affair,
　　　　　　　　　　of waiting to see what happens.

Escalation of surroundings should be stopped in each path,
　　　　　　　　　　by the taking of control:
　　　　　　　　　　by the soothing of the sea,
　　　　　　　　　　by the calming of the wind,
　　　　　　　　　　by the settling of the power grid and
　　　　　　　　　　　　　　　the telephone systems,
　　　　　　　　　　　　　under shields of divine protection,
　　　　　　　　　　　　　before damage can occur.

Escalation of surroundings see man suffering,
　　　　　　　　　　from what he thinks he cannot control,
　　　　　　　　　　　　　which is another lie from Satan,
　　　　　　　　　　　　　both widespread and believed.

Escalation of surroundings have occurred because of man,
　　　　　　　　　　surrendering his dominion,
　　　　　　　　　　over The Earth when in My garden;
　　　　　　　　　　and not believing he is now in a position to reclaim it back,
　　　　　　　　　　in righteousness and truth with The Freewill activity of man,
　　　　　　　　　　now also able to activate rejection,
　　　　　　　　　　　　　of what Satan is endeavouring to establish,
　　　　　　　　　　　　　before his period in the limelight fades into obscurity,
　　　　　　　　　　　　　　　for quite some considerable time.

Escalation of surroundings now have control by man made possible,
　　　　　　　　　　through The Pentecostal giftings with power and authority,
　　　　　　　　　　　　　arising from The Cross of The Christ—
　　　　　　as the miracles of God were attached to the proxy existence of man,
　　　　　　　　　　who did not recognize what he had received,
　　　　　　　　　　　　　with the difference it could make,
　　　　　　　　　by those who read The Word with understanding of The Truth,
　　　　　　　　　　with the reception of bequeathed intent.

Escalation of surroundings mark the defeatist ways of man under Satan,
　　　　　　　　　　　and The Established Ways of God,
　　　　　　　waiting for The Wise for the application of the reining in of control,
　　　　　　　　　　with The Words of Knowledge and of Wisdom,
　　　　　　　　　　and The Declarations as loved by God."

Blowing of The Wind

And I hear Jesus saying,
"Blowing of the wind dries out the mistakes,
        catches the falling tears of heaven,
        circles and implodes,
        ignites and carries forward,
        twirls and twists the flames,
        holds and harnesses the keenness to move forward,
            the keenness to siphon and protect,
            the keenness to validate the testing of the risks,
        of the forest where life forms trade in risk,
        when out upon a limb with fire and smoke below,
            and nowhere else to go,
            without an open means of escape,
            before the tunnelling of fire,
            within the vapours from the trees.

Blowing of the wind is at its worst for fire entrapment,
        when fanning the flames within the forests of the eucalypts,
        as animals do abound in feeding from the leaves,
        are not fast movers across the open ground,
        where wind is often the fanner of lost hope for embedded life,
        which is slow and troubled by the heat and smoke,
        to know not in which direction up or down or either side,
        where safety lies within a time frame to be sought and reached,
        as a slightly scorched survivor from within but another forest fire,
        from wherein many relatives did die,
        not to be seen again.

Blowing of the wind builds upon the fire base,
        builds in swirling the wind tunnels,
        where direction becomes lost,
        builds within a loss of identity where life can be made,
        marred or disfigured for a lifetime,
        as the ruins are viewed with dismay and lost hope,
        as the fire has come and gone;
        leaving nothing worth the picking up or sharing,
        from a past now burnt and lost,
        in being no longer open to review.

Blowing of the wind can jump across divides,
        as it sends the sparks before it as symbols of destruction,
        as it sends the forest litter to mix it with the sparks,
        when the result is well known to set:
        shades or goggles or masks upon the face,
        as covering for the eyes or unprotected hair.

Blowing of the wind strengthens with the gusts,
        strengthens with the bearings being constant,
        strengthens with the waving of any flags encountered.

Blowing of the wind is weakened by the advancing of a cloud base,
        sends a welcome message to the fighters and the thwarters—
                the strugglers,
            as called to be the deniers of the fuel,
            as fallen to the ground and dried,
            is everywhere abounding,
            is nowhere scarce and restricted,
            as rotting would have made it,
        in restriction of the fire hazard as witnessed in reality,
            and is now being fought by the willing,
            without relief from the heat and the oppression,
                of the smoke and ash.

Blowing of the wind cycles within its strengths,
        within a season on the land,
        cycles within its strengths when supported from the sea.

Blowing of the wind shrieks and howls in its distress at night,
        screams and splits the wood as it shatters,
        in the energy as building in the afternoon,
            with sunlight in excess,
            and the heating from the sea and plains,
            whereon majestic rivers choose to live and flow,
            with river boats going both ways with the passengers,
                as well as in the trading of the goods.

Blowing of the wind is not committed to a space-time curriculum,
                can alter its attack plan with sufficient will,
                can blow from all directions of the compass,
        when the wind meets with the approval of the wind source of the day,
            as it beats and cajoles its bounds into order for assimilation,
            by the coastlines with the onshore winds being stretched,
                in the testing of their strength.

Blowing of the wind can blow the windows in,
        can blow the giant trees down,
        can uproot their earthing roots,
        can topple with a crash and bounce,
            regardless of where the wind says it is to land:
            in finality of purpose and of life.

Blowing of the wind can hunt out the troubled and the weak,
the rotten cores as logged with partial decay,
which creak when bent by a testing of the vertical,
and its quest of affirmation in desiring to survive.

Blowing of the wind can be extremely strong and dangerous,
as it centres in a storm,
as it transforms into a hurricane,
as it starts to get a number,
as man's bits and pieces start to move around the sky,
with a definite rough landing foretold and understood,
now seen without the cushioning they first enjoyed,
when going sailing in the sky.

Blowing of the wind has head-on attacks with cameras to the fore,
has sideways attacks where the camera can jump
to the left or to the right,
at very little notice yet with very fast driving,
of the support crew in attention to pursuit,
as the camera rolls in seeing and recording,
the riskings of the day.

Blowing of the wind can end in the calmness of surprise,
of the fading away of the kernel of the storm front,
where the lightning strikes have died,
where the thunder claps have silenced,
as they both moved away.

Blowing of the wind felt the buffeting upon the camera car,
felt the shock waves and the bumps,
absorbed the smallest shimmy,
and yielded to the strongest oooh!
as the whole car moved across the road,
until a new trajectory gave fresh grip to the tyres,
with a swerve at speed.

Blowing of the wind is not to be taken lightly,
can be a very serious mistake,
when a storm appears in the overloading of the system,
in leaving everything as damaged,
and then dumped upon the scene,
as history has the records to retell."

My Content Study Aid

Coming of The Sea

And I hear Jesus saying,
"Coming of the sea is an instance usually of one of inundation,
along the shorelines of disturbance.

Coming of the sea varies with the season,
usually stays within the natural confines of its bounds,
between the high and low water marks as known and accustomed.

Coming of the sea can be a terrifying experience for visitors and guests,
can set the eyes to tears,
can set the mouth to utter what is on one's heart in unbridled fear.

Coming of the sea is one of forces accumulated in readiness to invade,
in readiness to overcome defences,
which will be insufficient for turning back,
the movements of determination,
which have gathered so to dwell within the day.

Coming of the sea does not issue invitations of inspection,
is busy enlisting waves which will not be beaten back,
which will surge in backing one another up until the walls are breached,
to see the water freely flowing,
to the low spots now unprotected,
from the depths of both concern and of how a disaster,
may still be averted or minimized,
from the water intent on being inbound,
on what it has attacked and is about to conquer.

Coming of the sea can overpower the might and will of man,
by volume by weight and by speed of entry,
where the little bit of retreating swirling water,
is quickly overcome by the volume,
which is speeding shoreward in mounting a fresh attack,
which now knows the weakest parts,
as it starts to move the cars as placed upon the streets,
while in the process of busy rinsing out the houses,
as selected for a soaking in this unwelcome free for all,
with the price to be determined by collection and assistance,
after the waterline recedes and the mud is left to stay,
with a fresh coating for the floors which needs to be removed with shovels,
spades and washing in the company of high pressure hoses,
accompanied by scrubbing brushes driven by determination,
with lots of elbow grease and perseverance.

Coming of the sea can keep coming in the daylight,
        can keep coming in the night,
        can keep coming until the storm centre is seen to waver,
                where the force shows inklings of diminishing,
                that which started in an increasing fury,
        as the rain lets up from clouds seen to be lightening by the hour,
                    yet still have plenty left in reserve,
                      to so show and do.

Coming of the sea is not eager to retire,
        wants to stay and rest upon its laurels,
        as a victory is uncovered with the morning light,
        where a city can be seen in submission,
            to a high speed invasion which did not hesitate in its thrust,
                and capture of the land mass,
            as placed before it for the onus of defeat.

Coming of the sea leaves turmoil in its midst,
        leaves deposits which cannot stay;
        leaves cars which are soaked in sea water and grit,
                which are now of little value;
        leaves low spots which will not drain and empty;
        leaves houses in need of pumping,
            from the filling of the basements with the residues,
                arising from the giftings of the sea,
            as the destroying of the contents completes,
                to have them all made worthless.

Coming of the sea is too massive to force a retreat upon it,
            requires patience with the drainage,
              with unblocking as required,
        with re-establishing of the flow channels once in use,
        but now no longer still inclined to function,
        until attention has been given to the angles at the corners,
        where the slopes of gradient do meet and intersect,
            and the sumps all need to be cleaned out.

Coming of the sea has made its mark upon the network of electricity,
        has left transformers and transducers probably still under water,
              and likely filled with sand.

Coming of the sea will not be easily forgotten,
        will not be easily forgiven as the curses flowed,
        will neither be prized nor rewarded,
            for the closing works of Satan,
            at the tail-end of his freedom.

Coming of the sea is becoming more frequent,
>as retribution mixed with unentitled vengeance,
>colours and distorts in confirmation
>of the semblance of satanic authority,
>now in its final stages,
>before removal from the scene.

Coming of the sea does not comb the wet and straggling,
>does not beautify the distraught and weeping,
>does not confirm the lonely and resentful,
>does not respond to replacement or repair.

Coming of the sea causes judgment with the call for help,
>causes deep concern as to means of prevention in the future,
>as to how a city can be rated as both dry and secure,
>from the ravages as seen to be vested in the surges of the sea,
>arising from the feeding of a Hurricane,
>with the energy as bound and released,
>from within the warm waters set free to do its mischief,
>with neither let nor hindrance,
>as it moves along a coastline or moves inland to stall and dump,
>or moving up and down in the sharing of a disaster,
>as borne and bred and heated into violence,
>while monitored at sea.

Coming of the sea is not as a result of an invitation,
>is not as a result of answered prayer to God.

Coming of the sea needs its progress to be stopped and blown to pieces,
>by the prayer appeals to God,
>by the proxy ministry of Freewill as bestowed and operational,
>by the overcoming of Satan and his cronies,
>where the coming of the sea has its threat dismembered,
>as disintegration showers the sea,
>with the residues of dissemination,
>from the protective prayers to God."

My Content Study Aid

_____
_____
_____
_____
_____

Forests Born in Fire

And I hear Jesus saying,
"Forests born in fire sign with the scorch marks on their trunks,
        sign with the death marks of the remains,
        sign with the sprouting of the seedlings from the fire.

Forests born in fire stand in need to initiate the rebirth of a forest,
                with the triggering of fire.

Forests born in fire await the triggering of a lightning flash,
          which can strike positively from a distance;
          without the immediate followup of rain or wind.

Forests born in fire have odours all their own,
      have odours of maturity,
      have odours borne of seed ejections,
      have odours borne of leaves,
      have odours born of the density of the scattered seedlings,
            as struck and birthed by fire.

Forests born in fire survive or perish in dry surroundings,
      make the watering last within the availability of insightful need.

Forests born in fire have cones which know how to scatter their birthright,
         in the heat of a fire field's awaited day,
         when the throwing of the seed heads,
            from within the cones,
         establishes their imminent readiness for release,
         as the flames below have climbed and touched,
            the triggers in the cones,
          which send the opening seed shells,
          on their way with projectile force,
        with a seed head which carries weight and speed,
          with the sense to ensure achievement,
           of the avoidance of the eyes.

Forests born in fire meet but do not matchup in qualifying for a fire,
      are to be independent and mature,
         before the cones will flare,
         before the cones will burn,
         before the triggers fire,
         before the seed shells will endeavour to dispense,
        on-going life through sending the seed heads down,
         through the lightish ash,

to make contact with the indenting,
of the earthen floor of resistance,
to the spot-heat as encountered,
but to be so pushed aside in landing,
as it sets itself to await for the refreshing showers of rain,
as they make possible to witness,
the sign of life in action in a forest,
which appears to be as bare as possible after fire,
yet where new growth sprouts the actuality of future trees.

Forests born in fire have a very risky life,
where they use a lightning strike,
for the ploughing of the fields,
where they use a fire storm to prepare and seed the sowing bed,
where they use a rainstorm to breath in the difficulty,
of attaching new life-in-waiting,
into The Earthen Soil of God.

Forests born in fire exist within a level of very special interest,
exist within a level where understanding fails the test of common sense,
exist within a level where an explanation restores,
the sense of balance with acceptance.

Forests born in fire have seen success right through the centuries,
have seen success where the odds did not appear to be in favour,
where the rain often failed the first the second and the third attempts,
to spit upon the earth,
as the forest so required,
yet was forced to wait,
for the trigger to complete.

Forests born in fire see the lightning and hear the majestic clash of symbols,
which carry through the forest as the birds take flights of evacuation,
yet there is life awaiting for the bringing of hope,
with expectation of fulfilment to the fore:
so the forest can drink and drink and drink and drink,
to so fill the thirst arising from the fire,
and the needs of the sprouting of the seeds,
each in their own little indentations,
to where the water runs in gathering,
for the starting of new life upon The Earth.

Forests born in fire have days and ways of waiting,
where the wind is slack as the forest wilts,
in the streaming of the sun.

Forests born in fire do not encourage visitors,
          do not want to see any matches lit,
          would rather wait for the storm fronts to appear,
                    with their flashes and their bangs,
               which are much more reliable,
               which are much less open to interference.

Forests born in fire tend to want it the way they have experienced,
          have no warranty to request a change,
             only want a lightning strike with fire every sixty years or so,
             where frequency declares a certain casualness of approach,
        yet almost certainly can guarantee success within a few years either side.

Forests born in fire should not be deliberately set alight,
          may well be its death knell if maturity is missing,
                  or the rains are out of season with the fire,
              so dryness brings the onset of the shrivelling,
                    and the lack of growth.

Forests born in fire usually have no river source there that can be tapped,
          usually are very short of rain to feed a stream or lake,
          often can not remember the last time that it rained.

Forests born in fire should not be expected:
                  to glow at night nor to smoke in daylight,
          should have no need to sound a siren,
          should not expect a water cart or tanker to attend the wayward flames.

Forests born in fire can exercise the beaters and the thrashers,
              when a fire is called without the lightning or the thunder,
                 where the undergrowth is mild,
              is still to pose the unlikelihood of a carried fire.

Forests born in fire know the starving of a fire site,
          know the concern when matters become out of hand,
          would create a sequence where a slight back-burn was possible,
                     controllable,
               and made a lot of sense.

Forests born in fire know that God is not far away,
          that the frequency of fire really does not pose a risk,
               either to life or limb,
               or the homesteads of the few."

My Content Study Aid

_____

_____

Lakes Running Dry

And I hear Jesus saying,
"Lakes running dry are catastrophes in waiting,
    are catastrophes just waiting to appear and restrain,
    are catastrophes spelling the end to water reticulation,
     to the plant growth as embedded in the fields of expectation.

Lakes running dry are threats of things to come,
      of threats approaching very quickly,
      of threats expanding which will not go away,
    are controls without restrictions,
    are excess takedowns without a payback in like for like.

Lakes running dry are dotted in the water catchments in decline,
    are noticed as the shorelines continue to recede,
   are victims of the farmers who gobble up all on which they can lay their hands,
       either rightly or wrongly,
     as the seasons pass,
     as the lakes are subjected to theft and dust,
     where the earth is left as cracked and parched,
      to be seen as having suffered,
       the loosing of respect,
      together with any reasonable ability,
       to meet and share demand,
      without destruction of the future.

Lakes running dry should condemn a nation,
    should incur restrictions designed for preservation,
    should not see the streams and river becoming uninhabited,
      to be forsaken by the fish life they used to carry,
      to ultimately,
      on the runs see breeding:
      for the canning of the food.

Lakes running dry are not appreciated until the loss is complete,
        and not likely to be recovered,
   as the siphoning off from streams and rivers are counted as a farming privilege,
    without checking that water can still maintain its route unto the sea,
      with the preservation of a minimum flow,
       to stop the algae blooming,
    while the water shed with its drainage is not subject to diminishing,
     with the loss of vitality and purity,
     as stock trample mud into faecal sludge contaminants,
     as they drink and browse without restraint,
     along what should be the pristine water's edge.

Lakes running dry should rebound on the users along the way,
with comparisons of water quality and volume upon reception,
and of water quality and volume as sent upon its way;
and of responsibility and accountability for the differences,
arising from the water's quality and volume,
as either lost or gained in its passage,
with its public ownership intact;
to be carried forward on its journey under gravity,
without the running of the pumps for the spraying of the fields,
with the incurring of the water loss under the heating of the day.

Lakes running dry can speak of mismanagement or theft,
at the intake level that never makes it to the lake,
as a diversion could be in place.

Lakes running dry are an insult to intelligence,
are an insult to the water resources of all who are downstream,
are an insult for the lack of care and motivation,
to maintain the purity of volume as received,
with the inflow to be the purity of volume as passed on in the outflow.

Lakes running dry should have their rainfall credentials checked,
for accuracy and comparison,
should assess the reasons for the excess of the drawdown from a lake,
so poaching is not included to distort results.

Lakes running dry see visitors decline,
see tourist loss of interest,
see water sports being weakened,
see boating being transferred to interests elsewhere,
see chalets and holiday homes no longer being used,
or kept tidy and presentable,
see vistas unmaintained,
see snowmelt as insufficient,
or as a diversion by an aqueduct to a generating dam or pumping ram.

Lakes running dry witness nature under attack,
signs of the interference of man,
where planning is amiss,
and so awaits correction.

Lakes running dry are not a pretty sight,
are not attractions which can be maintained,
are not of any worth once the last drop is taken,
when the sun is left to bake.

Lakes running dry may not have lapping water,
        may have an encirclement of scum,
                with a surface of coloured floating algae,
                which does nothing to enhance appearances.

Lakes running dry suffer badly from a lack of drinks,
        from insufficient glasses,
            mostly empty,
        as set upon the breakfast entry table,
            and at other times of day,
        where once saw replenishment well under way,
            and successful with the top-ups,
            from the surplus and the clean.

Lakes running dry are of significance to the support of bird life,
            and of the aquatic fast running out of breath.

Lakes running dry are not at all good news to the affected and concerned,
        to the sympathetic and the caring,
        to the failed management in exhibiting dismay,
           with attempts at correction,
           before the stress point goes beyond,
           the yardstick of recovery.

Lakes running dry are also mindful of when they are told of steam-stacks ejecting
            cooling water to the sky above,
        and contaminated water as pumped into the aquifers below:
            in further unchecked loss,
             of the clean and drinkable.

Lakes running dry do not seem to have watching crowds,
        as sentries for inspecting and calculating forward,
     do not seem to have a sufficient following,
        to impart a change of heart:
        to value what is there and of how it may be rescued;
           within where folk do dwell,
           as shops do struggle to survive,
      while hope and trust and faith all slowly ebb away,
      with a lack of urgency in attending to the nearly broken,
           before collapse is witnessed,
   and the dust begins to swirl as a monument to the unsatisfied greed of man:
        while God looks on in wonderment,
        as He sees them attending a static church,
        where solutions are neither sought nor counselled:
           or to be set upon a pedestal,
           from which shouting could be heard,
           at a surprising distance."

Rivers Without Feed

And I hear Jesus saying,
"Rivers without feed have experience with earthquakes which have changed the beds,
which have changed the sheets with the underlay of carpeting,
above the rocks and stones.

Rivers without feed can have it come and go,
are not snow fed all year round,
are rain fed on occasions,
have it bank to bank in a downpour when excess strikes,
to be gathered very quickly at short notice of intent,
where the instructions are to take it to the sea within an hour or so,
where the river delivers with the semi-circular staining of the sea,
while muddiness and turbulence both remain,
within the banks with a fast run,
where discharging carries all the silt out to the mouth,
which yawns in having seen it all before,
while salmon fishermen wait with their rods and reels and transport at the mouth,
for the water to revert to one of clarity,
and of being free from silt,
while the netters with their boats set to catch the fish,
lingering at the mouth,
as such gather for several days in which they will feed,
prior to a commitment to a hunger strike,
when joining in a run upstream,
to their breeding gravel.

Rivers without feed have over time brought the scoria down from the mountain sides
and hills,
have flushed it along the bed where stone islands have been formed,
where water can some times be seen seeping in between,
the loose fitting of the low level stones upon the bed.

Rivers without feed but with a steep gradient to the sea,
can often,
in setting up the downstream tumbling,
wash the rounded rocks right out to sea over the drop-off to the depths.

Rivers without feed although confounded with uneven river beds for vehicles,
usually have no water flowing to establish the validity of a bridge:
until a roaring torrent presents itself for inspection,
as it continues to rise to engulf the bed from bank to bank,
sometimes to also touch the underneath side of a bridge.

Rivers without feed have witnessed people stranded and unable to go safely home,
        when on horseback in the days where some feed-less rivers had no bridges,
      where a fortnight could pass before the water fell to a depth of two feet or so,
            in which a horse could struggle through without undue risk,
                    either to the life of man or to the horse,
             while crossing with a stick for the testing of the depth.

Rivers without feed are short in length,
        often are on islands,
        have flash floods to be navigated,
        often have concreted lengthwise dips centred on the road,
                  which warrants a slow approach,
             in case large rocks have been left across the road,
                  and need to be manually removed.

Rivers without feed often require a slow approach,
             with caution and with care,
        where speed is not attempted in the middle of the night,
        where bottoming of the vehicle may put strains
                    on stopping quickly,
        where caution remains until the light beams,
                   or the line of sight,
      can clarify exactly what may be found in the centre of the road,
                  with its warning notice.

Rivers without feed are difficult to judge with no foreknowledge,
      are difficult to prepare for when in a hurry,
             and distractions may be present,
             can lead to a disaster from a rock,
             just sitting in the way and looking round,
         if it is too large to qualify for passing underneath,
             without tinkering with what it's found,
        in the seconds it is both relevant and interesting.

Rivers without feed rarely make a splash unless it's raining at the time.

Rivers without feed sometimes need livestock rescuing,
             from the river beds with alacrity,
      when a possibility exists for their stranding on a stony sub-island,
             which may not be very large,
             which may be submerging by the hour,
             as the waters approach and build,
             prior to their leaving and their lowering,
                  of the risk,
        which could well have washed the small herd all off its feet.

Rivers without feed usually have no alarm systems,
                usually are monitored by locals,
                        can sometimes have a tractor at the ready with the chains or ropes
                                                for helping on the way.

Rivers without feed are not all that common,
                can generate a mess if there is a miscalculation,
                                if there is a stone thrown up which shatters glass,
                                if there is an injury which requires the help of others.

Rivers without feed cannot think,
                cannot make assumptions,
                cannot bend back the steel or aluminium,
                cannot heat so bends can be straightened out.

Rivers without feed can be difficult from which to recover,
                                when there is a face to face with others on the road.

Rivers without feed know the onset of misery and neglect,
                                when halted by a breakdown in a thunder storm,
                        the structuring of carelessness and stupidity,
                        the seeking of a thrill and memory,
                                                of what has just gone before,
                        that which could have been avoided with neither pain nor suffering.

Rivers without feed do not contribute to a cash-in on the stupidity of man,
                        already know stupidity is very common in assault,
                        already is aware of the outcome of a race between the amateurs,
                                who know not what they're doing on a wet race track,
                                where obstacles may be present and safety is ignored,
                can hardly complain for what they may encounter in the cross-winds of doubt."

My Content Study Aid

_____

_____

_____

_____

_____

_____

_____

_____

_____

Snow without The Ice

And I hear Jesus saying,
"Snow without the ice is the tail without the sting,
                is the tooth without the ache,
                is the catch without the hook.

Snow without the ice is the colour without transparency,
                is the covering without the risk,
                is the gradient without the fall.

Snow without the ice is the temperature without the chill,
                is the refrigeration with neither equipment nor the power,
                is the cold stuff required for throwing,
      or for rolling snowballs down a hillside or for building a visitor at the gate.

Snow without the ice is asking to be shovelled so a path is clear,
                is waiting for the snow plough so the road is clear,
                can see folk waiting for the sunshine so everything is clear.

Snow without the ice can become the slush and mud,
                where stepping takes both care and perception to traverse.

Snow without the ice can require the boots and shawl against a biting wind,
            can require access to a candle set to flame and flicker in a window,
                to so dress the scene for admiration,
      which is enhanced with external coloured lights in a season of the year.

Snow without the ice dresses and brings to mind,
           has music for the sleighs and bells,
           has settings of delight for all who profess they are children
                    still at heart.

Snow without the ice deserves a trip around a town,
          to see the conclusions as they have been drawn and stabled,
              as they have been drawn and fed,
              as they have been drawn and harnessed,
              so to pull and visit through the night of dreams,
              with an imaginary lookout kept for chimneys,
                  or faces at the windows,
             where noses may all be pressed to the glass,
                  as star belts can be seen,
                  as the clocks do tick,
                  as the beds do summon.

Snow without the ice sees everyone awaking to a vista of a wonderland,
hears children rejoicing at what they have found,
in a sock at the bottom of a bed,
await with much anticipation,
what may be carefully placed under a tree.

Snow without the ice can hinder the arrivals,
can impose some difficulties on delivery,
can open up the eyes in marvelling,
where all voices speak at once,
with their shows and tells,
as they go from seat to seat,
or sit upon the floor surrounded by the wrapping paper,
which has now served its purpose,
to lie there torn and shredded,
as disclosure breaks all open for inspection,
for a tryout with a smile,
as a 'thank you' is still seeking out,
the ears of relevance and love.

Snow without the ice is a very special time for children,
where the parents are not quite so sure of the blessings,
where in other parts it goes head to head,
up against the sunshine and the beaches,
with extended holidays as a timely consolation.

Snow without the ice sees objectives being attained,
sees new jobs being affirmed,
sees pending changes in the air,
with benefits for the families.

Snow without the ice changes situations all around the world.

Snow without the ice can still call up an avalanche,
can still block up a road,
can still put its finger in a spoke:
when the vehicles have no chains,
when the snow is deep and steep,
when the gripping is at risk.

Snow without the ice is not wise to await compaction with a frost,
is not wise to think the ice is not lying there in wait,
not to cling onto the road,
that it has not had time to build with effect,
with a potential disaster in the making,
where safety has its making as a vehicle stops,
as the chains are fitted,
as the journey can proceed,
now with surety of traction and of grip.

Snow without the ice can overcome the surges and the Skids,,
    can overcome the interlocking smacks and bangs,
        of tail-enders who cannot stop,
      who are driving too fast for the conditions of the day,
      who have not stopped to procure or to fit the chains,
        as necessitated by conditions,
     where common sense should speak,
     before the death or injury occurs,
      with its instance of regret based on current ignorance,
    as to the outcome of a delayed decision to ensure safety,
    with the introduction of the grieving which cannot be reversed.

Snow without the ice is best vested in an overnight stop within a camping ground,
    where a life can be assured it will still be alive in the morning,
     and not queuing in the surgical waiting room of a hospital,
      for news concerning an emergency operation,
      arising from travelling in the night among the snow.

Snow without the ice can test the driving skills,
     when stopping with excessive breaking,
        as the tailgate looms in front,
        as a slide is generating.

Snow without the ice can see a close call ending,
      in a run off into a roadside ditch:
     if it can be located in an instant or in fact is there,
        with any degree of certainty,
        under a covering of snow.

Snow without the ice can dispel the happiness,
     for the passengers in the vehicle,
         as it sideslips to avoid,
         as it tries to shed its speed.

Snow without the ice can bring silence to a vehicle as it finally is stopped,
     as it finally has silenced all those within the vehicle,
      where the seatbelts may have been empty,
    so unable to moderate the result of the violence of collision,
     with what was and is a threat to life.

Snow without the ice is like bread without the butter,
    is like meat without the chutney,
    is like a hamburger without the mayo.

Snow without the ice links and tests the stopping power,
      required for the preservation of life,
     where the skill of the physicians or the surgeons,
      should neither be tested nor sought,
        as to an outcome."

Storm Clouds of Menace

And I hear Jesus saying,
"Storm clouds of menace gather for a purpose,
    gather for iniquity,
    gather for destruction of the innocent and unaligned.

Storm clouds of menace carry the handiwork of Satan,
    carry disasters in a string,
    carry death and mayhem as the end result,
        which is not easily prevented,
   unless by a willingness to control under the authority of a proxy ministry.

Storm clouds of menace have no nice feature worth watching,
    are set with black clouds swirling,
    are loaded with black clouds rotating,
    are charged as lightning flashes are discharged,
     into the cloud base as it starts to pour,
    as the storm increases with the wind velocity,
   as people start to batten down when it almost is too late.

Storm clouds of menace can be recognized at once,
    can be abandoned by an active prayer life calling to account,
    The Freewill application as based upon demolishing everything,
      as worked for,
      with an upright stance.

Storm clouds of menace know all the clouds of Heaven,
    know all the clouds of Earth,
    know all the clouds of Hell.

Storm clouds of menace can identify and be whistled to in a change of direction,
     in a change of discharging water,
    in a change of the blustering of the wind shear,
    as it picks and swallows in a feeding frenzy.

Storm clouds of menace often assemble the eye out at sea,
    often collect to clutch the warmest to the heart,
    often despatch test pieces to the perimeter to see how they behave.

Storm clouds of menace mount to thrust their spears,
    mount to capture and insert the strong and piercing in attack,
    mount to batter and to blast that which cannot stand against the sea,
     yet can ravage and report along the shoreline of the sea,
      as pieces are parted,
      split and set asunder,
    distorted bent cracked and soaked as the games are played,
    while the game master does neither bother to count the pieces,
    nor to relegate them to the status of the kindling for an open fire.

Storm clouds of menace will not succumb to cajoling,
>will not succumb to threats known to be empty,
>will not succumb to the interests of My church.

Storm clouds of menace are exactly what they are called,
>are exactly aligned with the wardrobe of the demonic,
>are soon to be demolished by a leadership arrest,
>>with the confiscation of resources.

Storm clouds of menace come in multiple arrays,
>come in banked up layers of energy release,
>come in high speed inundations with the battering of homes,
>>as tattered and forlorn with fragments,
>>as seen on neighbouring lawns.

Storm clouds of menace can encircle and disrupt without intention to dismiss,
>can hang around for days in an environment of intimidation and of lies,
>where intent as stated is no indication of what will actually come to be.

Storm clouds of menace can mess with electricity,
>can blow fuses beyond repair,
>can crack and cause to leak the transformers getting soaked,
>can sequence the lightning bolts for where most damage will occur,
>>as flash backs burn and smoulder,
>>to upset the checks and balances.

Storm clouds of menace sharpen and gnash their teeth,
>vibrate and shake the foundations as they split and short,
>aim to blow the trees down within the path of injury with tears,
>where ambulances have difficulty in progressing through the streets,
>>now under water or blocked by trees,
>>or showered with glass and concrete blocks,
>>>falling from several stories up,
>where hospitals have emergencies several times an hour,
>>to struggle with the inflow with the time sheets,
>>as well as the seriousness of what they see.

Storm clouds of menace attach very quickly once decided,
>dissipate very slowly on departure.

Storm clouds of menace laugh at the casinos busy doing what they do best,
>in the wrecking of the lives,
>in the splitting of the marriages,
>in the syphoning off the legitimacy of the funds,
>in the tinkering with the charlatans,
>with the encountering of the dishonest,
>>as they magnify their thefts.

Storm clouds of menace crash and bang,
in response to their lightning running wild,
ensure no one gets to sleep right throughout the night,
ensure all are bleary eyed,
when the dawn is finally to meet its schedule to arrive.

Storm clouds of menace really do know how to menace,
with their clouds of overflow and flooding,
with their winds of wrecking and frustrating,
with their open-ended attacks upon the lean and the scared,
where traps still lie in wait,
with the flooding of the manholes and the drains.

Storm clouds of menace can move very quickly in their relocations,
can move miles in several minutes,
can change localities for the rainstorms in the twinkling of an eye,
with the assistance of the wind force pushing from behind,
as a low pressure system in the front is busy encouraging things along,
as the system churns,
as the system expands,
as the eye enlarges,
as the winds increase in strength in density and speed,
while the hurricane enjoys its life at everyone's expense,
being quite content to linger while the damage is completed,
with nothing left intact.

Storm clouds of menace can be fractured and broken up,
by a proxy ministry declaring in authority which lasts."

My Content Study Aid

_____
_____
_____
_____
_____
_____
_____
_____
_____
_____

Secreting of Supplies

And I hear Jesus saying,
"Secreting of supplies are often worthwhile accumulating when shortages are foreseen,
$\qquad$ when prices are likely to go rocketing,
$\qquad$ when deliveries are delayed or stop altogether.

Secreting of supplies are advisable when starvation may stare one in the face,
$\qquad$ when there is complete and utter dependency
$\qquad\qquad$ on the supermarket shelves,
$\qquad$ when reliability is uncertain and unconfirmed.

Secreting of supplies will not last for ever,
$\qquad$ will not meet the totality of offtake,
$\qquad$ can only meet a home with its expectations of its needs,
$\qquad\qquad$ for a certain period of time,
$\qquad$ becomes much more serious as weight loss is encountered,
$\qquad\qquad$ with tablets unable to be dispensed,
$\qquad\qquad$ to support the health maintenance,
$\qquad\qquad\qquad$ of the recent past.

Secreting of supplies then and only then become adjuncts,
$\qquad$ to the prayer of Faith for needs as met by God,
$\qquad$ where the critical and the shortages move into the divine arena,
$\qquad$ wherein are encountered the miracles of life support,
$\qquad\qquad$ and of how they are delivered.

Secreting of supplies are unlikely to last until relief arrives,
$\qquad$ as difficulties increase with shortages fully realized,
$\qquad\qquad$ and not being replenished.

Secreting of supplies pose problems with collection,
$\qquad$ of whatever still remains upon the shelves,
$\qquad$ may have need of walking shoes with baskets,
$\qquad$ as transport loses the fight for maintenance of the fuel supply.

Secreting of supplies may leave the pets all short and hungry,
$\qquad$ with rationing in force,
$\qquad$ with food that cannot be wasted after just a nibble,
$\qquad\qquad$ at the gravy on the top.

Secreting of supplies will bring the likelihood of raids,
$\qquad$ and straight out theft where injuries are possible,
$\qquad\qquad$ incurring a further need,
$\qquad\qquad$ in the process of defence.

Secreting of supplies are likely to invoke the process of defence,
from the unruly and the mobsters,
where torture to release delivery may well be on the cards,
as a possibility of behaviour in the gang modes of invasion,
where life restraints may well descend below the level of the animals,
as predators develop with their arms and enforcement methods,
to impose on a weary population.

Secreting of supplies are not easy to maintain,
where rubbish growth must be hidden,
or would declare what is being eaten from a stockpile.

Secreting of supplies may be in need of counter weapons of protection,
from marauding bands,
may be in need of an ongoing source of water,
with the burial of excrement,
when the water services are no longer operational.

Secreting of supplies requires an alternative means of warming,
the cans of availability,
and the boiling of the water,
when the lights do fail,
and TV no longer carries the news of the day,
when a generator is unavailable with the fuel and cabling.

Secreting of supplies can take up a lot of space,
may need the sacrifice of at least one car,
with a tarpaulin for the covering of the stack within a garage,
or the stripping of the inside of a vehicle,
so storage space is at a maximum,
both around and in a vehicle.

Secreting of supplies must keep a hand on common sense,
of the feasible with the needful,
with the quantified and the cost,
with the storage of the liquids and the solids,
with consideration of the perishable and the tinned,
where frozen may well not be even one month's solution,
when in a power grid transmission failure.

Secreting of supplies cannot be gathered when the need is known and active,
is best served wherein denial is still current,
and future need does not transmit concern,
for either supply or pricing.

Secreting of supplies may have practical aspects,
of specific product options being shared around,
among the trustworthy.

Secreting of supplies cannot easily be made dependent on a season,
> for supply of the fresh in quantity,
> when the actual season remains an unknown,
> while the capability of supply is not secured,
> for price or quantity or an ability to deliver.

Secreting of supplies should not arouse suspicion,
> should not set up a raiding target,
>> for a later period or time,
> should not convey an underlying area of concern,
>> in general conversation.

Secreting of supplies should visit bulk shops and stores,
> to see what they have on offer,
> with the dried foods and their storage,
> with the accompanying means of containment.

Secreting of supplies seeks the useful and the edible,
> after an extended period of time,
> where preservation is the main consideration.

Secreting of supplies is not a silly notion best told to the birds,
> is both practical and serviceable,
>> as early settlers soon discovered,
> after sea voyages committed to new colony beginnings,
>> yet with survival needs neither planned nor met,
> as starvation raised its ugly head,
> as it severely limited survival with the first winter encountered.

Secreting of supplies should be a means unto an end:
> of ensuring the survival of a family,
>> in the end-time of Faith and Grace;
>> in the end-time tribulation of man:
>> within the presence of the plotting of Satan
>>> with both his failures and successes;
>> of God as He encourages His Bride to purity,
> as His Wrath clears the involved in The Freewill destinies of default:
>> the vanquishing of the sin fields long established;
> in the reality of the glory of the coming advent of The King of kings."

My Content Study Aid

_____

_____

_____

Squeezing of The Raindrops

And I hear Jesus saying,
"Squeezing of the raindrops increase the intensity of the falling,
             decrease the distance of their separation,
             reduce the area of their wetting.

Squeezing of the raindrops bring an increase in their size as they meld together,
             bring an increase in their weight so they fall much faster,
             bring an increase in the downpour for when the heavens open.

Squeezing of the raindrops fill all the escape routes in the gutters of the roofs,
             fill all the kerbside channels with run-off from the streets,
             fill all the underground capacity to take it to a river,
                  see the natural landscape have its natural water
                        stolen from the land,
                  which previously was a supporter of the streams,
                     with the channellings of ditches,
                   on the fence lines where the cattle grazed:
                  into a large loss of rainfall catchment area,
                  as the homes were built and roofed upon their sites,
                  within the newly built streets and living quarters.

Squeezing of the raindrops concentrate the water flow so erosion may occur,
             so ponding can result,
             so the flooding of the streets can prevent their use,
          can be deep enough to threaten the soaking of the walls and floors,
         of the premises subject to their low level of elevation,
         for where sandbags are sought urgently to combat further inundation,
                  of the lawns and driveways,
             where drainage cannot swallow at the velocity required,
                  for clearance of the water flow,
                  to where it is intended.

Squeezing of the raindrops overcome the lack of water,
             dwindling as it rises,
             on the rainfalls of the hills,
             and on the snow fields with their mountain tops,
             where catchments are in place.

Squeezing of the raindrops treat the fields and crops,
             treat the hay fields reserved for their yield of hay
                  for harvesting,
            for use within the winter or at the farmer's discretion.

Squeezing of the raindrops can increase the size of hail,
      can increase the crop damage for a farm dependant,
            when he is least expecting it;
    as an orchardist can see an afternoon hailstorm bury all his hopes,
        for an annual income,
        which now has to be very closely watched,
        to try to make it stretch from the bank,
        unto the pocket,
        with the ongoing needs of family.

Squeezing of the raindrops can see the brightness of a rainbow,
           where the sun does fall as well,
     as the promise is reflected,
     as the colour order is remembered,
     as the jingle of a child recalls and repeats,
     as the flashes and the thunder revisit the storms of centuries,
        with their rain belts where the light is split:
     as a full grown marvel in pointing to the promise in the sky.

Squeezing of the raindrops can turn them into clouds,
      can vaporize and heat,
      can hurl and send them skyward,
         to where they can re-condense and cool,
         to travel on their way.

Squeezing of the raindrops is not as if there is a squeezing of an orange or a lemon,
      but the squeezing of a cloud has a similar identity
         as the parent of the raindrops,
      can feel the initial squeezing of the raindrops
         as they are at home,
         within the confines of a cloud.

Squeezing of the raindrops can leave impressions to be gained,
      can record the impressions of the fall,
      can search and find within the dampness of The Earth,
        the single most constructive life force as involved,
         within the triggering of growth to everyone's advantage,
           with freedom from sustained neglect.

Squeezing of the raindrops can cause The Earth to toss and turn,
        The Earth to whirl and to submit,
        The Earth to circle and depose the masterminds
          with the cherry pickers,
      as seen standing by the side lines yet ready to withdraw,
          from the fields with the fledglings,
           still waiting for assistance,
            yet won't react to help.

Squeezing of the raindrops try not to frequent The Candles of The Lord,
     can catch and bring the heat with a sizzle to the grill,
       when approaching from the rear;
     can seek and turn the rain drops back into the steam,
     so to be taken up and mixed with the vapours,
     as witnessed and declared when first taken from the cloud.

Squeezing of the raindrops can leave stains upon the tools,
     can leave corrosion marks on hand,
     can leave the evidence of the cracking of the shells.

Squeezing of the raindrops can verify existence,
     can strengthen the arm which wields the sword of honour,
     can bring maturity of thought into the well of
       the morning light;
     can seek and find the outlook for analysis,
      the way forward in perception,
      the effort which rewards without encircling:
      the concepts which are the backbones of the truth,
      the conversion factors which are the carriers of Faith,
      the sustainers of the way forward without a relapse
       into a backward step,
     the majesty and forthrightness of God,
    when seen within the resting place of God,
    where meditation rules advancement into The Holy of Holies,
    and The Son streams the sunlight into the surroundings of each day,
    where Grace prevails and is accessible,
      to bring glory to the outcome into an enquiry as to truth,
      with an ongoing confirmation of belief,
       in the welfare of the outflow of The Love of God,
       in the homeland as preserved in readiness,
        for birthright claims and habitation,
      within the points of the compass on The Earth,
  and The Will of God as it yields a fresh security on the completeness of
       The Holy Land,
      as promised and restored,
      in all its fullness of its beauty and its preservation,
     as The Ways of God are finally made known,
       in completed declaration of the truth,
     as it leads into the destinations of finality and longevity,
   where God holds the keys to the maintenance of life upon The Earth,
     as understanding increases through the ongoing calls,
       of both man and of God."

Freeing of The Fuel Pumps

And I hear Jesus saying,
"Freeing of the fuel pumps is an event worth commemorating,
in the history of powered transportation.

Freeing of the fuel pumps has been a long time in coming,
has had many forms of prevention or of ineffectiveness,
has been head to head with the cartels with satanic influence,
in protection of excessive profitability,
under the guise of price control or of discounting a price,
which has already been recalculated,
on supposedly variable cartel costs,
which always ends in 99c to the amazement of no-one,
but the gullible,
who sometimes wonder aloud why this should be so;
as established to include potential discounts on the day,
and even higher surpluses on four days of the seven,
deemed by the cartels to be the days when discounts,
are said to be inactive and cannot then be claimed,
with a minimum purchase set,
so some vehicles must be very nearly empty to qualify,
which again controls the input of any discount,
where consistency applies,
where a true free market has no reality of a pure existence.

Freeing of the fuel pumps is not meddling with the market,
rather it is a fixing of corruption with cartels established and in place,
rather it is a supervision which they all fight to prevent,
rather it it is a correction of the price at which they should be selling,
when with comparison within the global market.

Freeing of the fuel pumps should see prices only changing in going up or down,
to meet the new costings arising,
from the quantities pumped for export by producers,
from any change in shipping costs attributable as valid,
within the cartels' access to their own tankers,
as sized and shaped,
to be used for delivery vessels for refining,
within a home bound market place,
where the local costs should be marked down,
in compliance with the findings of compatible delivery systems;

such as the picking up of the daily milk,
from within the individual dairy sheds,
as placed upon the farms,
or the delivery of fuel types beyond cartel control,
where costing may be competitive with the quoting for the business,
such as the supply of aviation fuel to the airports across the country,
or to other big consumers wherein the roads are sealed,
as they have first hand knowledge,
of the delivery costs incurred.

Freeing of the fuel pumps is a battle for supremacy,
between the ruthlessness of the cartels,
and the helplessness of the end-of-line consumer,
with a pocket or a purse still only clinking,
against the change to be saved,
until a small total can be financed,
as the minimum acceptable,
as discounts bite the dust,
to become irrelevant and inapplicable to the task at hand.

Freeing of the fuel pumps will neither cause them to beg nor frown,
have no real interest in where they are poked or seen,
have neither a motive of being just nor of pumping at a fair price,
into the tanks of minimums,
where top-ups give no substance to the offered discounts,
and hope they'll just go away,
or not come in the first place,
to be bothered by the queuing for the change.

Freeing of the fuel pumps witnesses extra containers being carried,
extra containers so a discount may be encountered,
extra containers so the volume will be proved to be sufficient,
before the pumps cut out to call them full,
as discounts walk away on a journey where selfishness prevails,
in confirming money is the objective,
however it is gained by the intrinsic greed in overcharging,
or by even more so in vanishing discounts already added on,
which will only add to the take if they can be disqualified,
because minimums are not reached,
because surplus gouging prices have no need to be legally reduced.

Freeing of the fuel pumps should stop the padding of the prices,
all the way down the chain of the linked ownerships,
of business entities:
from the crude within the well,
until it splashes on the inside of a vehicle's fuel tank;

where the taxes have been minimized in the country of delivery,
where there are already large credits to deduct,
from the eventual trading profit,
as declared and claimed by foreign tax payments,
which are unable to be checked or verified,
as they turn taxable profits into a carried credit for a loss,
where consumers are seen to pay with little or no understanding.

Freeing of the fuel pumps are still prisoners of the system,
are following instructions arising from automation,
can be subject to change when bonuses or records are at risk,
when participation in a national share-out of a prize take,
within the staff for the effort rendered,
may leave the faces blank in wondering,
of how it first accumulates,
and to where it finally goes,
as money to promotions of someone's unbidden fancy,
of that which was first stolen,
from the customers who searched,
and had to very carefully count,
in not realizing some was being stolen,
had no right to be forced to leave the safety of their keeping,
to roll across a counter of deceit,
to feed a hapless greed,
without any moral justification and a total lack of accountability.

Freeing of the fuel pumps is a target within the sight of God,
which will neither be long delayed nor overlooked,
as markets so collapse,
as alternatives are developed,
which will remove the cartels' concepts of charging,
as it now exists."

My Content Study Aid

_____

_____

_____

_____

_____

_____

_____

Stocking of The Shelves

And I hear Jesus saying,
"Stocking of the shelves is not an automated process,
   takes a lot of time and effort,
   when a shelf is emptying,
   or when there is a query on an empty one not yet replenished
        with its ticket.

Stocking of the shelves varies with a season,
   varies with the offtake,
   varies with the shelf space to be found for new products to be stocked.

Stocking of the shelves leaves a large surplus behind of a lot of cardboard cartons,
      of various shapes and sizes,
       with the finishes as preferred,
       by the makers of the contents,
     as just recognized with the passing of the use-by dates,
      which are unlikely ever to be read again,
    as they all end-up in a large recycling bin,
      where it does not matter if some get wet,
      from their stay in the rain upon the pavement.

Stocking of the shelves goes on even when the supermarket is full of customers,
    where some trollies need to be reversed or moved over to one side,
    where some trollies are not controlled within the borders of
       a left-driving country,
       or of left-walking on a footpath,
   or even in the consistency of the aisles within the supermarkets.

Stocking of the shelves is fast and fastidious,
    as they enter from the large storehouse out the back,
    as the produce is running short in specific items,
      which now are required to be replenished,
      from the frozen and the cold,
      from the plastic wrap as fitted for the searchers,
       seeking the various presented quarries,
       which may think they are hiding behind,
       the frontage of glass counters:
       behind which appears the sliced and diced,
       to be served up as valued contributors,
       to salads or to dips,
    or to the sliced meat components,
    of the lamb or beef or pork,
    with the stuffed and cooked chickens,
    with the whole and half pork hams and the flavoured sausages,
    which have all sacrificed much,

for the prime spot of displaying,
the delicatessen delicacies,
before those who stop to hunt:
that which is chilled or cold or warm or hot,
but serve their missions well,
in establishing their flavours,
and their scents with the pickles,
and the desires of colour and of taste,
wherein they are sorted and waiting to be served,
up to someone who can imagine what the taste buds will encounter,
when they are called to account.

Stocking of the shelves concentrate on all aspects of living,
with the family of varied tastes and wants,
as decided by the age,
of the one for whom they are intended;
of pet food for the birds and dogs and cats,
with specials on demand and litter as required.

Stocking of the shelves is a little difficult,
when the fruit and vegetables,
want to high-tail it across the floor,
to follow the example of just a single orange,
who was dropped and decided to make a run for it,
to then collide with others in another loaded tray,
who obviously also thought it was a very good idea,
as they followed along behind,
without any other thoughts,
in encouragement for the others:
for all the customers to be stooping to the floor,
in catching what they could,
and in leaving all the others what they could not catch,
but watched,
as they rolled away without a sense of stopping,
or even slowing down;
to start hiding where they should not be.

Stocking of the shelves is a very repetitive task,
is a somewhat thankless task,
can continue throughout the night with a change in shift.

Stocking of the shelves has a challenge,
in the opening of the cartons on a trolly,
one at a time starting from the top and working down,
with another trolley in which to place the emptied cartons,
as they come to hand to be quickly flattened,
at their folds for compression.

Stocking of the shelves is an ongoing job,
 does not have stepping stones to conquer and progress,
  only has the night owl to overcome and not to tire,
  only has to stand in support of a second job,
   which is found to be needed and worthwhile,
  only has to follow directions for the layout,
   of both the storehouse and the supermarket,
 so the simple does not become the complex,
 and the layout is not unexpectedly changed,
  by a meddler or an ignorant,
  who know not what they're doing,
   as they fill the freezers and the chillers,
   with whatever takes their fancy,
   as they do not understand instructions,
   for the maintaining of the system,
 with the various categories,
  as set within the rows,
  except for the premium sales points open to selection,
   at both ends of the rows.

Stocking of the shelves has long hours involved,
 has long hours of keeping things together,
 has long hours of opening cartons,
  of placing the contents correctly for selection
   by consumers,
  of being steady and assured,
 in not dropping denting or shattering the items,
 when they happen to slip when being placed,
   on a high-reach shelf,
 or had some which were knocked over on the shelves,
   throughout a night of tiredness.

Stocking of the shelves may require selecting and the assembling of pre-orders,
 with each item with its costing and its weight if necessary,
  and of being error free,
  in the gathering from the shelves,
  without undue delay,
 from the orders compiled in readiness for delivery,
  to the doors of customers,
  within the cycle of completion,
  and on the frontier of self-help,
  well-stocked in emphasis of choice."

Dealing With The Loss

And I hear Jesus saying,
"Dealing with the loss is sometimes very difficult,
               sometimes does not make much sense,
               sometime leaves a mess behind,
               sometimes takes a long time to clean up.

Dealing with the loss can require additional help,
          can use an extra pair of hands,
          can build upon the status as retained,
          can insert what is missing and in need of an adjustment.

Dealing with the loss can run around in circles,
          can be slow to perceive the needs,
          can be blind to what is evident to others,
          can be an area of concern to others with their hearts aligned and pumping.

Dealing with the loss can take weeks or months or years,
          can bring vibrations with the updates,
          can enlist the aid of the skilled and informed,
          can rotate the problem and inspect it from all sides,
          can exchange ideas in arriving at a settlement,
          can speed up the desired results by using the latest equipment in support.

Dealing with the loss is far from being a waste of time,
          is far from not affecting the future way of life,
          is far from not fulfilling the concepts and the effort,
                                 as invested in the past.

Dealing with the loss is not an immediate necessity,
          is not a cure-all for the feelings,
          is not a means of escape from familiar surroundings gone astray,
          is not a fix for the harassments of the mind and soul and body,
                                 arising from a lack of sleep.

Dealing with the loss can create a new day of achievement,
          a new day where the sun does shine,
          a new day where the contacts are helpful and understanding,
          with the shadows now moving into the past.

Dealing with the loss can move possessions back and forth,
          can move possessions from the sunlight to the shadows,
          can pack up the memories which are the basis,
                              of frustration and regret.

Dealing with the loss is a day by day progression,
          is a time scale for release,
          is the chewing on a cud which does not see the grass.

Dealing with the loss can feel the hugs and kisses,
        can stand and quietly weep,
        can sit and fall asleep.

Dealing with the loss can forget to give attention to the meals,
        leads to survival on the liquids and the snacks,
            on life within a tea or coffee shop,
          which does not activate what was lost,
          which no longer desires to be opened to review,
          which closes and assures the conquering of the nightly fears.

Dealing with the loss can clean an environment,
            in which the living can exist,
        can remove the ties to memories established in the past,
          where the tears still dwell within the eyes,
            with attempts to invade and move onto the cheeks.

Dealing with the loss can see some memories removed,
              from the walls of rooms and passageways,
        can see the familiar and the loved committed to a storage shelf,
              where it can stay,
          to not inflict the past upon the present or the future,
          to so fill them with regret for promises not kept,
          as opportunities were lost and cannot be recovered,
            while in an overseen arena filled with life.

Dealing with the loss can be a blow unto the soul,
        can be a stamp upon the spirit,
        can be a further loss of life of a body in rejection;
       all of which can be avoided when accepting of The Love of God,
          of The Sacrifice from Heaven,
          of the effort made to re-establish The Redemption of man,
          of The Commitment of The Father,
          of The Commitment of The Son,
          of The Commitment of The Holy Spirit—
          of The Three-in-one—
            all three fully committed to The Salvation of man.

Dealing with the loss also needs to deal with Satan,
          to keep all within the perspective of common sense,
            within the reality of mortality,
          to ensure Satan is deprived of his objective,
              in the detaching of a soul,
              for a change in ownership,
          to consider as to who is the best leader to follow:
          Satan with his cult of intensive evil and degradation of man,
              within the destiny of default—

to be spent in eternity in Hell;
or Jesus with His retinues of His committed followers,
in discipleship within the light of Glory—
and a destiny of choice with God within Eternity,
in the settings of His gardening and love.

Dealing with the loss has huge ramifications as to how or why or when,
for the future development of an individual,
in both the physical and the spiritual,
with the choices to be made or ignored,
with the appropriate results.

Dealing with the loss can be within a time frame of emergency,
can be with surroundings of serenity,
can be within the convulsions of sickness and illness of disease,
or the glow of health with lack of pain and difficulties,
as the light does shine the way into a superlative way of life,
where the freedom of Freewill rewards the actions,
as acquired unto commitment due for honouring;
rather than the emulsion of The Freewill mixes,
with the demanding of respect.

Dealing with the loss needs to achieve finality within the plains of existence,
within the foresight of movement in the here and now,
and also in the here and hereafter:
as the sharks of man are consumed by the sharks of man,
or as the dolphins of man play and rejoice within the dolphins of man,
with complete and utter immunity from the restricted sharks of man."

My Content Study Aid

_____
_____
_____
_____
_____
_____
_____
_____
_____
_____
_____

Purchasing Power Eroded

And I hear Jesus saying,
"Purchasing power eroded is government theft in action,
        is the shaming of a nation,
        is a loss to the elderly,
        is the theft of the living standards from the nation at large,
          and those among the elderly who spend more,
          than the superannuation of entitlement if any,
        which is linked to maintaining equality of value,
        with the actual inflation rate for the year,
        with the degree to which it is higher or lower
                than the target inflation rate,
        which is an official government set level,
          for the reserve bank of government to establish,
          in bringing about a reduction in the annual cost of funding,
              its long term borrowed foreign debt.

Purchasing power eroded clashes with morality,
        clashes with the lack of trust to be placed upon a government,
        who has no right in law to steal and take,
        without a taxation law enacted,
      or an infringement within the law surrounding the revenue dept,
          which would empower them to deduct,
           from the savings of the people.

Purchasing power eroded is a servant of the time period,
        is a slave to a twelve month period coming under scrutiny,
        is the victim of analysis where millions are at stake with little
              in reserve.

Purchasing power eroded sees the cheaper cups and mugs exhibited in shops,
          with a Made in XYZ imprint on the bottom,
             by way of declaration,
          sees the cheapest of everything with a history,
      of being birthed within the technology of a would be giant,
      sees the implications for a nation of being bound to a wayward giant,
      with apparently unfriendly aspirations in the surrounding seas.

Purchasing power eroded puts an added glint upon the cheapest,
        says goodbye to those with quality and design,
           which can no longer be afforded,
         from within the historical manufacturers.

Purchasing power eroded signifies a switch to numbers built on cheapness,
a switch to numbers built on simplicity of design,
a switch to numbers where the price no longer
controls or contributes,
to the beauty of design at the potter's hands.

Purchasing power eroded indicates the passing of an era,
where beauty and craftsmanship were the forerunners,
in the guarding of collections,
where prices were irrelevant if settings scened:
the perfection of technique.

Purchasing power eroded sings a sad song of the ending,
of a dance of joy and happiness,
now replaced in solitude by the hop the step the jump,
as flattened by the spreadeagled landing in the sand.

Purchasing power eroded is all about the numerics of supply,
is all about the numbers to lay before consumers,
of very little taste but where specific packaging,
may be sufficient to entice,
so to swing the day.

Purchasing power eroded has an effect on shopping,
shares and shows on increasing prices,
where the cafes and the supermarkets ring the changes,
by the day on sandwiches cakes pies and drinks,
without regret or embarrassment,
for what people are asked to pay.

Purchasing power eroded must have an end result,
most probably in witnessing the scarcity,
behind a huge explosion,
where the gradual and the incremental,
burst into a surge of happening,
which rockets from control,
which surprises all and sundry,
as prices start to double by the month,
as they pick up all the tricks from those in South America,
who have learnt by the hard way of rising prices,
mixed with shortages.

Purchasing power eroded gets to win no sympathies,
gets to stay isolated and impoverished,
as the food disappears from the shelves,
while the queues are forced to wait.

Purchasing power eroded once saw wheelbarrows transporting money,
for a single loaf of bread,
could see bank notes being overprinted,
as the notes were further monetized,
could see economies fail and fall to pieces;
as The Left would tax and take from those who have struggled,
to make ends meet,
to see it given to 'the idle' and 'the deserving',
because they have not worked,
for as the rogues abound so shall the funds be used,
as the unworthy politicians keep dipping,
into the cash funds until there are none left,
as hunger breaks the threads to the protection of any food,
seen to be stacked in sheds or warehouses,
or seen to be hidden under lock and key.

Purchasing power eroded can move the field of purchasing,
from clay unto the plastic,
from moulding unto stamping,
from being retained in usage,
to a short life as a plastic,
without significant weight or ongoing interest.

Purchasing power eroded sees plastic keeping purchasing power retained,
as the one and two dollar shops sees cheapness attractive,
to the parents and the youngsters,
when scribbling in a book with plastic or wax crayons,
with coloured ball point pens,
where items are designed to appeal to the parents of the young,
for amusement purposes which should ring the safety bells,
when rolling on the floor in play.

Purchasing power eroded requires a welcomed change in governance,
where justice should prevail on scenes of mockery and usurping,
in the deprivation of fair and honest rewarding,
for the effort,
in assembling the wares for the purchasing cycles,
within ongoing and personal dwellings,
where money holds its value,
is not to be discounted by the year,
after being subjected to governmental theft,
from those who are the most dependant,
as the savings are caused to diminish by the bankers,
who are no longer trustworthy nor truthful in supposed righteousness,
which now has no basis in the facts where inflation rules."

Prayerful on The Knees

And I hear Jesus saying,
"Prayerful on the knees is a desirable place to be found,
                is the opener of a wonderland of access,
                is the conversation pit where man and God decide to change the world.

Prayerful on the knees is the meeting place with perfection,
                is the meeting place for the fullness of all knowledge,
                is the meeting place where the fluency of tongues interact,
                        with wisdom for the benefit of man.

Prayerful on the knees is a signpost to the stars,
                is where the humble start to feed,
                is where significance comes to be transferred,
                is where majesty is welcomed,
                is where understanding ushers in the love fields of God.

Prayerful on the knees is where the heart of man discovers the heart of God,
                is where the proximity of angels can be felt,
                is where The Will of God is easily found in confirmation.

Prayerful on the knees has no better stance for man,
                has no better stance for knowledge to be transferred from the light,
                has no better stance to teach to the youngsters of the light,
                has no better stance to see within the families of God.

Prayerful on the knees has a supplicant being taught,
                has a disciple in tuition,
                has a language being practised,
                    from the gifting box of God.

Prayerful on the knees is the best place to learn and to acquire,
                    the blessings of man within the gifts of Pentecost,
                        where tuition is the key,
           as yearning supplies the answer,
           as practice does the polishing,
           as fluency in the tongues of heaven,
           opens all the doors which were previously closed and locked,
                    when practice was in progress,
                    while access was not granted.

Prayerful on the knees is not a play position for the puppies,
                is not a reaching to be noticed,
                is not a copycat aware of all which is going on,
                is neither the place nor the posture for silent meditation,
                  when approaching the spirituality of The Holy of Holies.

Prayerful on the knees is suitable within Communion,
>> is suitable when within A Prayer Field,
>> is suitable when The Heavenly is interacting with The Earthly.

Prayerful on the knees is One on One with God,
>> is not a posture to be taken lightly,
>> is not subjected to a time limit imposed.

Prayerful on the knees can ask for the covering of God,
>> for the healing of the tired yet still a non-forsaker,
>> for a two way conversation within the environments:
>>> of Righteousness of Trust and of Truth with Faith.

Prayerful on the knees can bring down a house of cards,
>> can change the weather map of a locality,
>> can lead to the staircase of advancement,
>> can introduce familiarity with the gifts to kings and queens,
>>> as well as to princes and to princesses,
>> both on the run and learning the complexity of their callings,
>>> before The Throne of Grace.

Prayerful on the knees is the prayer grounds for release,
>> is the prayer posture of a humble spirit which seeks the ear of God,
>> is the posture appropriate for the honouring of God.

Prayerful on the knees sees the angels gathering round,
>> sees messages being recorded,
>> sees accuracy superseding speed.

Prayerful on the knees uplifts and beholds,
>> speaks and listens,
>> receives with understanding the content as embedded,
>>> in the wisdom shared by God.

Prayerful on the knees opens the door to the counselling of God,
>> opens the door to a possible rebuke,
>> opens the door to ongoing praise and worship,
>> opens the door to where sickness is eschewed,
>>> from within the sphere of health,
>>> with well-being to the fore.

Prayerful on the knees is not a chattering situation,
>> is not for the nonsense of a child,
>> is not for tears sent seeking sympathy,
>> is not for irrelevant explanations,
>> is not for anything other than the Faith-filled Truth.

Prayerful on the knees is as if within a confessional box with God,
        where Grace may be part of the agenda for recovery,
        where forgiveness is placed on the timeline set for expiry,
        without any further delays from self-pity or accusations.

Prayerful on the knees should arise and shine,
        should hug and welcome,
        should smile and recognize,
        should expand and greet.

Prayerful on the knees should not be in an up and down mode,
        should be static until the subject matter is made known,
                and dealt with,
        to the satisfaction of both man in repentance,
          and of God who brings Grace unto the table,
        with counselling as needed for growth to be re-established,
            in an ongoing life.

Prayerful on the knees does not beg the question,
        does not grovel in the dust,
        asks with simplicity of expression in sincerity with ongoing Faith.

Prayerful on the knees may be searching for the words,
        should not be spoken to in case of damaging the thought patterning,
        as brought before The God of Love and Redemption,
        for the injured and all so seeking help.

Prayerful on the knees should arise with a smile,
        should know matters are under due consideration,
        should know the outcome will comply with The Morality of God.

Prayerful on the knees does not need to be repetitive when circumscribed by the trivial,
        can attend to and overcome the worries of the past,
        and the mistakes of the present,
        with the outlook for the future,
        within the presence of The Living Loving God:
        of both man and all of His creation."

My Content Study Aid

_____

_____

_____

_____

_____

Being Lost and Found

And I hear Jesus saying,
"Being lost and found sets a seal upon an adventure of survival,
            sets muscles back to work,
            sets clothing deposited in the laundry basket.

Being lost and found sounds like: a stray within a 'mapless' city,
                 a walk beyond the 'signposting' of the bush,
                 a floating in a 'drifting' boat,
                 a 'drive' into the wilderness where a battery failed.

Being lost and found discovered it is easier to become lost rather than to be found,
           it is easier to become hungry rather than to find a meal,
           it is easier to become cold rather than to stay warm,
           it is easier to become signal-less rather than to pick up
                                       a sound.

Being lost and found has a desert island semblance,
           when one is neither lost nor found,
           but somewhere in between.

Being lost and found does not require a compass in the first part,
           does require a team in the second part.

Being lost and found can arise because of initial stupidity,
           can be finalised by death,
                 or even more stupidity:
                 with a complete and utter lack of knowledge,
                       as to the best foot forward,
                       or of how to promote a rescue,
                       before the warmth does fade way.

Being lost and found depends upon the circumstances of the lost,
           and the forward expectations of where the found will be.

Being lost and found is not happy through and through,
           is not happy in the difficulties,
           is not happy in the finding of the routes or where the huts have
                                       been put,
           is not happy in the walking of a city as it is getting dark,
           is not happy when at sea and the motor will not start,
           is not happy with the kindling when there are no matches,
           is not happy with a car when the battery is exhausted,
                       with not another one in sight.

Being lost and found whistles up the wind,
           erects an umbrella,

puts on a jacket without a hat,
dons a seat belt or a vest.

Being lost and found is not a concept for a battery revival,
is not the simplicity expected for a city,
is not the trailing through the bush,
is not the watching of the shoreline recede into the distance.

Being lost and found is at home within the qualified,
is at home within the links where the greens stick out from the bush,
is at home for when the postman calls then carries on to
the next address,
is at home when the sea saws up and down with an onshore wind,
is at home with a blanket or two in the back seat of a car.

Being lost and found can extend over about a week,
before it is called off within a residential area,
can search with the sniffers in the bush of silence to the calls,
with the overflights looking for a stationary vehicle on a roadside
or a lay-by,
with the checking of the hut shelters,
with the storm warnings all at sea in a bouncing boat.

Being lost and found waits another day for the sun to rise.

Being lost and found can be complex when intent remains unknown,
when direction is debatable,
where roads are lengthy and uncertain,
where a boat is unlikely to be washed up with a life still preserved.

Being lost and found calls but is not answered,
shouts but is not heard,
fires a shot with just an echo,
sends up a flare which receives no answer in the mist.

Being lost and found witnesses the cold quietly creeping up a street,
sees the dangers of hypothermia appearing for consideration,
as the wind does gather strength,
sees a parked car starting up and turning round,
sees the winking of a light at sea which proves to be a false alarm.

Being lost and found hears a knock upon a door within a street,
in asking for directions to a place for the night;
sees a weak and flickering light from something parked within,
a lay-by in the countryside with its coming gloom;
sees a down-hill striding is possible with meadows in the distance;
can spot the lights along the shoreline,
where hope is more than evident.

Being lost and found has people worried and still searching,
    has people in tears and frightened of results,
    has queries unable to be answered from available information,
    has the waves in background as they splash and surge.

Being lost and found waits another day for the sun to rise.

Being lost and found is depending on being found,
    is depending on someone reporting in successfully,
    is depending on the covering of the search areas,
        according to the motivation with the means as used.

Being lost and found puts search parties lives at risk,
    made worse by a lack of information,
    as to from where and when they are expected to return.

Being lost and found takes time to become organized,
    to set up the search patterns,
    to lay down perimeters,
    to arrange the searching numbers with their capabilities,
        and closeness to the scenes.

Being lost and found expects results sooner rather than later,
    where experience rubs off onto the selection of direction,
        and eventual destinies,
    where shelter may be targeted and found.

Being lost and found saw the shoreline lights becoming closer on a sandy beach,
        until the boat touched bottom,
    and someone slowly climbed from the boat,
    to then proceed up the beach to a lighted house,
        where a telephone was quickly rung;
    the batteried car was likely discovered by a mail man,
    on his twice weekly run who gave a lift into a township,
        where a garage would have been the first port of call;
    the meadows were soon reached,
        and followed to a homestead in low lying hills,
        where a welcome was right at the door,
        and another telephone was rung;
    the one walking in a city finally caught a taxi with a radio,
    to be taken many miles to where the scenery again
        became familiar,
    as a family prepared a homecoming for the lost now found,
    to greet and to celebrate with the news they had received,
    as they eagerly awaited the missing one returned."

Stopcocks Without Water

And I hear Jesus saying,
"Stopcocks without water are specific in their use to anyone moving,
>>> beyond the realm of water,
>> are specific in their use for organic liquids in control,
>> are specific in their use for maintaining flow rates
>>> proportional to demand.

Stopcocks without water may speak of new installations,
>> may speak of hazards still not cleared,
>> may speak of buildings still not fireproofed.

Stopcocks without water are not fulfilling an objective,
>> of controlling water on the move,
>> of ensuring the availability of both need and usage,
>> in the pipes through which it travels both slowly or at speed.

Stopcocks without water may be servicing oil or gas,
>> whether natural or petroleum refined,
>> where the viscosities do vary with the tankers involved:
>> from petrol grades to aviation fuels to diesel and to heavy
>>> fuel oils,
>> for the servicing of general vehicle transportation,
>> in the air on the ground and on and in the seas and oceans,
>>> with the bunkering of ships with the underwater,
>>> and the fuelling of the aircraft of the skies.

Stopcocks without water control the spraying of the heated bitumen,
>>> for the sealing of the roads.

Stopcocks without water are the valves on the lifelines,
>> of industry around the world—
>> of steam as venting to the sky,
>>> or as venting from The Earth;
> for the usage as determined by the association with the generators,
> running both day and night with the ongoing demands of industry,
>> and the servicing of cities with the harbours,
>> and the agricultural countrysides of farmlands at large,
>> and bringing food to where the hungry are awaiting,
>>> for the gathered and the grown,
>>> the mixed and the baked,
>>> the bottled and the pouched,
>>> the raw and the cooked:
>> as they use the relevancy of the stopcocks,
>>> for the flow rates as needed,
>> and hence determined for their jobs at hand.

Stopcocks without water service milk in all its guises,
until ending on the packing floor as a powder derivative,
in a shipping bag.

Stopcocks without water brings milk into the tanker,
serves it well into a factory,
keeps it in a tank awaiting processing,
for later distribution with the starts and stops,
when creating the ones for the retail outlets,
with domestic purchasing and use.

Stopcocks without water service the widespread needs of man,
as it measures and decrees the portions for delivery,
from a tanker on the road with its hose,
which makes it possible and clean.

Stopcocks without water should not discharge into a stream or river,
should not discharge into a paddock or a field,
should not treat as waste what someone has preserved to keep,
while someone else has spoilt and labelled waste,
best suited to disposal by the transportation,
which is under way.

Stopcocks without water do not want to handle,
the produce from an on-farm cooling dairy vat,
which is out of order,
which is non-compliant with the standards as required;
to curdle the unnecessary,
to be concerned with the whey.

Stopcocks without water still need water for the rinsing,
and the draining of the milk tankers,
as well as for the clean-down spraying,
from a pressured hose into a drain of supervision,
so it is not released into a waterway for contamination,
with either a working-strike excuse,
or a breakdown in the internal processing equipment.

Stopcocks without water do not often fail,
are consistent in what they are asked to do,
with a satisfactory result.

Stopcocks without water with refinery deliveries from a shipping drop-point,
in a regional tank farm installation,
test their daily commitments to service,
often are committed to long hours and distances,
where mixed weather in all its wintry turns,
can well affect completion of their tasks and schedules.

Stopcocks without water are not the subjects of debate,
> are not items of concern,
> within the lines and pipes,
> or at the end of hoses.

Stopcocks without water do not often bring embarrassment,
> are not often on the schedule for replacement,
> are not often the cause of maintenance,
>> upon a tanker and its loads.

Stopcocks without water should neither be fiddled with,
> nor played with,
> when there is no indication of a fault in the turning off or on,
> when there is nothing dripping onto or marking,
>> the environment in which the tanker operates.

Stopcocks without water rarely have alarms coupled to assess their ins and outs,
> rarely have alarms with any significant indicators
>> of effectiveness,
> of operation beyond perhaps just a flashing light,
> where smell is probably more immediately effective,
> in indicating an ignition source requiring serious,
>> and urgent attention when safety is imperilled.

Stopcocks without water can selectively spray upon the road,
>> even with water for dust and compaction control,
>>> on a hot or sunny day.

Stopcocks without water are the unbidden slaves of industry,
> are the sharers and the dividers,
> are the deliverers and the restrictors,
> are the supplicants and the masters in the encouraging,
>> of the payment of the outstanding bills.

Stopcocks without water are the enforcers without friends,
> when times are tough and cash flow is diverted,
> from that considered past due and waiting for a payment:
>> to start the stopcocks flowing again,
>> with embarrassment avoided."

My Content Study Aid

_____

_____

_____

_____

Heating With Alternatives

And I hear Jesus saying,
"Heating with alternatives all require a heat source,
                            even if a pet which is taken into bed.

Heating with alternatives are not easily divided into options for consideration,
                            often are left hanging in the balance,
                            often are costed and left upon a kitchen bench,
                            often are ignored and rated against a candle.

Heating with alternatives is dependent on the season,
                            is dependent on the quantity and the type of heat involved,
                            is dependent on the watchers and the waiters,
                            of those who seek the heat and desire to have a say.

Heating with alternatives can use a hot ring or an electric jug,
                            can wait for an oven to reach its settings,
                            or share the rest in lying back within a micro wave,
                            as it heats and waves a stick,
                            after sending its target to going round in circles.

Heating with alternatives can be as simple,
                            as a couple of iron gas burners,
                            with hose links couplings into:
                            the top of a mobile gas canister.

Heating with alternatives should be based upon simplicity,
                            upon size and shape and weight,
                            with the time to cool down after use,
                            and with a wind shield,
                            if the flames are sensitive to draft.

Heating with alternatives requires safety first and last,
                            requires fuels to be safe in storage and replenishment,
                            requires usage to be simple and obvious,
                            with the pots easy to remove or to inspect,
                            while stability is not at risk,
                            while manipulating hot or boiling utensils with the food.

Heating with alternatives does not want steam with condensation,
                            does not want spluttering with oils,
                            does not want carelessness in handling,
                            does not want to see first aid kits in use.

Heating with alternatives must keep track of which is hot or cold,
                            must separate the potentially dangerous,
                                        from that considered safe,

must be disconnected safely when usage is completed,
and all is washed up in readiness for the morrow,
as it brings another day.

Heating with alternatives does not put on non-punctured cans to simmer,
must first release the potential build up of internal pressure,
and neither forget nor overlook,
the progress of a meal.

Heating with alternatives should neither see nor hear pops or spurts,
from liquids misbehaving in sachets,
yet neither pierced nor made safe,
as temperatures go reaching for the boiling point,
as steam can puff and pressurize a bag,
to scald the skin without any warning to beware.

Heating with alternatives cannot afford to rush,
need to handle a power outage with great care,
with switches in the circuitry in the off position,
with the realization that the only source of lights,
other than the candles with their matches,
or a torch which cannot be recharged,
or a portable emergency radio with its battery:
together with a winding handle on a built-in generator,
to recharge the battery,
are those within the headlights of the vehicles,
wherever they are parked.

Heating with alternatives may require an emergency 240 volt generator,
to stretch out the time the food is frozen,
or to access a washing machine,
or a natural gas fire in a lounge with electrical ignition,
or a studied circuit board with the efficiency,
of LED lighting to the fore.

Heating with alternatives can expose choice to trials,
can bring satisfaction to the core idea,
can invert the need to carry on once success is established,
and satisfaction is achieved.

Heating with alternatives can have a solution sought,
for a household in the winter,
who is living as if within a refrigerator,
who know in the summer a string of sleepless nights,
and tiring days as bound within the summer heat,
where coolness is forgotten,
not to be easily attained.

Heating with alternatives requires very careful thought,
          can have a lot of blame placed at the feet of house builders,
          who know not how to build a home fit for year round habitation,
          who know not how to control the temperatures,
                in that which they have laid before man,
                and stated it as fit for use.

Heating with alternatives opens the trapdoor of the ceiling,
          uses cavities within the roof,
          for importing air for correction,
          which does not first have to struggle,
              in overcoming the potency of a tin roof,
              in the sunlight and fully exposed to the heat of day.

Heating with alternatives should seriously investigate,
          the clay tiling of the roofs,
          long since used in the past,
          before the chase after money became the craze,
              of changing to the cheapest,
          with ineffective insulation so comfort is assured,
          without the big heat transferences,
              downwards in the summer,
              and upwards in the winter from roofs,
        all the same dark colour on their upside surface,
        which carried no recognition,
        of the radiation attributes from a coloured surface,
            as it indicates a lack of care or concern,
            from the builders of monstrosities,
       where beauty has long been edited out,
       for the sake of speed and the cheapening of the end result,
      where the cities are dark and foreboding,
     and where joy and light and colour are the first to be banished,
           from the scene followed by dissatisfaction,
     with the loss of happiness as the heat and cold felt suffering,
       in living with what really is just a dark grey tin hut,
          without a heating or a cooling equilibrium,
          as occurs in the cheapest of materials,
      with no variations in the colour schemes
      or the external coverings,
     where future maintenance is just postponed until a later date:
     while attractiveness is no longer relevant or desired,
          as a signpost of a caring builder."

Demand For Lighting

And I hear Jesus saying,
"Demand for lighting is not an easy one to grant,
   requires a lot of technology to put it on a switch,
   require a lot of knowledge to maintain it in a state,
       of being operational and safe.

Demand for lighting can be disclosed as a kerosene lamp with a wick;
   can be an incandescent kerosene lamp burning vapours,
        within a shroud;
   can be a battery within a torch;
   can be a battery within a car;
   can be a battery with a hand-winding mechanism,
    for charging within the use of a battery,
    or a radio for inward contact in an emergency perceived,
      where public outages have left,
      all inbound receivers off the air.

Demand for lighting can be very high,
    but unable to be satisfied,
   can be very insistent,
    but too late to be eased.

Demand for lighting cannot bring a current impossibility,
   into the presence of existence,
   without a time spent on first finding the fault,
     and then repairing it as needed.

Demand for lighting can be both advancing,
    with the onset of the night,
    and retreating with the onset of the day.

Demand for lighting does not vilify the workers,
   does not speed up the time until a restoration.

Demand for lighting can be quite excessive,
    when a whole city goes down,
     and there is no magic switch for reconnection,
      at the bottom of the heap.

Demand for lighting can call out,
    to the trapped in darkness,
    in lifts between the floors of the high-rise buildings,
     may have an early rescue:
      if a hospital is fitted with cut-in generators,
      to carry the sustainability of a new load,
       in a chain of circumstances,
       from which the loading does arise.

Demand for lighting can be after,
    a complete and utter black-out,
      from where working pieces can be and are retrieved.

Demand for lighting can open the gates to criminals,
    can start them on their sprees,
    can expose the electrical failures,
      with the repositories of the physical.

Demand for lighting can see movement to where lighting still occurs,
    can see lighting with a flicker,
      where candles have been lit,
      where generators have been started,
      where some are remaining unaffected,
       as the street lights circuitry remains in operation.

Demand for lighting does not quench the thirst,
      as others open up or close up,
       according to their partitioning of the day,
      as shops and offices and factories,
       can have their lights running from many hours,
        to all day at a time.

Demand for lighting tries to meet the needs of industry,
    to meet the needs of commerce,
    to meet the needs of governance,
    to meet the needs of residential,
    to meet the needs of tourism and accommodation.

Demand for lighting does not screen out the haphazard and the unkempt,
      the graffitied and disfigured,
      the stupid and the foolish,
       as they circumvent or ignore the law,
        they choose to flout.

Demand for lighting focuses strongly on the maintaining of a service;
    focuses strongly on a beach night with a lantern,
      of fishing with a rod and reel as the tide advances;
    focuses strongly on a party long since planned with invitations,
      as an urgent search for lighting,
      leaves much to be desired,
      with the music flattened and remaining unplayable.

Demand for lighting does not serve the mathematics,
    of chance with win or lose,
    where lose is clearly seen as the biased numbers of the night.

Demand for lighting is not signed up for insurance against a power failure,
        is not seen as worth the effort,
        is left out in the wilderness where the cut and thrust plays out,
            where such possibilities are not considered likely to occur,
            where faces are upset,
                as the party gets harder and harder to get started,
                without the lights or sounds of a party seen in progress.

Demand for lighting makes it difficult for fancy dress,
        makes it difficult for a 21st,
        makes it difficult for a wedding feast,
        makes it difficult to organise a dance,
        makes it difficult to celebrate a birthday of the years,
            or an anniversary where meaning has been mostly lost,
            and somewhat irrelevant to folk sitting around,
                    with memories galore,
            when conversation is at a premium either to encounter,
            or to start in earnest with laughter and happiness,
                    intermixed with joy.

Demand for lighting has not seen searchlights in the sky,
                looking for lost balloons with baskets,
                has not seen any balloons with baskets,
                has not seen any balloons at all.

Demand for lighting cannot recall the last time this occurred,
        which may not have been,
            so all encompassing for the day involved,
        which may not have needed,
            such heights of access,
            as had been expected to be available,
        which may not have been seeking,
            the compliance of the media with reporting capabilities.

Demand for lighting was needed for a film set,
        was left with the gloom and stumbles,
            did not hear the voices carrying very far,
            or the tap dancing of the shoes.

Demand for lighting would seem to need reserving,
        would seem to need renewing,
        would seem to need recalling,
                for that which has proved to be:
                the missing and defunct,
                from one right out of the book."

Docking of The Ships

And I hear Jesus saying,
"Docking of the ships requires much skill and experience,
        requires positioning with care and full attention to the task at hand,
            with the pilot in command.

Docking of the ships signifies the end of journey,
        signifies an approaching time of rest,
        signifies a completion of the task at hand.

Docking of the ships bequeaths instructions carried out,
        bequeaths an impact on the future,
        bequeaths gratitude for what was enabled to be done.

Docking of the ships highlights the thoughts and the commitments,
        the successful needs and the ignored wants,
        the timeframe of activity with the ploughing of the waves.

Docking of the ships turns a page of history as a record of the past,
        turns the desires of the hearts into reality of existence,
        turns the ignorant and the indifferent into the longing and the caring.

Docking of the ships tie up with righteousness and truth shining from their bows,
        tie up with faith and grace still impacting on the waves which followed,
        tie up with peace and satisfaction seeping from their pores:
            into the hearts of peace,
        with the knowledge of improvements now standing tall and free.

Docking of the ships did not see the waves following them back home,
        saw them breaking off to go and feed the world,
            with knowledge and with wisdom,
            arising from the effort of The Master,
            seen ending in success.

Docking of the ships carry home more than that with which they departed,
            when they left to go and search,
        more than they could imagine in the forecastles of companionship,
        more that was laid at the feet of the authorised and chartered,
            than could be carried in the arms.

Docking of the ships left the shores as world changers packed with novices,
        returned to them as world beaters loaded high with overcomers.

Docking of the ships saw the ways of man and the ways of woman,
            as encountered at the end-point of the journeys,
            to the very distant shores.

Docking of the ships bring adventures home for retelling to the kinfolk,
  bring knowledge retrieved from what they saw and touched,
  bring wisdom home from what they heard and felt.

Docking of the ships saw theft decrease,
      as influence was spread upon the waterfronts,
  saw violence decline,
      as belief structures were modified,
  saw lies becoming obsolete,
      as truth nurtured new beginnings.

Docking of the ships witnessed abroad the purging flames of heaven,
      the falling of grace upon the needy,
      the reverberations arising from the truth,
          as it spread faster than the lies.

Docking of the ships left earthquakes behind them at their ports of call,
          arrived without the fanfares,
      departed with crowded jetties inundated with the saved and contrite,
          and seeking a return.

Docking of the ships sees the indigent across the seas,
      now standing strong and knowledgable,
      now gathering and discussing,
      now enjoying and abandoning,
    the idolatry of the past as birthed within a then lack of faith,
          and at the will of man.

Docking of the ships carried the colours of The King,
      carried the end result of faith within millennia,
      carried the strength of commitment,
      carried that which could not be overcome by evil power,
          or influence born of force.

Docking of the ships was a cry day for the valiant,
      as they hugged and kissed,
      as they left what was their temporary home,
    now homeward bound with families clustering around,
    eager to hear the news and all that was encountered,
    on the ways that were opened up to be taught,
          within The Will of God.

Docking of the ships hears the trumpet call to all who made it possible,
      within the enclave of the committed,
          as it sailed away;
      now hear the call of parentage with the siblings
          and the grandparents,
    as they stand upon the docks a second time,
      in the welcoming of a well-earned return.

Docking of the ships is a moment filled with wonder,
where no eyes are dry,
where all faces carry a watery smile,
with hankies to the fore.

Docking of the ships bring love and friendship home from across the seas.

Docking of the ships sees gravitation to the groups,
as they disembark to much excitement,
in fulfilment of a much awaited day.

Docking of the ships hears the cameras getting ready to record,
sees those pausing on request,
sees new friends being welcomed into the family groups,
as the shutters click,
to access and keep safe The Miracles of God.

Docking of the ships puts luggage in the sheds,
carries mementos of remembrance,
to share in the stories soon to be forthcoming,
as excitement builds in readiness for the sharing,
of such that God achieved and was seen to do.

Docking of the ships are looked back at with the lingering smiles of familiarity,
with fun times now within the memory boxes,
are looked back at with the memories,
of where they all went to speak and share,
of future outcomes arising from the days at sea,
yet unimaginable at present as happenings to be recounted,
for assimilation into the storybooks of history,
of love exposed to all and sundry who did stop to listen,
to understand the message,
as brought to become an enlightenment to families:
which will change the lifestyles,
arising from acceptance."

My Content Study Aid

_____

_____

_____

_____

_____

_____

Living Under Duress

And I hear Jesus saying,
"Living under duress holds over half the world in its thrall.

Living under duress hides the shadings of the shadows,
        hides the nerve endings of the sensitive and prolonged,
            of the bewhiskered and the bald,
            of the covered and enforced,
        of the secretive and hidden from the sunlight of the day,
          where reactions are extreme and seen to be inhuman,
       in comparison with the environmental restrictions imposed,
              upon the birthright freedoms,
           as stemming from the inheritance of man.

Living under duress is imposed without remorse,
      is concluded by rebellion in the streets,
        where death and mayhem often are introduced,
         by those in power and wanting to stay with that they did not earn,
           but captured from the gullible and the believing,
          of a better way which has not yet come to bear,
      without acquiring the means to depose impressed authority,
            from the chains of command and violence,
             together with the necessities of life.

Living under duress sees rockets in the sky,
      sees the rocketing of buildings occupied by families,
      sees guns blazing and pointing at civilians,
      sees death hovering just around a corner,
            of the unknown but waiting.

Living under duress puts lives at risk,
    makes it difficult to obtain sufficient food for the young and the dependant,
          ensures opposition cannot bring a change,
            to the treatment of the people,
            and their surrounding situations,
        where gunfire can be incessant,
        where only the unwise dare to stray outside.

Living under duress can be a life of tunnels and of tunnelling,
      can be a life of counting heads to see which ones are missing,
      can be a life of begging for a little bit of sustenance,
               to help see out the day,
              or to help a child to sleep.

Living under duress sees relief columns,
                              consistently captured by an unfriendly power,
                                        whereupon it is sold,
                                 or taken to the highest bidder,
                                    or eaten by their own,
                        which prevents the hungry and the undernourished,
                                from receiving any form of life support.

Living under duress can be one of continual noise,
                        can be one where lighting does not exist,
                                        and darkness is intense,
                        can be one where thirst is not addressed,
                              where sips are scarcely managed,
                                        by weakened forms of supply.

Living under duress can have enforcers at every corner,
                                        where such live in an environment,
                                 of where there are neither shortages of food,
                                        nor of how it is acquired.

Living under duress smothers out the caring and the kind,
                              smothers out the rescuers and the helpers,
                              smothers out positions of safety and security,
                              smothers out the shops and stores.

Living under duress makes it difficult to escape,
                              leaves all the numbers ticked and cross-indexed,
                              leaves the details known and filled in,
                              leaves references alive and followed up in detail of suspicion.

Living under duress links suspicion to a trial,
                              links a trial unto conviction,
                              links conviction into imprisonment without a time set for release.

Living under duress knows of few occasions,
                                 where suspicion links to a verdict of innocence and release;
                                 probably had distant relatives who well knew the ropes,
                                        and pulled the right strings.

Living under duress sees children clambering on tanks,
                              sees children carrying guns,
                                        they can scarcely lift or aim,
                                        but know how to fire.

Living under duress has people following behind,
                                 with their heads down and avoiding eye contact,
                                        for selection as a target with a lesson,
                                 or as a marksman who may well be inclined to miss.

Living under duress has people seeking a defence to the violence and the hurting,
to the jumbled and the lies,
to the nonsense and exaggerated,
to the patterned for deceit and
corruption in the government.

Living under duress sees people avoiding walking on toes,
sees people downcast and afraid of looking up,
where someone always stares with a frown;
which moves and twitches at the mouth.

Living under duress has eyes on eyes which are not good to emulate,
which are not good while bending down to tie a shoelace,
which are not good to attempt to hail a taxi at short notice,
where handles can be locked,
and a prisoner achieved,
without the will of the driver to release or to deliver,
to the secret police for an interview,
of both intent and contacts on the grounds,
of lingering and looking at the sky.

Living under duress knows the roads and streets to torture,
knows the techniques of pain and lack of breath,
as near death experiences,
which have very slow recoveries.

Living under duress count the days to meat,
count the days to bread,
count the days to baby milk to be mixed up with the paste.

Living under duress senses when an apple may role across the counter,
senses when the leftovers are left at one end for self help attention,
to what's there:
without recrimination or a snatch back trick employed.

Living under duress can be escaped with friends and knowledge,
leading to a chain of circumstances with release across a frontier,
where help and freedom reigns.

Living under duress is not of God,
sees the devil playing catch-up with torture rings at large,
for dismissing job seekers from the queues at factories,
to which it is most likely they will not return."

My Content Study Aid

Sourcing of Fresh Water

And I hear Jesus saying,
"Sourcing of fresh water can be incoming from a city or a town supply,
with chlorination treatment prior to delivery,
and the water is boiled or taken straight from a tap,
in preparation for a drink,
whether hot or cold.

Sourcing of fresh water cannot be falling with the rain,
where it is contaminated with the dust,
cannot be sourced from a roof catchment area,
where birds do perch and linger,
on a gutter or a peak.

Sourcing of fresh water cannot be found running in a river,
cannot be found flowing in a stream,
for these are now contaminated by man's spreading of his viruses,
imported from other tourist supplying nations,
to what were once pristine environments.

Sourcing of fresh water is now virtually impossible to find,
in the outdoors scenery of bush and forest,
as the rivers flowing water down to the sea,
now have visitors fishing and wading and swimming,
in the headwaters of the rivers,
in their search for trophy trout and salmon,
where their upriver antics bring viral sickness to
the downstream areas,
where the water is now permanently contaminated,
and cannot be restored,
to the quality as it once used to be.

Sourcing of fresh water is best from artesian water,
which has flowed through underground gravel,
in downhill filtering from the mountains,
where the snow did gather and the rain did fall,
in the freshness of the air.

Sourcing of fresh water can be pumped from a covered well,
where things and sediments alive or dead cannot fall in,
to leave their souvenirs.

Sourcing of fresh water as bottled water appears to be an unknown for its treatment,
for viral life whether tested for or found,
is selected from the flowing spring-heads across the countryside.

Sourcing of fresh water seems to be promoting the water quality,
    as it is seen to flow from underground,
      and pressurised aquifers,
        and in so far as they are put to commercial use,
    in transmitting groundwater for bottling to the market place,
    where the demand is great and volume offtake is extensive,
    and growing very quickly for both national use
          and international export,
          within the watch of God.

Sourcing of fresh water is a worldwide hunt,
      goes underground as both purity and quantity is sought,
    is a worldwide resource for increasing,
      the spread of life for growth of food.

Sourcing of fresh water should have a check put on,
      the quality of what is left to discharge to the sea,
      after the electricity has been dam or lake generated,
        from the water as encountered.

Sourcing of fresh water is the quest for the uncontaminated,
        that still found to be immune,
    from oil fracking or radiation or waste products injections,
    to so confound the damaging of the aquifers at varying levels,
        within the crust of The Earth,
    to the extent that they too are threatening to become,
         unusable by man.

Sourcing of fresh water may have its solution lie,
      within the expansion of the process of extraction,
        of fresh water from the sea,
      with the aid of solar energy to heat,
        and to condense the steam,
      as an ongoing flow of stable sterile and pure water,
        resulting from the harvesting of the surplus,
        of the seas and of the sky.

Sourcing of fresh water would then be searching instead,
    for a nation with a seafront,
    or with the permitting of a seawater pipeline to convey it,
        to a hinterland,
      where the sea does not reach,
    or a river is very large and can be tapped in substitution,
        as a source.

Sourcing of fresh water may have simplified solutions,
                          with the arrays to catch the sunlight,
              may benefit the desert lands,
                          with the high sunlight quotas,
              may benefit man as investment constructions and running costs,
                    no longer have to bear the brunt of being oil-fired,
                                or trusting to the nuclear option,
                    as water would again be seen flowing,
                          into that which could become,
                                as if the future gardens of Eden,
              in these end-time days of faith and grace,
                          with the inclusive technology gifts,
                                to the inventiveness of man.

Sourcing of fresh water sees the patents multiply as demand increases,
              sees the common sense approach,
                    where commercial interests of cartels:
              should not be permitted to have a stranglehold,
                                on the life blood of man,
              should not be permitted to auction off the rivers and the seas,
                    as they convey and support the life cycles on The Earth,
              should not be accepting of watching the rivers die,
                          before they make it to the sea.

Sourcing of fresh water is a monument to the ingenuity of man,
              is a signpost of a victory at sea,
              is a master stroke in bringing life,
                          to fresh oases around The Earth.

Sourcing of fresh water will set The Earth to bloom:
              where new cities are established,
              where there is food available to meet the need,
                    as generated for the future population centres,
              which changes and liberates a tie to the monster of starvation,
                    and the assumed lack of space deemed suitable,
                          for development and growth.

Sourcing of fresh water is a key note for discussion,
              is the keynote for progress and security,
              is the keynote to expanded life within the future,
                          to so be grasped by both man and God,
                                as partners in The Sun."

My Content Study Aid

Hunting Out Ingredients

And I hear Jesus saying,
"Hunting out ingredients speaks of a recipe being followed,
                                    whether of explosives or of food.

Hunting out ingredients can take you to a bulk shop or a supermarket,
                        to a butchery or a grocer or a corner store,
            or to a cast of dice where the immigrants do shop and are yet to settle in.

Hunting out ingredients can be quite time consuming if variants are similar,
                    and choice is somewhat difficult for an end-game of success.

Hunting out ingredients sees prices going up as quantities decline,
                sees a victory prolonged in the honest purchases
                                    without exaggeration,
                    and yet a thoughtful look offered in retrospect.

Hunting out ingredients is time consuming for the specialists,
                is stressful for the assemblers,
                is scary for the testers.

Hunting out ingredients is relatively simple once completed,
                    when accuracy and locations of supply are then known,
                            for future use of such resources.

Hunting out ingredients is a call down on a blow down,
                is a fracturing of settlement,
                is the missing of a pin.

Hunting out ingredients seeks the preserving rather than the opened,
                seeks the retained rather than the closed,
                seeks the found rather than the lost,
                acknowledges the kept rather than the thrown away.

Hunting out ingredients hurls the ignited,
                closets the second best,
                wanders after the mislaid,
                throws it at the guilty and confessed.

Hunting out ingredients sees the battle worn and scarred,
                lifts up the damaged and forlorn,
                tidies the fastidious and careful,
                passes out on the cruel and horrid.

Hunting out ingredients knows the best from the worst,
        knows the captive from the cheat,
        rounds on the liar and dishonest,
        silences the wounded and the screeching,
        overcomes the bashful and reserved,
        seconds the silent and the nervous,
        hides the brave and injured,
        helps the active and unafraid,
        invigorates the tired and resting,
        keeps the valued and ongoing,
        measures up the tall and unflattering,
        surrounds the dangerous and fateful.

Hunting out ingredients composes the piecemeal and the tragic,
        the hunted and the followed,
        the scared and the impulsive.

Hunting out ingredients has enough to make a cake,
        has enough to satisfy the hungry and forlorn,
        has sufficient to turn the back and charge,
        has enough to hear the pipes and laugh,
          to hear the drumbeats and the pauses,
          to be marshalled to stand upright with the victor's shield.

Hunting out ingredients has both searched and found,
        has both conquered and dispatched,
        has calculated and drawn the living straw,
        has memorised and is heading for a gathering to decide a battle,
        has invaded and conquered fear and bravado,
          is the victor in the camp,
           and inspecting of the status,
             of what was whirled and is no longer active,
             of what was twirled and ended in a back,
               of the fleeing and the scared,
               of the young and frightened,
               who know not which way to run.

Hunting out ingredients posts call outs on the standards,
        post the cuts and thrusts onto the wounded and the moaning,
        posts the iniquity of man in separation,
             into the life of liberty and gain.

Hunting out ingredients knows what composes the ingredients of war,
        what manages the call to victory,
        what hides and does not reclaim,
            the scene of loss and desertion.

Hunting out ingredients means encircling the runaways,
        of attending with a knife blade to the cowards and the dying,

to locating the hurt and the brave,
the injured and the silent,
the heroes and the successful,
the wise and the silent,
who have seen and encountered it all before.

Hunting out ingredients is the final dressing of the battlefield,
the uplifting of the dead,
the counting of the killed,
the picking of the tags,
the scrawling of the ingredients with their names,
which will not blend in to another cake,
or the oven known as Hell.

Hunting out ingredients sees the fraternity of brotherhood in action,
with the deftness and control,
with the inspection and allocation,
with the handling in readiness for transporting,
to the bounds of lost and found.

Hunting out ingredients witnesses the end of daze,
witnesses the end of envy,
witnesses the end-point,
where there are no further rights or wrongs,
but just the rites of burial and loss with interment,
in The Bloodstained Earth,
on which they were born and lived,
but could not befriend the critical with a future of equivalence,
and a share with the informed and battle hardened,
as to what was just and fair,
as to what could be supported,
as to what should be forgotten,
as to what is best left and ignored,
and so put to rest.

Hunting out ingredients always has an end-point for the targets,
always has a total kept and polished,
on a shield of life surrendered,
always has a cost to pay,
in the achieving of freedom from restraint,
in the achieving of freedom of decision making,
in the achieving of an unimpeded walk with God,
in a time of expectancy,
where love can be rejoined to faith and grace,
can continue to reign and to hold fast,
to all that is right and justified,
and is valued in a life."

Searching For The Available

And I hear Jesus saying,
"Searching for the available can be a disappointing one,
    can encourage very few,
    can segregate the willing from the silent for the activities of God.

Searching for the available requires consistency of appeal,
    requires explanations of intent,
    requires the prospects to be satisfied with the rewards of God.

Searching for the available can be found in families devoted and enthusiastic,
    can be found where bloodlines are familiar names within the services of God.

Searching for the available awaits the response of volunteers,
    awaits the absence of excuses,
    awaits the eagerness to go,
    awaits the arrangements for the family,
      to make the time scale both possible and rewarding.

Searching for the available is finding the gold among the gravel,
    is finding jewels ready to participate within The Will of God,
    is finding the unorthodox stuck within the orthodox,
      in not knowing the best way to serve.

Searching for the available has a very handsome pay back,
    for those who put their hands up in seeking an adventure,
      under the auspices of God.

Searching for the available are gifted with the memories,
    are gifted with the abilities,
    are gifted with the knowledge,
   are gifted with the inheritance of The Cross on an emphasis of Freewill,
   are gifted with the days of Pentecost and the acquisition of knowledge,
      of wisdom and of tongues.

Searching for the available loves those with fluency in tongues,
    as they understand the value implicit in their acquisition,
    in bringing forth The Reality of God into the lives of many,
    where the on-site evangelists receive the hugs,
      and the recipients receive the gifts,
    The Loving Living God would have bestowed,
      on His people of commitment,
   with their new found knowledge as understanding dawns,
      in opening up,
   the endowments of The Cross with the new destiny of choice.

Searching for the available is a call unto the committed:
>>> those who do not want to be the seat warmers and the stationary,
>>> who want to be active and energetic as they,
>>>>>> in their proxy ministries,
>>> gather in the would-be sheep from the wilderness,
>>> as God is introduced on a personal basis,
>>> of how He came taught suffered and died,
>> so man could join him both in mortality in the here and now,
>>>> and later to advance into eternity,
>>>>> within The Company of God,
>> and all He has prepared for those who now have an entry in:
>>>>> The Lamb's Book of Life.

Searching for the available has an incredible flow-on to the effectiveness,
>>>>> of The Outreach of God.

Searching for the available enables the messaging of the multitudes,
>>>>>> with a message of Good News,
>>> the messaging of the ignorant with that,
>>>>> of which they have not heard,
>>> the messaging of the bound of Freewill,
>>>> and wanting to be freed:
>>> into a home of Righteousness and Truth,
>>>> of Faith and of Grace released—
>> as His people join the ranks of the overcomers,
>> as they come into the forgiving light of Christ.

Searching for the available leaves significant impressions,
>>>> encounters those who would like to go,
>>> but are uncertain of their own abilities,
>>>> and of what they could achieve.

Searching for the available encounters the doubting and the hesitant,
>>> the want to's but the nervous,
>>> the should I's and the querulous,
>>>> who are really seeking confirmation,
>> that their innate commitment could also be acceptable,
>>>> for them to join in and go as well,
>> where the harvest field is white and waiting for the reapers.

Searching for the available can set these minds and souls at rest,
>> can be assured they are wanted,
>> can be assured there are places for them,
> where they can speak and testify,
> where they can speak the words they find within their mouths of God.

Searching for the available heightens an awareness:

of the concepts subject to a struggle,
of the concepts where the lies are rampant,
of the concepts deemed important by God,
yet without the support or confirmation
available from man in all his guises.

Searching for the available turns up the concept of abortion,

and the shallowness of man;
turns up the concept of willingness to attempt to sell,

a proxy ministry to Satan,
to convert a church of God into a haven of iniquity,
where neither vows nor promises exist,
in not being brought before an altar of significance,
together with the distortions of what should be,

the unwavering truth of Faith;
turns up the concept of replacing the morality of God with the ethics of man,
where the ethics are weak and subject to additions and alterations,

depending on the end-time and the counsel,
on the locations and the voices as shouting for attention,

all of which are completely meaningless,
in their applications and self-interpretations,
especially when being brought before the rule of law;
turns up the concept of the truth,
where lies contaminate with passage as the truth,
where the truth within the morality of God,

has been established for millennia,
having served man well,
with humanity to the fore and the protection of the innocent,
where the lies of make-believe and dishonesty will fall before:

the wall of Righteousness reinforced by Truth,
with personal accountability of Freewill,
before The God of man who saw to the death throes of The Cross,
as it could no longer conquer that for which it was renowned."

My Content Study Aid

_____

_____

_____

_____

_____

_____

Quarantine of Needs

And I hear Jesus saying,
"Quarantine of needs has indications of far too many:
>>> attempts to put them to one side,
>>> attempts to schedule them ahead,
>>> attempts to justify delay,
>>>> to leave to a later date and time.

Quarantine of needs moves them to a list,
>> casts a very careful eye looking for the potential for deletions,
>> regards them all as necessary but with no urgency to purchase,
>>> or to borrow or to build upon a signal of intent,
>>>> with a will or won't.

Quarantine of needs is formed because of the viewpoint at a turning point,
>> because of the hedge rows hiding accumulation,
>> because of the many aspects to the clearing of the past,
>> because of what counts specifically in the shuffling of the funds.

Quarantine of needs rises in uncertainty,
>> settles with an estimate apportioned for a purchase,
>>>> to be tightened by the costing arising,
>>>>> from a confirming question.

Quarantine of needs arises from the foresight of the future,
>> from the foresight of the broken which will be unable
>>>> to supply,
>>>> to the projection of demand,
>> from the foresight of the management,
>>>> of that which is likely to be unavailable,
>>>>> for varying periods of time,
>>> with a resulting disruption to both a home and refuge,
>>> arising as the tribulation of man from within the wrath of God,
>>>>> in vengeance for the calls upon Freewill,
>>>>>> without due cause;
>> in the end-time shaping of the pathway of ascent from mortality,
>> as it leads up the conceptual gradient into the welcome to be found,
>>>> in an entry of significance within the initiation,
>>>>> into all the fields of specialties,
>>>>> to be found within eternity.

Quarantine of needs has the solutions all put aside and stored,
    until the necessity to use becomes of first grade importance,
    to open up a new threshold of existence,
    where preparation is the key for the combating of the past
        the present and the future,
    as the declarations have called to set apart,
    the cleared and coming dangers with the solutions thereto,
    as appearing in the list of needs still to be acquired,
        borrowed or shared with neighbours,
            in the maturing of concern.

Quarantine of needs should not be all that complex,
    should carry the tins into the dawns ahead,
    should try to vary the dry grains as they are milled,
        and set every 4 months or so,
        when the moths don't fly,
    should try to keep the instant coffee and the tea leaves dry,
        and sealed in readiness for immersion,
        for the presenting of the drinks.

Quarantine of needs can summarize and cope,
    can enlist and keep,
    can Freewill and hope.

Quarantine of needs varies from home to home,
    varies with the contents presently available,
    varies with the facilities which may have to be pushed or pulled,
        into an ongoing and working commitment,
        to what they should be doing.

Quarantine of needs speaks of future shortages expected,
    speaks of booking and holding,
    speaks of encountering and keeping,
    speaks of visiting and checking,
    speaks of maintenance and operating,
    speaks of attention to and understanding of what needs to
        be repeated.

Quarantine of needs seeks release from the encumbrances,
    seeks a larger tub from which the water will not slop,
    seeks a bigger jug which eases where it pours,
    seeks a more trustworthy teapot,
        which neither spills nor drips from the spout,
        in the preparing of the tea.

Quarantine of needs is the separation of the likely to be called into action,
    is the call to assistance when services are no longer reliable,
    when chance inserts its spoke into a doubtful outcome,

when the culprit does not heat and declaims responsibility,
when the seasoned has not ripened until the wasps descend,
when the apples are all growing and the codlin moth is held at bay,
when the apples are all ripening and the codlin moth has missed its day.

Quarantine of needs sees them all lined up,
and let folk wonder what could be the purpose,
sees them at the pump-head with the bottles cleaned and rinsed,
with the splashing of their filling of the water bottles,
as it mostly all goes in,
sees them in the kitchen,
where the shelving is all primed and loaded,
and waiting for an unloading 'go'.

Quarantine of needs sees the preserved fruit all bottled with their seals and tops,
see the large crock pots filled with salted layers of sliced beans,
sees the large crocks with water and preservatives of choice,
for the keeping of the eggs,
for six months or so.

Quarantine of needs settles on the dried fruits of sultanas raisins dates figs and bananas,
with nuts of all sizes and shapes,
as shelled or otherwise,
and sealed to be kept where the storage room is cool.

Quarantine of needs can see the need for diesel or for petrol in their storage cans,
where safety is assured as the generator runs,
or as the LPG Gas stoves do heat and sterilise the water,
as stored and and kept for eventual use.

Quarantine of needs will need to cover the outage of the services,
until they can come back on line,
with working mechanisms to restore the services,
to the way they were before.

Quarantine of needs can mend the broken security,
can mend the lack of water,
can mend the source of power,
can see to the maintenance during the shortfalls of supply."

My Content Study Aid

_____

_____
_____

_____

Protecting of The Garden

And I hear Jesus saying,
"Protecting of the garden is a forthright endeavour,
      is building on a high plateau,
      is constructing among the snow and waterfalls,
      is returning to the warmth and comfort of the median.

Protecting of the garden is the end result of ages:
        from the settling of the dust,
        from the crowbars spent on leverage,
        from the cyclones of resistance,
        from the apex of construction,
        from the peaks intended for the summiting,
          by those who dwell therein.

Protecting of the garden is seeing it in order,
      is seeing it blooming and at peace,
      is seeing it at its very best,
      is seeing it through the eyes of God.

Protecting of the garden is not one of chivalry,
      is not one of selfishness,
      is not one of too much supervision.

Protecting of the garden is one of love and thoughtfulness,
      is one of abatement and selection,
      is one of jurisdiction and of holiness maintained.

Protecting of the garden includes:
      all of the bridal party with entries in The Lambs's Book of Life,
      all of the survivors of correction from the tribulation,
      all of the strangers who have long been settled in,
      all of the visitors invited for a time of verification,
         of what they have seen and heard,
         in the night time of reconciliation,
         and their adjustment to the facts.

Protecting of the garden includes the shining of the morning dew,
      includes the tidying of the pick up and the drop off points,
      of those who come and go to the parts which catch their interest,
        for a closer examination of the content.

Protecting of the garden has many facets held in steadiness for presentation,
      has many sections which should not be divided further,
      has many attributes of placement and of peculiarity,
        which should stay where they are put.

Protecting of the garden is one of protecting from deterioration,
        to ensure it stays as it should be so,
        to see that items do not change or suffer from interpretation,
            or a close up study of the features.

Protecting of the garden exposes the caring and maintaining of:
        an environment of stability;
        an environment where the qualified and the keen,
        the committed and the valued,
        the rescued and the sought after;
          all have the tendency to leave an impression,
            however slight or small or large,
            on what they see or do,
            within a time frame of inspection;
            as they move and carry among,
              or just sit and rest,
              in their being beside or on,
              that wherein they live.

Protecting of the garden is not a restrictive oversight,
      is not a surplus form of governance,
      is not a call unto either pride,
        or to too much sensitivity.

Protecting of the garden is to see it loved and used,
        to be left just so as it is encountered,
        with the decisions of perfection to restrain,
        what may be considered as light-heartedness,
          or casual carelessness,
        in the brush pasts which impact to varying degrees,
            upon an eternity,
        from what could be described as just plain wear and tear.

Protecting of the garden is an ongoing attention to the details,
      is an ongoing consideration of the effects of perseverance,
      is an ongoing summation of the effects of the passers by,
    with the touching and the feeling of the skin textures of the coverings,
          together with the bending over or the step up,
          to enable the smelling,
           of the forthcoming scents and odours.

Protecting of the garden is ongoing and continuous,
        as frameless for the largest states of both art and life.

Protecting of the garden is not an endeavour built on shallowness of activity,
      is not an endeavor designed to fall or to collapse,
      is not an endeavour which may have to be rebuilt,
      is not an endeavour which cannot outstay the time-smiths of eternity,
         with all that is implied and claimed.

Protecting of the garden does not seek,
>> has no need to restore,
>> will neither shrink nor fade away.

Protecting of the garden is not from attacks of evil intent where immunity does reign,
>> is not from stray projectiles floating free within an universal scene,
>> is not a semblance of a museum declaring what is not.

Protecting of the garden has already had a very long existence in the sight of man,
>> has already impacted on historical authenticity,
>> has already been built constructed or composed,
>>>> from within the resources,
>>> of what exists as an ongoing continuum.

Protecting of the garden is a home within a home,
>> is a home outside of time,
>> is a home beyond any need for repair,
>> is a home whose existence does not have an end-point,
>>> which can be targeted or achieved.

Protecting of the garden is in the oversight of God,
>> is in the journeying capabilities of the mortal and indigenous,
>>> of the committed and the blessed,
>>> of the resourceful and the understanding,
>>> in the belief structures of concept and reality.

Protecting of the garden is not a call to arms,
>> is not a call to action stations,
>> is not a call to the repelling of invaders.

Protecting of the garden is one of maintaining the state of that which already is,
>>> of keeping it in pristine condition,
>> where rubbish tins or bins are not required,
>> where rubbish can no longer lay claim to an existence,
>>> on a basis of eternity;
>> where God regards the overall and says that it is good."

My Content Study Aid

_____

_____

_____

_____

_____

_____

Access to The Seeds

And I hear Jesus saying,
"Access to the seeds is often an envelope inside an envelope,
        is often the damp inside the wet,
        is often the sprout inside the shell.

Access to the seeds often starts with the seed heads poking through,
        the seed heads poking up into the sunlight,
          with their baby roots investigating access,
            to the water and a thirst for growth.

Access to the seeds is not a time where length exceeds the height,
        is not a prospect worthy of a ribbon,
            when not growing as expected.

Access to the seeds cannot be continued indefinitely,
        can only be a starting point for a vegetable as sought in green,
            and has not been played with,
        in establishing a sortie into the colour bands of variants,
        or of a flower into a turbulence of colour and of scent.

Access to the seeds can determine what is planted by a farmer,
          a gardener,
          or some one else with a piece of land.

Access to the seeds creates time to plot and plan,
      time to select the choice,
      time to place the where and when.

Access to the seeds permits a close up study of their strike,
      a close up study of their establishment,
      a close up acquaintance with the weeds,
        as they join the struggle for survival,
          beside that which has been planted,
        as they are desperate to join the race,
        but are yet to experience a dreaded termination.

Access to the seeds can bring multiple rows into alignment,
      with the spacing as it should be,
      can expect the growth of beans exactly as they are planted,
      in a zig zag and a diamond formation,
      down the row made by a shovel,
        so the sprinkling goes with peas,
         so the scattering goes with radishes—
         the speed kings of the circuitry,
         of both the strike and growth unto maturity,
         in six or seven days.

Access to the seeds should enable the guarding from the birds,
>>especially of the peas,
>>as they poke their heads above the ground,
>>to wonder where they are,
>>>just to find a hungry beak,
>>>which limits the potential of success.

Access to the seeds also likes access to a hose,
>>>with a high speed fine droplet spray,
>>>which soaks but does not scour.

Access to the seeds can be quite gratifying,
>>as the seed lines appear within their rows,
>>>>on cue as to the day marked for their appearance,
>>>>on their scenes of fellowship.

Access to the seeds is in the hands of God,
>>is in the environment wherein the seeds do multiply,
>>in readiness to be spread upon The Will of God.

Access to the seeds are built upon the years of growth and tending,
>>are best remembered for the forest giants,
>>>for the Redwood cedars with their circumferences and heights,
>>>for The Mount of Olives in Jerusalem,
>>>>where the olive trees have truly amazing ages of survival.

Access to the seeds grows over time,
>>grows with the spreading of man,
>>grows with the love for all of the vegetation of creation,
>>>as it has come and flowered throughout the ages of The Earth,
>>>to all be so seen and wondered at,
>>>when with an eternal pass of access to Eternity,
>>>and the gateways to the green seasons of The Earth.

Access to the seeds are named yet remain unknown to man,
>>>in his current years of life,
>>are lodged and placed yet remain unseen by man,
>>>in his present time upon The Earth,
>>are listed and viewed by The Strangers and The Neandertals,
>>>>with historical relationships to Eternity,
>>>who lived within the distant past of dinosaurs,
>>>all who witnessed the world as it changed,
>>>>in preparation with the deposits of reserves of oil and gold,
>>>>as held in readiness for their discovery,
>>>>>thereby to enable the onward development of man,
>>>>>with the distant readiness in marking,
>>>>>the promised birthrights of Abraham,
>>>>>in bringing forth The Stars of God.

Access to the seeds leads into The Milky Way,
            leads into the fragments of division,
            leads into the establishment of gates.

Access to the seeds can only be traveled within the authority of God,
            can only be inspected close up,
                        with life preserved,
                        with familiarity of the power of God,
            can only travel intergalactically with the approval of God.

Access to the seeds is kept and protected by God in His wisdom,
            is discussed and explained from within the oversight of God,
            is linked both to mortality,
                        and to the insight granted from within eternity,
                                    when under the ministry of God.

Access to the seeds is for the travellers with confidence,
            is for the ability to transfer the travel modes of God,
                        into the reality of the travel modes of man,
                        when under the ongoing guidance of The Living God,
                        complete within His Sanctuaries of existence,
                                    and of outreach to the stars,
                                    as seen by man,
                                    and as created by God.

Access to the seeds demonstrates the naivety of man both in his disbelief,
                        within his feelings of certainty somewhat astray,
            and in his commitment to the truth,
                        still existing in the world of mortal incompleteness,
                        prior to the gaining of access to eternity,
                        with the completing of the schooling of man,
                        who knows his parentage back to his Holy origins,
            now to be within the fluency of the wisdom fields,
                                    of the tongues of God.

Access to the seeds establishes the wisdom base of man,
                        within The Glory of His God,
            as understanding dawns to so be carried forward,
                        within the functioning of knowledge,
                        within the expanded intellect of belief and structure,
                        for The Servicing of Life within The Eternity of God."

My Content Study Aid

_____

_____

Backstop to The Heating

And I hear Jesus saying,
"Backstop to the heating lies within the prayer fields of God,
                    is not reactive to the childlike efforts of man,
            witnessing their fellows running around in circles and achieving very little,
            with their inept mutterings of climate change as if it were a daily occurrence.

Backstop to the heating is in the need for prayer,
                    in the absence of the need for understanding of the cause.

Backstop to the heating knows nothing will be corrected by a chasing after gas,
                        by attempts to minimise down into decline,
                        that which feeds the forests and food chains of man,
                        in an on-going cycle of the ups and downs.

Backstop to the heating is the correction of the direction of the gulf stream;
           is the adjustments to the undersea upheavals;
           is the resetting of the equilibrium disturbed by the undersea earthquakes,
                with the resulting tsunamis which batter on their nearest coasts;
           is the heating of the seas so cyclones and hurricanes,
                      can form at sea and drift onto the cooler land,
                which shorts out the up-flows and encourages the down-drafts.

Backstop to the heating requires knowledge of the trenches of undersea locations,
                          which have been blocked,
              which are redirecting the marine currents to one side or the other,
                    as they participate in breaking up the flow.

Backstop to the heating can be investigated and be stopped;
              can have the known warmest currents examined,
                      to affirm where they are going;
                whether they are losing the heating potential much faster,
                  with their drops in temperature,
              from among the ice caps and the seashores:
           where the ice is fast disappearing and reluctant to return,
           where undersea volcanic vents are now blowing,
           steam up from the ocean floors to dissolve the floating ice.

Backstop to the heating sees the atmosphere gain points,
                which is not unduly dramatic from the initial surge,
                which started all the fuss confusion and exaggeration,
        at the youth level which took it all very seriously as they fell in love,
       with what they thought they were capable of doing to so save The Earth.

Backstop to the heating is within the capability of man to reverse,
        when understanding dawns and genuine activity commences,
        despite the howls and cries fed into the microphones,
            as the not-so-young babies are gathered,
     to cry all together without understanding as to what has really happened,
          in the wider climate scene and of how it may be fixed.

Backstop to the heating knows the ignorant support,
        of the multi-media lambasting the governments of the world.

Backstop to the heating is simple and capable,
        is silent and compressing,
        is fusion and of sealing,
        is movement and restraint,
        is clearing and restoring—
            all which is within the sea-bounds of The Earth,
        which man can only resolve by taking his courage to the seas,
        where his strength of purpose can be realized,
        as it clears the blockages in the ancient channels and trenches,
        with their valleys and their volcanic vents.

Backstop to the heating finally has a nuclear solution to the problem of the heating,
        requires nuclear detonations to be placed in critical areas,
        on the sea-floors for softening up the blockages,
        as brought by the slush and mud of landslides,
   large enough to block and to divert the flow of the currents of the centuries,
   large enough to demolish and destroy,
   large enough to seal and to prevent,
        the diversions of the waters of the seas,
        where heat carrying capacity is all important,
            as to where it goes and why,
            as the heat analysis of the seas of The Earth,
              is reflecting underwater changes,
              in direction of the current flows,
          with their warmer impact on the colder areas,
              where water temperature is sensitive,
         and could mark or mar the existence or otherwise,
           of an ice field in the making or the breaking.

Backstop to the heating is nuclear detonations carried out for a set purpose,
            in The seas of the Earth,
     with the capacity to really make a difference in temperature location,
         via the flow rates and the temperature charting,
         in the areas appearing to be at risk,
         in being heated above the normal of the centuries,
             as evidenced within the past,
      and where less than one degree up or down,
     can change the long term viability of the present ice pattern,

as destined to be changed when without intelligent interference,
and the solution as prepared for and in being held in trust,
for the days when it was needed to reduce the excess flow rates,
in directions bringing change and loss of heritage,
and the extinction of some species,
where the temperature change lies in wait,
to defeat their living quarters,
with access to their feeding grounds,
with which they were and are familiar,
in the lifetimes of their long and distant past.

Backstop to the heating employs nuclear techniques,
of restoration and application to mend a broken jigsaw,
of confusion and of mystery,
in wondering what the problem actually is and how it came into existence.

Backstop to the heating knows the only other solution is to simply wait it out,
to accept what is likely to be yielded up,
and whether and how long it will take for the ocean and the sea flows,
to become effectively re-established in the old channels as used for millennia,
and whether these will be re-instated and go to completion,
or new undersea channels will be cut and modified,
as the surrounding land temperatures become affected,
by a new series of sea and ocean flows;
where the prevailing winds will change in alignment,
with new rivers being formed as the rain fields are borne,
so dry lands again become both lush and green as the flows are set,
whose effect has an affect which calls for push for push,
is yet to be re-ascertained and projected in its fulness into a future of concern.

Backstop to the heating has an awareness of the end-time strengthening a decision,
where it may be better to wait out the coming of the second advent,
with the rebirth of The Rejuvenation of The Earth,
which has been a long time in prediction,
with an expectation to turn The Earth around,
for a new beginning on the dawning of a new day.

Backstop to the heating has further references worth the reading,
with an understanding so knowledge may be arrived at,
as it carries the wisdom of God to man,
which is somewhat conditional but the objective is important:
as to which way the winds will blow and bring rain,
as to which way the oceans and the sea will establish the new fisheries,
where those used to plenty will have lean years,
while those used to the leanness of the seas will hang their nets on the other side,
to experience the fishing of new grounds and reaches,
as they become established to so bear their fruit."

Waylaying of The Pet

And I hear Jesus saying,
"Waylaying of the pet knows its own way home,
          knows the scents within its home,
          knows the scent of those who come and go,
          knows the scents as found wherein the pet does live and feed.

Waylaying of the pet meets and greets,
          recognises and maintains friendship or acquaintanceship,
          within the family of which the pet has joined.

Waylaying of the pet is best not done by strangers,
          as defences will be activated,
      with apologies being non-existent,
     which may not be thought applicable to who thinks they are dominant,
      in the meeting of the minds with an interruption,
          to the journeying of the pet.

Waylaying of the pet can be a kidnapping exercise in reality,
      can be a life threatening experience in the planning,
      can be only one moment of distraction,
          for an escape to be successful,
          into a world of unfamiliarity,
      where wandering may result in bringing forth care and attention,
      where a veterinarian may stop to read a chip.

Restoring of a pet is a time of happiness and appreciation,
     is a time of both-way recognition,
          as the pet so badly missed yet hopeful of a return,
          to the family without an undue delay.

Waylaying of the pet speaks of nefarious intent,
      speaks of the ill will of removal,
      speaks of a desire to re-establish the membership of a family,
          wherein they were reared with both food and lodgings,
          in an area of attractions and of interest.

Waylaying of the pet is not the objective of the pet,
        which is to maintain the lifestyle of the familiar and the caring,
      is to sustain the choices and the freedom,
        the investigative and the homely,
        the encouraging and the doubtful,
        the visiting and the guests,
      the unusual with a new scent to be acquired and remembered,
         for the future as a part of that within a home-life,
          as it develops and is accepted,
          in the folklore of the pet.

Waylaying of the pet is not to be a repeat occurrence,
>> where cameras record the visitors,
>> with their vehicles lengthwise down the street.

Waylaying of the pet is not the establishing of fear,
> is not the secreting in captivity,
> is not the walking of the pet,
>> with a connection to the hand or wrist.

Waylaying of the pet is not depriving it of freedom,
> is not laying poisoned bait,
> is not the dismissing of integrity of approach,
> is not the carrying of a stick,
> is not the shouts of anger,
> is not the interference with its meals.

Waylaying of the pet is the temporary or permanent denial of its home,
>> with an interruption to its progress:
> of preventing its return,
> of abducting it to be sold,
> of its feeding and enticing,
> of taking it away from the surroundings of its home.

Waylaying of the pet should not be spoken to,
> may encourage it to stop what it is doing and not restart,
> may cause it to approach or follow in the lee,
>> should not be subjected to a distraction,
>> which gathers its attention in a watch and wait,
>> or causes it to run away to be quickly out of sight.

Waylaying of the pet could be fierce and warning of approach,
> could be a defence active for the company,
> could be because of a disease which should make it unapproachable,
>> from which it is best stayed well clear,
>>> and completely out of reach;
> where a snarling drivelling bite requires immediate medical attention,
>>> before it is too late.

Waylaying of the pet exposes man to attitudes of petting and affection,
> exposes man to wrong assumptions,
>> about friendliness and acceptance,
> where the pet is unknown and should not be trusted,
>> with an outreached arm,
>> which may have always carried a stick,
>>> even as a training tool,
>>> which the pet had come to hate.

Waylaying of the pet should leave the pet exactly,
>> as the pet was first encountered.

Waylaying of the pet should not lead to an attempt to feed,
>> or bring it close,
> should not lead to an attempt to put a collar on,
> should not be an excuse to place a chain upon a collar,
>> which does speak of theft.

Waylaying of the pet can be a group of two or three,
> when they are best avoided to be given a wide berth.

Waylaying of the pet should not be attacked with a pepper spray,
> which can instigate an immediate and violent defence reaction.

Waylaying of the pet is not a samurai warrior in waiting,
> is not a practiced attacker,
> is not at the forefront of a fight,
>> where a watering hose is the best means of defence.

Waylaying of the pet has a memory for mistreatment,
> where a growl can be a caustic warning,
> where a beating in anger leaves the residual signs of a whipping,
> where the skin and bone appearance speaks of long term neglect,
> with what was once a pet but is now an ex pet,
>> very cautious and scared to approach,
>> or to a one-sided attempt to befriend,
> with its interest in man long gone as an unwilling experience,
> on which the sores do fester,
> and an approach to man has long been stripped away.

Waylaying of the pet should not be assumed an approach is possible,
> should not be assumed an approach is desirable,
> should not be deemed as practical by either the caution of the pet,
>> or the willingness of man."

My Content Study Aid

_____

_____

_____

_____

_____

_____

_____

_____

_____

Seeking of Success

And I hear Jesus saying,
"Seeking of success is issued with a selected intent of limiting the objective,
of not being measured as a gatherer of wealth,
of not falling into the trap that more is better,
of not moving in the circles of comparison,
of not walking in the shadows,
of those still striving to achieve.

Seeking of success is more concerned with personality,
of family growth,
of sensitizing the seeker to the truth within a life of righteousness.

Seeking of success is an ice cream with the children,
is a night out with the family,
is the sharing of desires and hopes for the future.

Seeking of success does not take much finding,
is there for all to see when the captain of one's life,
is the spirit seen to be in charge,
of the leading of the soul.

Seeking of success does not mean that penury is faced every day,
does not mean that being broke,
leaves no money in the pocket,
does not mean that the future is looking very bleak,
does not mean that payday is seen as insufficient.

Seeking of success can have a leisurely stroll within a park,
can work high up in the sky,
or low down in a basement,
can be tuned as a multi-millionaire,
where investments turn to gold,
or as one who can say,
'I am comfortably well off and have all I want within our family,
and especially with our combined journeys,
into where our God will take us,
with Righteousness and Grace and where Faith and Commitment,
attend us with our journey into our twilight;
within the livelihood of Truth and the walk with God;
into where He will take us as we accompany Him,
on an everlasting adventure under His provisioning.'

Seeking of success does not need a blindfold,
does not need a guiding hand,
does not need advice on business acumen.

Seeking of success needs attendance at the work place,
>for servicing of the work flow,
>where rejects are minimized,
>where supervision has no faults to find,
>where the time frame for procurement is both known and authorized.

Seeking of success can have a vision for the future,
>can have a target in the work place,
>can have a target in employment,
>can have a target for the climbing of the ladder,
>>into the surroundings of seniority.

Seeking of success is not a function of the overtime,
>is not a function of simulating others,
>is not a function of competing for the best seat in the house.

Seeking of success can be an upward trend,
>can be affirmed by management,
>can be an attention getter for the sequel to a service.

Seeking of success varies with the weather for outdoor production,
>on a site known for its outdoor safety and reliance,
>on one another as production is compared,
>for gloss and shine and smoothness of the edging,
>where score marks are forbidden,
>and timing is essential.

Seeking of success attends to the marked and chipped,
>to the bent and damaged,
>to the unpolished and the dull,
>where finish is essential and the rims are circular,
>where polishing the dull is essential in its thoroughness,
>as they stand upright but alone.

Seeking of success does not involve climbing mountains,
>does not involve deep diving in the seas,
>does not involve the exploring of underwater caves.

Seeking of success can be a simple 8am - 5pm commitment to reliability,
>a commitment to the work ethos,
>when moving in a factory,
>a commitment to the standard as raised to honour,
>the work standards as achieved and verified,
>in the time frame of a day.

Seeking of success does neither manipulate nor squander,
>does neither smear nor besmirch,
>does neither pick on nor pander to the ins and outs,
>of factory communications when they are noised abroad,
>for comment and discussion.

Seeking of success is not just a rainstorm in a cup,
rather it is more like an SUV* in a swimming pool,
in which it cannot float,
while the sides are very narrow,
but the pool is deep and drainable.

Seeking of success does not get caught up in nets:
either tennis or fishing or ones across the orchards,
does not attend to the banking of a surplus,
and how it was obtained,
does not attend inspections,
yet wonders how the charlatans can so keep the books in surplus,
while open to inspection and to validation.

Seeking of success achieved can be seen,
as a nail being driven home with a flourish,
can be seen as a family running free,
and unemcumbered by the past,
can be experienced as debt free,
from credit cards and money lenders associated with property,
as bought and sold and bought again on the low points,
and the hight points and again on the low points,
all pointing to success and understanding,
with the money in the bank.

Seeking of success is not a lifetime dream,
should stop when enough has topped the target,
and there is sufficient in the kitty,
and all the cats are happy and content.

Seeking of success has no need to boast,
which just calls to the attention of the beggars,
who want a piece of pie which they have never earned,
but to which they think they are entitled,
and cannot understand rejection of their dishonest pleas,
and false statements of provision.

Seeking of success is good to have a fence of stability,
and freedom around the family home,
to defend it day and night from the brotherhoods of knaves,
and villains who regard such with much envy,
and would like to know what is to be found inside,
the protective ring of Righteousness and Grace."

Scribal Note: *SUV Sports Utility Vehicle

Modelling of Drama

And I hear Jesus saying,
"Modelling of drama opens up the avenues of expression.

Modelling of drama expands the intellect of man.

Modelling of drama shares the interface of expectation.

Modelling of drama exposes a very large budget for production.

Modelling of drama brings the skytrains to The Earth,
     fills the carriages with spectators and guests,
     travels the star routes of the infinite,
     accompanies the beautiful and mature.

Modelling of drama starts the curtain rising,
     has the stage already set,
     has the players and the actors in position,
          with their lines of wisdom and of style,
          which are acceptable to God.

Modelling of drama should have playwrights of ability,
       playwrights of experience,
       playwrights of knowledge matched to understanding.

Modelling of drama should not promote the craven or the distorted,
     should not cheer for the works with satanic backing,
     should not rejoice at the downfall of man,
         or those intent on displaying a murderous intent.

Modelling of drama should not glorify the black heart brigade,
     should not chortle at the smutty jokes,
     should neither uphold nor praise the besmirched by man.

Modelling of drama speaks of style and presentation,
     speaks of growth in understanding,
     speaks of the exalting of the praiseworthy,
     speaks of determination to complete and shine.

Modelling of drama requires the base of competence in language,
        with enunciation and clarity of thought.

Modelling of drama should avoid the smutty and the uncouth.

Modelling of drama should retain the ideals of grace with the fervour of endeavour.

Modelling of drama has a wide scope of application and of meaning,
       without the need for either the sly or the sinister.

Modelling of drama has the backdrop of the stage,
     has the perspective of life,
     has the simulation of reality,
     has fixation on the delivery and timing.

Modelling of drama has an outreach to an enthusiasm for the good and cheerful,
        has an attachment to the gowns and makeup,
        has the period costumes for venturing into the past,
            so the past becomes alive enjoyed and understood.

Modelling of drama can seize the stage and shake it,
        can use the stage and warm it,
        can manipulate the stage and freeze it.

Modelling of drama can show what is no longer there in existence,
           of what occurred in another time and place,
           of the effect it carried and how society was changed.

Modelling of drama has many variations,
        has many sources of resourcefulness,
        has many bars of music and of songs,
        has many capabilities within the fields of poetry and mimicry,
        has many options in the field of dancing,
            when skill and timing are to the fore.

Modelling of drama has promoters everywhere and married to the theatres,
        has scriptwriters kept busy in the sparks of creativity and originality,
        has the patrons sitting waiting patiently for the next attendances,
           at the finished and considerate performances,
            for the interested and intrigued.

Modelling of drama is the events of life,
           which happen so quickly or in private,
           they have not been seen as placed before,
           the patrons of a theatre for enjoyment of or instruction,
            on a recent situation.

Modelling of drama has a lot of leeway with the truth,
        has a lot of freedom with the facts,
        has a lot of rewrites prior to being regarded,
           as having a finished script which can be allocated,
            to the reality of the stage and/or film.

Modelling of drama has its time set for the considered apportioning,
           of actors and of actresses with their appointments,
            for assessment at a reading.

Modelling of drama can be successful or otherwise,
           when passed into the hands of those,
           who must bring the written words to life,
           who are likely to carry the responsibility,
            for the outcome of the presentation,
           with all the preparation which has gone before.

Modelling of drama has its stewards of the keep,
      charged with preservation of the present,
        as it moves into the past,
      charged with the establishing the records,
        of the changing voice of society,
          as it moves across the bounds of income and of education,
            together with the poverty of life,
             where affordable opportunities were rare,
               soon to be left far behind,
         in being seldom able to be taken up or exploited,
         in the living and advancement for the day:
     where remorse was too expensive to carry forward as a burden,
        so all had no alternative but to move on,
        into what the morrow would be bringing to reveal.

Modelling of drama has the records of recent times,
     has the records of the singing and the playing of the music,
     has the records of the acting with the films,
     has the tracking of the playbacks from the chips*,
     has the records for display upon the phones of man,
        from throughout the world for the imparting of knowledge,
      for the images from the lowest dregs of humanity,
         as Freewill is misused and misapplied,
    to so be held accountable with bookings for the destiny of default:
         unless some changes occur without undue delay,
        so grace may be seen as being influential,
        with the reinstatement of faith and trust and truth,
        so these four can return with Righteousness,
          to the forefront of the lives so affected,
          and as known by God."

Scribal Note: *chips*, A tiny wafer of semiconducting material used to make an integrated circuit; a microchip.*

My Content Study Aid

_____

_____

_____

_____

_____

_____

_____

Hiding of The Stores

And I hear Jesus saying,
"Hiding of the stores is only needed when living within a prospect of a raid,
    when living within the outcry for food,
    when living within the circumstances close to starvation,
    when living close to insufficiency with the empty supermarket shelves.

Hiding of the stores is best when the address is not smothered in suspicion,
    when the address does not have empty cans strewn at the gate,
    or spread across a lawn by a playful pet.

Hiding of the stores should attempt to minimize an electricity bill,
    should attempt to not use the lights at night,
    except for candlelight with matches.

Hiding of the stores do not last well,
    when underneath a bed,
    when in a wardrobe in the hall,
    when located in a bedroom wardrobe,
    behind the dresses and the clothes,
    when located in a roof cavity,
    which can be clambered into with a powerful torch.

Hiding of the stores can be in the garden,
    if the marks of grass disturbance are not too obvious or new,
    are best placed in the garden areas which have been freshly tended,
    for their weeds,
    where there is no clash of appearances,
    and no reason for disturbance visible or left,
    within a culture born of carelessness and urgency,
    where the suspicions are aroused by the outlines,
    on the gardened earth,
    with empty cartons in the garage,
    where gas standbys are displayed,
    scattered round with facilities to heat or cook,
    when the power goes off,
    not to return later in the day.

Hiding of the stores fit well around the flower beds of delight,
    fit well within the circling of the fruit trees,
    fit well around the orange trees of little stature,
    fit well within the planting boxes of the roses and the freesias,
    fit well within the edging flower strips,
    as well as out round the edging,
    of the boundary board fences.

Hiding of the stores does not create a vacuum,
                does not mend a broken fence,
                does not fill a gap that is too large to mend.

Hiding of the stores needs a nose for hiding trouble,
                    a nose for not overstating the obvious and the marked,
                    a nose which can smell the gaseous or the nauseous.

Hiding of the stores is best done at a height,
                        where the searchers are looking down.

Hiding of the stores depends on size and weight,
                      where overloading is a give away,
                      where all will end up being stripped.

Hiding of the stores can be done within an unknown boat,
                            at a different address,
          can be done under a tarpaulin in a back yard,
                  where a few cartons are relabelled,
                      as a second grade cheap undercoating paint,
          can be done in a park where a sack can be deposited,
                      in the water on the edging of a pond or lake,
                where the water is not clear and the ducks abound.

Hiding of the stores does not require a lot of space,
                  does require an estimate of how long the hiding period should be,
                          when lives may be dependant,
                          and security is necessary.

Hiding of the stores can be in travel suitcases,
                    placed up on the top of the garage cupboards,
                  out of the way of casual interest,
                  or stuck to the backing of the pictures on the walls.

Hiding of the stores can be placed in a gravel dump,
                      on the side of a road,
                      or in the herbage surrounding it,
                          which would mask its presence.

Hiding of the stores can be in a black plastic bag,
              which is thrown into a stream underneath a culvert,
              which could be multiplied as required,
                  and the vehicle has mud or cloth or paper scraps,
                  as gathered by the wind at the front and back,
                  to be casually entangled on the obscuring,
                          of the number plates.

Hiding of the stores can be inside the rims of old tyres,
                  as used for weighing down a compost heap,
                      which may not contain much compost.

Hiding of the stores can be as single tins,
        at the bottom of clay pots charged,
            with the holding of a plant,
      or inside in the toilet cisterns,
      or on the book shelves of a library,
          out of sight behind the books.

Hiding of the stores can be underneath the upturned rubbish,
      from a wheelbarrow with the gardening waste,
         in a corner where its damp and wet.

Hiding of the stores can be outside in a rubbish bin,
      near a down pipe filled with water,
         for a thirsty summer garden,
    can be at the placement of single tins of different sizes,
      in a garden area with a complete ground coverage,
      of violets poppies cacti or other plants known for,
         their effective creeping coverage,
         depending on the season,
        where there should also be a check,
        that there are no casual glints of tins,
        protruding from The Earth.

Hiding of the stores could also be a pile of empty random bottles,
      in a corner of the backyard,
      where the good ones are found by burrowing underneath.

Hiding of the stores can be placed within and underneath,
      an old blanket in an outside plastic pet shelter,
      in which there is protection from the rain and wind and sun,
      where the lumps and bumps are tucked well out of sight.

Hiding of the stores can have tins of appropriate size,
      placed end to end around and in,
      the roof's edge guttering of a home,
      which will store many tins over time and out of sight,
      with the help of a step ladder to reach where one can feel,
      or an external wooden table,
         on which standing is sufficient,
         on a sturdy wooden chair,
         for both placement and recovery.

Hiding of the stores should use the most vulnerable,
        as the first and foremost for consumption."

Setting-up The Toilet

And I hear Jesus saying,
"Setting-up the toilet is for when the toilet does not flush,
        for when the water is in short supply,
        for when the water needs to be used elsewhere.

Setting-up the toilet will need to be on the long drop principle,
        of a deep hole in The Earth,
        if intended for an ongoing usage;
     or the purchase of a small chemical unit as used in mobile situations,
        with the instructions as included for the functioning,
        with the chemicals as required,
        for treatment of the residue.

Setting-up the toilet is best done with the chemical unit,
        with ease of use and tidiness,
        and the absence of the odours.

Setting-up the toilet completes and is operational,
        is clear and understandable,
        is accurate and to the point.

Setting-up the toilet is neither difficult nor messy,
        is neither time consuming nor wasteful,
        is neither furtive nor secretive.

Setting-up the toilet is available for immediate use,
        can be kept and used inside until,
        an emptying is required outside,
        whereupon a simple hole suffices.

Setting-up the toilet is not a glossy affair,
        is both practical and down to earth,
        is both simple and safe,
        is hygienic and should be free from germs,
        is tolerant and circumspect.

Setting-up the toilet does not need an outside light,
        once the disposal method is understood,
        and operational in the daylight.

Setting-up the toilet is not at variance with custom,
        is not at variance with the system,
        is not at variance with its ease of use.

Setting-up the toilet is simple and systematic,
        is practical and certain,
        is operational and at ease.

Setting-up the toilet is not dependant on the reading,
     is not dependant on the positioning,
     is not dependant on the urgency,
     is not dependant on the recovery of decorum.

Setting-up the toilet is straightforward with easy access,
     requires initial supervision of a child for the certainty of process.

Setting-up the toilet soon overcomes any nervousness of detail,
     soon overcomes any strangeness of a change,
     soon overcomes any lack of familiarity
         and of the sequences involved.
Setting-up the toilet does not take very long when siting,
       accessing,
       dispensing,
       and the activation of the chemicals.

Setting-up the toilet does not carry undue risk,
     does not threaten to spill or overturn,
     does not succumb to difficulty or desertion of the inexperienced.

Setting-up the toilet is straightforward and comfortable,
      and does not need a chaperone.

Setting-up the toilet with a hygienic cleanup afterwards water is not needed,
      but do rub the hands in a dispensing germicidal cream,
       soon to be absorbed so safety is assured."

My Content Study Aid

_____

_____

_____

_____

_____

_____

_____

_____

_____

_____

_____

Rustling in The Tins

And I hear Jesus saying,
"Rustling in the tins is a very strange noise,
          means there is movement in the tins and the tins are empty.

Rustling in the tins arouses curiosity.

Rustling in the tins arises from the wind,
        an earthquake,
        a small animal alive,
          and probably having a playful investigation,
        or an alarm trap which has been deliberately set,
          and now been sprung,
          from the hanging tins.

Rustling in the tins can be at head height or at ground level,
          depending on where they have been hung,
          and out of drafts.

Rustling in the tins will have created an instance,
          of surprise and caution and possibly a retreat.

Rustling in the tins will not happen a second time,
        unless further traps are laid either in advancement,
          or in retreat along a corridor or walkway,
          through unfamiliar territory.

Rustling in the tins can have the same effect,
        when stacked in an inverted V,
          waiting to be knocked over by an unwary foot,
          advancing in the dark.

Rustling in the tins can be as a result of a trip wire or a piece of string,
        waiting to be triggered for a cascading stack of empty cans,
        from a height with an odd rock or stones or marbles,
        included in the mix to establish the clashing,
      of the cans as a difficulty in having an unimpeded prowl,
        in quietness down an internal passage way,
        which will arouse a microphone or camera,
          to yield a quick retreat,
          with a record of the happening.

Rustling in the tins is an effective means,
        of protecting from unhindered damage,
          or from theft.

Rustling in the tins can save a lot of recovery work,
        of re-stacking and stock checking,
          in an orderly manner.

Rustling in the tins can cause more anguish to the interlopers,

> as they start to hurry in their creeping,
>> and their whispering,
> as they encounter more alarms at random,
> as they try to exit through the recent means of entry,
> as external alarm bells start to ring for attention,
> as nervousness prevails.

Rustling in the tins can expose a gang of two or three,

> to the lighting of the circumstances,
> to the locking of partitions or divisions,
> to the unexpected bringing of confusion to an initial setting,
> which seemed at first to be quiet and helpless.

Rustling in the tins can be scary and intimidating,

> can start them fighting shadows,
> can raise the possibility of them attacking one another,
>> in defence from ghosts.

Rustling in the tins has created insecurity and a tendency to flight.

Rustling in the tins has brought what was thought to be,

> the known and safe from interference,
> into the unknown and uncertain,
>> of what may happen next.

Rustling in the tins can turn the lights on and address the invaders,

> with a call to surrender as they are surrounded,
> to walk out one at a time with their hands up,
> so no-one is likely to get hurt.

Rustling in the tins awakens the movement cameras,

> which call out the pre-recorded locations,
> of where they would have been seen and photographed.

Rustling in the tins can call a guard to duty,

> can call for support,
> can sound the call to arms,
> can handle the armed and the cocksure.

Rustling in the tins does not have to beat a retreat,

> is more than likely to encourage it in others,
>> with no right to be there.

Rustling in the tins can have drenching cans above,

> with heavy cans both falling and spraying contents,
> left and right amidst the darkness of uncertainty,
> or a torch beam spreading light with reflections,
> through the windows for the arousing of suspicion.

Rustling in the tins when they are spread and fallen,
   can bring tripped falls to those hurrying down the aisles,
     when they are no longer clear.

Rustling in the tins can place potential thieves:
    among the triggers and the traps,
    among the alarmed and waiting,
    among the patient and rewarding.

Rustling in the tins have sources to enhance security,
   have resources linked to one another,
   have the fields of retribution with the gates wide open and ready,
     to be padlocked with the caught inside.

Rustling in the tins is far from a good idea to go,
    to disturb the unknown-in-waiting,
    or to risk it it for a potential time in gaol.

Rustling in the tins is not a fire hazard in the making,
   is not an ignition source which brings any satisfaction,
    except to increase the reward for information,
    where mates may not be able to be counted on,
     to keep their and their girl friends' mouths,
      all tightly shut for ever.

Rustling in the tins can be the start of a disappointing night,
   can be an echo carried into the future,
     which will spoil the enjoyment of a life,
  can lead to tattoos upon the body which would carry their own warnings,
     in advance of an uncouth life.

Rustling in the tins can be unsheafed in readiness,
    for more powerful resources which will trip and fell,
     with leg chains locked on the legs,
     awaiting the arrival of authority,
    together with accountability in the shadow of Freewill,
     misapplied in action with a price,
      waiting to be paid.

Rustling in the tins can start a whirlwind,
    in the lives of the-not-so-innocent,
   can bring changes to the detriment of their existence,
    which would not otherwise occur,
   can upset the applecart for any future plans or hopes,
    as opportunity and happiness both attempt to escape,
     out past the rustling in the tins incurred,
     where the evil influence can so stain a life."

Breaking of The Glass

And I hear Jesus saying,
"Breaking of the glass requires some force misapplied,
                   unless within an emergency for a fire alarm or similar.

Breaking of the glass does not settle a dispute,
           does not mend the broken and the damaged,
           does not bring cheer unto the saddened or disheartened.

Breaking of the glass may be a sign of celebration at a wedding,
           may be a sign of excessive jubilation or excessive frustration,
           at the way the events have gone when frustration has moved,
                   beyond the boundary of control.

Breaking of the glass can be the cause of much alarm,
           can begin a threat against high valued items,
           can be an attempt to acquire that which does not rightfully belong.

Breaking of the glass should start to ring alarm bells,
           in a distant station where security is paramount,
           with arrests being quite frequent as the ultimate result,
                   for the reason of alarm.

Breaking of the glass is done with an objective,
           is done with a reaching for the best,
           is done with speed and foresight,
           is done with expectation of the noise and summoning,
           is done in the hope of a getaway in time,
               with identities still unknown and unable to be placed,
                   within a court of justice.

Breaking of the glass continues with the getaway being successful,
               with the gloves and masks fulfilling their functions,
                 for those charged with their detention,
               with the recovery of the stolen and usurped.

Breaking of the glass encounters no difficulties until they reach their hideaway,
             to take time to see what they have gained,
             of how the value has declined to just one fifth,
             of the value as defined so recently when on display.

Breaking of the glass is the start of dissatisfaction not easily foreseen,
           speaks of a lack of criminal experience:
             of the loss of value when moving to the valuation,
             of the pawn shop with the fear of recognition,
             or just the fencing of the loot to whoever shows an interest,
          when offers may be even lower when recognition is almost certain,
             and stones will need to be removed from their settings,

to even be recut and resold as bare stones,
in the raw and in need of being set.

Breaking of the glass shows in the prices being offered,
shows in the prices being refused,
shows in the prices able to be lifted,
in going to a foreign shore.

Breaking of the glass does not reward the inexperienced or unaware,
of the going prices for jewellery of note,
as such is put on hold within the industry,
where authorities await reports that it has been seen,
or offered,
or be open to inspection.

Breaking of the glass may see the cheaper items sold,
where bulk can upgrade the total and identity is difficult,
or may well be suspected but without proof,
of prior ownership.

Breaking of the glass does not create instant wealth,
poses weeks or months of the risking of arrest,
or the closing of suspicion of involvement,
both backward and forward into time,
as the underworld does chatter and discuss,
while some jewellers with the heavies,
are attempting to find the easy money,
where an offer cannot be declined,
because of the likely repercussions to the health and safety,
of all known to be involved:
as an encouragement to sell,
to cut their losses,
as the dreams do start to fade away.

Breaking of the glass does not have happy endings at the end,
can end up with broken limbs or fingers,
or seriously disfigured faces,
or a wounding shot within the back,
which immediately draws suspicion to involvement,
when accompanied by a death promise,
for anyone who talks.

Breaking of the glass can become the pariah which no-one wants to touch,
can find the jewellery is too hot,
is too dangerous to even feel,
can find the foreign trip is all that they have left,
where the prices are also falling in the shadow of the rumours,
of the pricing as pitched at home.

Breaking of the glass has become a curse which is difficult to clear,
      has become well-known and sensitive to names,
      has begun a search so the names can be checked one by one,
        for involvement and the residing place,
        of all that was taken,
        partially cashed in,
        to later be stated as gone and not recoverable,
          or hidden under a cactus in a desert,
          where the digging was easy as the sand,
          provided a covering that would not draw attention,
            to any passer-by.

Breaking of the glass starts to bring the common sound of regret,
            in the voices round the table,
      of how the values fell,
      of how the offers smacked of collusion and of greed,
      of how the dreams were shattered by the onset of reality,
      of how it is falling around the ears of those responsible,
        who have wagered and appear to have lost,
        what was once upon the table,
        and spelling riches for everyone who participated,
        to potentially score a fortune in the making.

Breaking of the glass walks a one-way street,
      walks the talk of feasibility with enthusiasm and belief,
      encounters the reality as a place where the wolves do feed,
            with very little left for the cubs,
            who have been at play,
            and need to be taught a lesson,
        which they should remember beyond the spluttering,
        of the what ifs and whys and the question as to,
            where the final money went,
        where nothing but blank faces look,
        both surprised and guilty of the teaching of a lesson,
          as to how these things are done,
          when carried out by the professionals,
          and not the sons as raw recruits."

My Content Study Aid

_____

_____

_____

_____

Counting Down The Days

And I hear Jesus saying,
"Counting down the days is an eye upon the future,
                is an eye aware of the future,
                is an eye caring for the future.

Counting down the days has an eye on both the season and the objective.

Counting down the days has a value attached to time,
              has a value as an incentive,
              has a value which should not be wasted,
                          or frittered away without reward.

Counting down the days is not very difficult,
              is done quite often when something should not be missed,
              is there as a means of support to achievement.

Counting down the days carries its own reward,
                in escaping from a clock,
                in not being bound to a system longer than is necessary,
                in being able to count off the finality of success.

Counting down the days keeps the days with allocated effort,
              keeps the days with saturated ability of progression,
              keeps the days in validation of each one's existence.

Counting down the days runs across the battlefield and wins,
              runs across the surroundings and matures,
              runs across the mud and the mire to come out,
                        in the sunshine and the warmth.

Counting down the days is a measurement which controls distractions,
              is a measurement which assures the gaining of a target,
              is a measurement which ensures a release.

Counting down the days does not succumb to illness of the nose,
              does not succumb to phone calls of enquiry,
              does not succumb to invitations to attend the modest or the trivial.

Counting down the days has a mindset on commitment,
              has a mindset on completion,
              has a mindset on a victory of a short term gain.

Counting down the days can be fortuitous in freeing up the future,
              can be fortuitous for the expansion of the negative into the positive,
              can be fortuitous in enabling acceptance of an unknown challenge,
                        which fits within a way of life.

Counting down the days sees the minutes tick away,
              sees the hour hand moving forward,
              sees the rising and the setting of the sun.

Counting down the days sees the jumping out of bed when the clock calls for attention,
sees the grasping of a chance of advancement,
when the time is ripe and ready,
when the lights have moved from the yellow and are showing green,
when the body is charged and capable,
of doing what is asked.

Counting down the days summarises the not so distant past,
highlights the interruptions,
or when tiredness chooses to interfere,
brought conjecture on the scene,
as to whether the endpoint was achievable,
with its measure of importance,
with its assessment of validity for concerted effort,
with its reappraisal of what has been achieved,
in a shortened space of time.

Counting down the days sees the eyes alive,
and glistening with enthusiasm,
as the target approaches closer day by day,
as to whether progress is sufficient to be assured,
of being able to tick the box of completion and of satisfaction,
in the reviewing of all that has been finalised,
and readied for release.

Counting down the days sometimes sees the sunset meeting with the sunrise,
sometimes sees the sunrise mopping up the sunset.

Counting down the days invigorates the targeting of progress in a bottle,
of progress with fidelity,
of progress with intuitiveness,
of progress where finality is recognized,
and approaches to be capped.

Counting down the days is as if walking down a tunnel,
is like acknowledging the light at the end—
is getting bigger with the passing of each day,
is as if the cloud burst of intensity of feelings,
is well on the way to invading the body soul and spirit,
with the reward seen basking in the sunlight,
of a brand new day.

Counting down the days affirms the truth as blended in the plans,
affirms the grace as measured and applied,
affirms the field of righteousness with its applicability,
of directions to the highway of success.

Counting down the days witnesses no leaks appearing within the system,
        sees it is watertight and safe,
        sees it is bright and ready for a trial,
        sees there is neither porosity nor a clawing back of progress,
                which would steal the target of fixation.

Counting down the days can picture the ploughing of a field,
        the ploughing of the waves,
        the ploughing of direction which is straight and true.

Counting down the days has no requirement for a net,
        has no short circuits with a bounce back,
        has neither a surplus of the varnish nor the paint.

Counting down the days sees mothballs being removed,
        sees support trestles being checked,
        sees runways being prepared for the splashing of success.

Counting down the days has a bottle of champagne for the launching of ability,
        for the launching of perseverance,
        for the launching on the tide of circumstance,
           in the honouring of Freewill.

Counting down the days is fast approaching zero,
        has no bomb burst in the sky,
        has no fireworks exploding on a skyward trip,
        has no need for another bottle of champagne.

Counting down the days brings satisfaction to the fore,
        expands the field of admiration for the finished work,
            as taken to completion,
            without undue delay.

Counting down the days can witness,
        the bringing of the hands of man,
        into the servicing of the hands of God.

Counting down the days has a trip prepared,
        has a trip which has been held in expectation,
        has a trip resulting from a promise.

Counting down the days is approaching the end of time,
        is approaching the signals for accountability,
        is approaching the signalling of completion,
      where the workshop is tidied-up,
      where the workshop has fixated on completion,
      where the workshop has completed all which was set before it,
          to now display the glory of completion,
          with all which is intended for a new beginning.

Counting down the days should be able to see what is on its way,
>> what is affirming of its coming,
>> what has been planning far ahead,
>> what is about to start the sorting and the sifting,
>>> of the for and against.

Counting down the days should be prepared and ready,
> should be correct and waiting,
> should be onside and certain,
> should be contained and expectant,
> should be consistent and established,
> should be knowledgeable and committed,
> should be excited and joyful,
> should be rejoicing and affirming:
>> of all who have gone before.

Counting down the days will witness the changes underway,
> the changes awaiting affirmation of degrees,
> the changes ranging from the treetops of the living spaces,
>> to the roots of the onward life or death of man.

Counting down the days is difficult for those not knowing where or when to start,
> should be reading of the season,
> should be witnessing the proximity,
>> with the destinations of the trainloads of merchandise,
>>> as they are moved to no-ones benefit,
>> but that of the so-called elite,
>>> who worry only for themselves,
>>> with their marshalling of resources,
> in the concurrency of growing opposition,
> with a change addressed to the discerning of belief,
> with righteousness in charge as truth comes to the fore,
>> as the key to accountability changes hands,
>>> within the governance of both power and authority,
>>>> in which time can be extended,
>>>> to which there shall be no end."

My Content Study Aid

_____

_____

_____

_____

_____

Recovery in Sight

And I hear Jesus saying,
"Recovery in sight replaces dismay with hope.

Recovery in sight replaces would-be loss of faith with burgeoning expectation,
        replaces paucity of existence,
                with the realms of plenty,
        replaces the indebted with the debt-free,
                  and thereby freedom from the claws of money,
            which have imprisonment as their business guidelines.

Recovery in sight should shoot down all the children birthed of money:
           as debt is vanquished from the speech of the godly and the justified,
           as debt is hurled back,
                from all to where it has been spread,
                by the satanic forces working overtime,
                      to both entrap and to enslave,
                  to disrupt the lives of those who know not:
                    what they are getting into by the day,
                    to later regret it by the nightfall,
                when it seems to be too late with signatures attached.

Recovery in sight sees the benefits arising,
           sees the benefits making themselves felt and appreciated,
           sees the job opportunities increasing with enquiries,
           sees the conditions improving with the calls,
           sees the paydays becoming worth the effort,
                as they change from being insulting,
                to a fine and honest reward with holidays intact,
                to sometimes lengthened within a jurisdiction,
                  of that as known and loved by God.

Recovery in sight should not encourage debt increase,
           should not envelop life with the decision making,
                  as to whether or not it can be afforded,
                  in the income as available.

Recovery in sight is not a time to play catch-up with the smiths or jones,
           is not the time to overuse the credit cards,
                to turn the molehills into mountain tops,
           as the sharks make the money readily available,
                knowing full well there will soon come a day,
                when accountability comes knocking at the door,
                as repayment is required while further borrowing,
                  is not on offer any more.

Recovery in sight is not the time to lash out on a new car,
        is not the time to spend on doing up the kitchen,
        is the time to repay debt before the threats exist,
                and the money all dries up;
                as it becomes difficult to replace,
          as borrowing rates go through the roof:
          which is ready to collapse under the load,
          which the roof is carrying and trembling to maintain.

Recovery in sight can often be a bone of contention,
          in a war from selfish politicians,
       who only consider the effects on their chances of re-election,
       and not the benefit to whom,
       rumour has it,
       they are supposed to serve:
            both in honesty with integrity of purpose,
            and with righteousness in terms of behaviour;
            and of respect and honouring,
            from all which issues from the mouth;
      while what they do with their hands is something else again—
      where collusion is born,
      where self-aggrandisement serves no one but themselves,
       as the rules guiding propriety are cast aside to be ignored,
        as the oaths are broken willingly and with foreknowledge,
              and so cannot be repaired,
        as honesty and integrity become the scarcely-ever-mentioned,
        as they become undeservedly the shamefaced jokes in trade,
       as their hidden wealth illegally increases,
       as corruption spreads continuously upon a mountain top of lies,
       as the smiles upon their faces are not there for their electorates,
             are there because of an internal warmth,
            of what they are achieving for themselves,
         which are no longer carriers of,
             or reflectors,
             of the truth.

Recovery in sight should see bottlenecks disappearing,
       should see trade accelerating,
       should read the truth within the folds of newspapers,
          where there is no bias,
          and integrity is seen to govern—
            in avoidance of the trash and nonsense,
          which is so dishonest cold and unwelcoming,
            it cannot even be the source of heat,
          to so light a fire within a grate.

Recovery in sight is indicated when the price of homes and property,

are starting to rise in value,

are there because of reassurance,

from the behaviour of the market place,

are there because of ready availability,

of money from the lenders,

are there because of the attractiveness,

of being able to afford and finance a home,

in which to live without fear of reparation,

or of damage by a financial storm of intransigence,

which will not go away,

but has no application in the absence of a debt.

Recovery in sight can invite a little shopping,

can invite Father Christmas,

can remember a birthday on a card.

Recovery in sight may stretch out to a new dress,

may reach out to a tie,

may bring a pet on board from the SPCA,

may stretch to a family holiday,

where the stepping stones to the doors are not gold-plated,

or aimed at sparkling in the moonlight.

Recovery in sight can hear music playing,

can see theatres showing,

can see parks inviting,

can see the seashore catering,

can see the sports playing,

all in their venues of existence,

where common sense does rule,

in the sharing of resources which play into the night,

yet ignores the so-called games of chance,

which pays no one but themselves.

Recovery in sight is also about the blind,

should approach the love and care of God,

with a simple request as from the heart,

to repair or to initiate a recovery of sight:

of that which has been lost or damaged to so affect a life.

Recovery in sight can be healed by God,

through a sincerity of appeal to He who cares and knows,

the makeup of a body however it is damaged,

for the sourcing of a miracle in declaring The Reality of God,

as it brings Glory to The Son so He can bring Glory to The Father,

from within the lives affected as brought forth for healing attention,

through The Living Loving God."

Rebirth of Baking and Delivery

And I hear Jesus saying,
"Rebirth of baking and delivery is welcomed by the sunrise
as it follows the early morning,
is welcomed by the starting of a new day with the needs in store,
with the capabilities of completing those which are required,
with the speed and practice borne of consummation,
of many days of affirmation of the knowledge base,
as acquired and used.

Rebirth of baking and delivery sees the welcome signs of the making of deliveries,
of the restocking of the shelves,
of coping and of overcoming the tear stains
of the not too distant past.

Rebirth of baking and delivery sees bread returning to be sold,
with varieties to which the customers have familiarity,
with their favourite loaves.

Rebirth of baking and delivery signals of recovery and addresses what is missing.

Rebirth of baking and delivery recognizes the slicing and the bagging of the bread,
recognizes dependency on the time,
recognizes the necessity to get the delivery wheels a-rolling,
recognizes the time set for arrival and unloading,
of all which had been ordered and delivered as so sought.

Rebirth of baking and delivery sends the smell of newly baked bread,
into the arbours of a shop.

Rebirth of baking and delivery receives a very warm welcome,
from all the hands available,
from all the hands eager to assist in the download to reception.

Rebirth of baking and delivery has hopes of matching supply to demand,
of ensuring there are no hungry faces still looking at empty shelves,
of having residual loaves available right to the end of day.

Rebirth of baking and delivery has time for the buns,
still linked together in 6's 9's or 13's to form the baker's dozen.

Rebirth of baking and delivery sets food again upon the tables,
the tables of recognition of that which has been placed upon them,
for the breakfast of the day and the mid-day lunches as prepared,
in serving the rolling appetites at large.

Rebirth of baking and delivery completes the round of delivery,
witnesses loaves being made available,
to those who choose to visit and to purchase from the bakery,

where the bread is still slightly warm,
is still exuding its own personal aroma,
to the surroundings of the early morning's bake.

Rebirth of baking and delivery has a repetitive but honest starting to each day.

Rebirth of baking and delivery has numerous recipes to follow,
has numerous alternatives to catch the eye,
has numerous attractants for the taste buds,
has numerous people munching,
on the productions of the morning,
as placed and laid around.

Rebirth of baking and delivery sees fuel no longer in short supply,
sees the limitations with obstructions gradually being removed,
sees the prospects for the future quickly returning,
to what was regarded as the normal.

Rebirth of baking and delivery has staff back at work,
has production steady within its daily expectations of demand,
has satisfaction and excitement at the first loaves out of tins.

Rebirth of baking and delivery recuperates and recovers,
analyses and suggests,
frequents and responds,
monitors and sends,
counts and achieves,
wraps and stacks,
greets and rejoices.

Rebirth of baking and delivery is back to its supply chain,
of the staple backstop of the centuries.

Rebirth of baking and delivery nods wisely in recognition,
of all they have been through,
and have had to overcome,
before the bread could flow again,
to be restored back to its previous standing,
where quality has not deteriorated,
where it meets with fine approval of the baker's skills,
as it rushes off the shelves,
both in trust and to satisfy the hunger,
seen circling in inspection.

Rebirth of baking and delivery resets the clock of both time and motion,
of both new and old,
of both quantity and access,
of both baked and quality approved.

Rebirth of baking and delivery sees the flour mills milling,
          sees the farmers sowing,
          sees the crops in preparation for a new dawn arising.

Rebirth of baking and delivery stops the hunger in mid-stride,
          stops the hunger without the firing of a gun,
          stops the hunger without the siphoning of fuel.

Rebirth of baking and delivery establishes the broken past into the welcome of the future,
          consigns the past into the basket of difficulties,
          now overcome and ready to be buried.

Rebirth of baking and delivery is quickly followed,
          by all within the food chain,
          as comprised from both the local and the imports:
          where nature can grow a little better somewhere else.

Rebirth of baking and delivery resets the standard for supply,
          resets the movement of both quantity and quality,
          resets the operation of verifying the stops and starts,
        in the completing of a delivery round with drop offs as required.

Rebirth of baking and delivery puts the seal upon recovery,
          puts the key of satisfaction into the lock,
             which tumbles as it churns,
             to leave the dough to rise,
                within the walls of readiness,
                so ensuring all is well.

Rebirth of baking and delivery reinstates:
          what has been available to man since time immemorial,
          where skill and contingency reign to ensure such so remains,
             upon the menu as served throughout the ages,
             as it is still remembered so by God."

My Content Study Aid

_____

_____

_____

_____

_____

_____

_____

Scavenging for Needs

And I hear Jesus saying,
"Scavenging for needs speaks of desperation in a search,
             speaks of lack of success within the expected sites,
             speaks of a mystery as to where they could be found.

Scavenging for needs can be various and time consuming,
             can be a failure and unrewarded,
             can be secreted and difficult to find,
                          in complementing one another in their applications.

Scavenging for needs are difficult to define,
             are obvious when found,
             are not so certain when attempting to compile a list.

Scavenging for needs takes alert eyes to the rubbish sites of the tips,
             can make enquiries of those who think of themselves
                                        as the professionals,
                          in finding the gems as hidden within,
                          what finds itself arriving at the tip.

Scavenging for needs is not good on the best of days,
             is not attractive to the nose,
             is not drawn to the big machines which push shove scrape and dig,
                          to cover that which has been deemed as waste.

Scavenging for needs finds it difficult to search:
                          in the presence of the compactors,
                          which crush and crumple all within their touch,
                                        as they push it out of sight;
                          in the presence of the rain which wets and stains,
                                        as it disintegrates the paper;
                          in the presence of the sun which heats and rots,
                                        as the flies are invited to attend;
                                        while the rodents wait until the night.

Scavenging for needs is easiest and most rewarding,
                          when limited to the supermarkets as well as,
                          the large retailers of their merchandise.

Scavenging for needs can be frustrating if the brand or type or action is unknown,
             can be rewarding when viewed on display,
                          with variants open to selection.

Scavenging for needs can be a way of life,
             can be a way of deprivation,
             can be a way of collecting and of selling used plastic bags.

Scavenging for needs does not bend the knee of the wealthy,
>> does bend the knee of the beggars and the gatherers,
>>> in the picking up of what is thrown away with very little value,
>>>> either attached or recoverable.

Scavenging for needs must not be confused with wants.

Scavenging for needs has a very high priority,
>> within the lives of those who stand in need,
>>> of those who search to find,
>>> of those who try to accumulate,
>> what can be sold to the reclaimers in their world,
>>> still seen as being completely untouchable,
>> by those who are forced to walk and work:
>>>> the dumping places with the tip zones,
>>>> as known and used by man.

Scavenging for needs can sometimes end in a small bonanza,
>> when a piece of jewellery is found,
>> yet with the true value never known,
>> but only guessed at as such will entice someone else to purchase it,
>>>> by way of a little bonus to the finder.

Scavenging for needs does not turn the world upside down,
>> can be a daily occurrence for the needful and the poverty restrained,
>> can be an ongoing turning over and examining,
>> can be a saving of an unknown as put aside for the advice of another,
>>> who is better informed from a much harder,
>>>> and longer experience.

Scavenging for needs also covers the younger or the older,
>> brothers and sisters as deserted by the parents,
>>> who could not afford the upkeep and so dumped them,
>> on the doorstep of the watchman's shed,
>> who allowed them to stay and try to find a living,
>> with its needs within a cabbage patch of mockery,
>> which holds no-one to account for the waste food,
>>> all used and found either as a mixed-up messy surplus,
>>>> or as both stale and second hand.

Scavenging for needs concentrates on clothes,
>> sometimes has to settle for the rags,
>> with holes and stains and tears as they were ripped and torn.

Scavenging for needs are far from being prim and proper in their presentation,
>> are far from holding out a hand with anything deemed to be of value,
>> are far from certain as to from where the next meal is coming,
>>> and whether it will make them sick.

Scavenging for needs stops to eat when a morsel has been found,
cannot risk it will be wrenched away to feed a bigger child.

Scavenging for needs sees the crawling and the flyblown,
sees the hatchings and the grubs,
sees the introduction to the edible in taste but the horrible in appearance,
as the experienced eat with their eyes shut,
in pretending things are not really as bad,
as they seem to be.

Scavenging for needs can tour the back door kitchens of the super-rich,
with a second-hand bag to see what they can garner as a meal,
from the cook or the dishwasher who both know,
what was left upon the plates to still be available,
for a brother or a sister and hopefully all three,
as a bag is extended in silence,
to wait hopefully for a response that helps.

Scavenging for needs can be difficult to carry,
when generosity is the order of the day,
for the kitchen staff in charge of disposal;
can see the offering of several paper bags,
filled-up and maybe spilling over.

Scavenging for needs can end on a happy note for those,
who will share in this unknown feast,
who will take it in turns to dip and see what they can recover,
from a walk along the kitchens of the homes,
where they are never invited to go inside,
yet know that God is also there."

My Content Study Aid

_____
_____
_____
_____
_____
_____
_____
_____
_____
_____

Counting of The Days

And I hear Jesus saying,
"Counting of the days can be a pleasant pastime,
          can be a link into a hobby,
          can be from excitement of an appointment fast approaching.

Counting of the days has an end in sight,
          has a total of significance,
          has an ability to make both ends meet with success,
                    as the time draws to a close.

Counting of the days awaits understanding of that to which the count refers,
          awaits at the forefront of events,
          awaits within the parallels of history,
          awaits upon the scenes of recompense,
          awaits within the throne of grace,
          awaits upon the coming of authority at last,
          awaits upon the scheduling of The Father and The Presence of
                    My Spirit.

Counting of the days does not call for repetition,
          does not call for a recount,
          does not call for the time date of creation.

Counting of the days bears upon the sad and the crying,
          bears upon the scared and the unrighteous,
          bears upon the unjustified and the unappreciative,
                    of their own Freewill.

Counting of the days bears upon the fluency achieved within the tableaux of the stars,
          as has been gifted on the days of Pentecost;
          within the circumference of creation,
          within the radiation of the energy,
          within the white space and the black space,
          which follow one another as freedom is obtained.

Counting of the days neither mimics nor stultifies,
          neither encroaches on nor aggregates,
          neither uplifts from nor downcasts to.

Counting of the days neither encircle nor capture,
          neither spit not hoick,
          neither simulate nor copy.

Counting of the days is a law unto itself,
          is a behaviour pattern waiting to be adopted,
          is an outline protecting information,
          is an accumulation of activities waiting to be joined together.

Counting of the days leads into the future,
>> neither dwells upon the past nor the present,
>> is concentrated on the approaching of the future,
>> with its effect upon the present on arrival.

Counting of the days introduces difficulties for man,
>> for which man should be prepared,
>>> should be well warned and ready,
>>> should be prepared to cope,
>> to seek the overcoming,
>> to not turn the back to flee,
>>> so there can be a stabbing in the back.

Counting of the days relies on common sense,
>> where panic is not all engulfing,
>> where panic does not attempt to rule the roost,
>> where panic does not prolong an experience of a lifetime or,
>>> indeed,
>>> an experience of millennia,
>>> where panic does not attempt to procure,
>>>> what common sense cannot.

Counting of the days does not attribute the counterfeit,
>> does not count both up and down,
>> does not approach with lies,
>>> will need to strain the truth with particularity,
>>> without either exaggeration or dismissal,
>>>> or a thump upon the back.

Counting of the days should check to ensure the guards are up and in place,
>> should check the validity of a hedge of protection,
>> should check the knowledge base for The End-time Will of God.

Counting of the days should breathe more easily when there is a genuine reliance,
>>> upon a close relationship with God.

Counting of the days is neither distorted nor delayed by a foreign imposition,
>> by the advancing of the heathen,
>> by the warlords of both the east and the west,
>> by the selfish and the greedy,
>> by the liars and the cheats:
>> where a surprise awaits with the discovery of
>>> an onset of a nil effect.

Counting of the days leads into what has been warned of in the past,
>> leads into what is certain to be encountered,
>> leads into the quagmire of man's mess within his time and self-election,
>>> on a throne of an evil incarnation.

Counting of the days does not verify the base load,
>>just indicates proximity with the need for attention,
>>just signals of the certainty of a coming storm,
>>>where life has been already threatened and ignored,
>>>as to any obvious change in attitude,
>>>which could impact on the end result.

Counting of the days ends with accountability for the curtaining of Freewill,
>of the pretence that nothing matters,
>that morality is no longer a requirement with a lifetime attachment to a life,
>that the sequences of achievement are secondary to the will of man,
>>with his fixation on his own scale of standards,
>>as arising from the argued evil ethics of man,
>>with his ongoing taking of the lives without remorse or hindrance.

Counting of the days terminates at the gates to the sin fields of The Earth.

Counting of the days does not prolong or harbour.

Counting of the days does surround and cut short,
>does round up and convict,
>does shorten and remove,
>does stop and not reclaim,
>does remove and eliminate the contaminants of The Earth,
>>>from within the whole of His creation,
>>>as witnessed over centuries,
>>where man has not been worried,
>>>by his lack of standards,
>>>for the guiding of his actions,
>>>as arising from his own Freewill.

Counting of the days collapses the house of cards,
>collapses the seedy and the criminal;
>deletes the murderous and the injurious,
>>the violent and the disdainful,
>>the vicious and the selfish from their walks of life.

Counting of the days introduces man,
>>to his days of accountability,
>>before the theatre of creation within the morality of God.

Counting of the days settles up the pleadings of the innocent,
>>>the suffering in being overridden by the immorality of man,
>>>in his wielding of his power and misplaced authority,
>>>>upon all within his scope,
>>>>such as the innocence of a would-be child,
>>>>when within the hands of God."

Victory Over Sleep

And I hear Jesus saying,
"Victory over sleep is not always wise,
   can lead to tiredness and lifelessness of activity.

Victory over sleep has its time of importance,
   has its time of keenness of application,
     where victory is important if not critical,
     where supervision is necessary and cannot be foregone,
     where control is essential and must not be underestimated,
     where success is paramount and should not be put at risk.

Victory over sleep has its sequences of the critical,
     which must be initiated accurately,
     with close attention to the details.

Victory over sleep can both exist together within the harmony of the body and the spirit.

Victory over sleep is not a nightmare in the offing,
   is not the surging of the waves,
   is not the raising of a flag,
   is not the loss of faith,
     of truth or of common sense.

Victory over sleep does not include the tossing and the turning,
     does not include the ups and downs throughout the night,
     does not include the interruptions of the pets within a room.

Victory over sleep stretches out the night,
     increases productivity for a time lock with concentration,
     sees the dawn arriving with the seeds of expectation,
        as sown for the coming day.

Victory over sleep does not count the snores,
     does not count the coughs and sneezes,
     does not count the cups of tea or coffee,
        as rendered through the night.

Victory over sleep must deny the eyelids closing,
     must deny the comfort of the bed,
     must deny the setting of an alarm beside the bed.

Victory over sleep is a matter of the will,
     is a matter driven by importance,
       will be a matter of regret,
         if it is not achieved:
         with inspections not ticked off,
         nor counted through the night.

Victory over sleep should be prompt and not lingering,
        should be an accurate objective,
        should be well worth the while of apportionment,
          when mixed with the other ingredients,
        included for success where stirring and blending within a time frame,
              are the architects of the structuring,
              of the crystal structure in the making.

Victory over sleep is a recurrent need,
        while production remains critical and essential,
        as a component in the building of a working model.

Victory over sleep has a row of sleepless nights,
           and of napping during the daylight hours.

Victory over sleep inspects what has been achieved,
        with the sizing of the crystals,
        expresses disappointment if they are not as intended—
          with the need to be redone,
        until they have reached conformity at last.

Victory over sleep has the lights shining all night long,
        has the cot and blanket remaining empty,
        has the electric jug remaining near the boiling point,
           as it is set to the retaining of its heat.

Victory over sleep is something one can become used to,
        is something where the loss of sleep,
          becomes of less importance,
          as the eyes stay open longer,
          without the need for refreshing,
          or of rubbing the eyelids into a form,
            of acceptable behaviour.

Victory over sleep places no emphasis on tablets,
        places no emphasis of employing such assistants,
        places no emphasis on trusting that,
           which would prove to be untrustworthy.

Victory over sleep does not admit to yawns,
        does not admit to bleary eyes,
        does not admit to partial closures,
          with a fast opening much wider stance.

Victory over sleep admits the difficulty of endeavour,
        admits the insurance of commitment,
        admits the keen interest in crosswords and of puzzles,
          with a word base which is easier to track,
          or the reading of a book which holds the interest,
          of the intellect without capturing the soul.

Victory over sleep is as if a mussel in its shell,
              where movement is at a stand-still;
      is as if a cat taking its catnaps,
          that can hear every word;
      is as if a nodding head becoming more drowsy,
          until a start refocusses attention on that which is at hand.

Victory over sleep can be within an environment of chaotic noise,
      can be where concentration is to the fore,
             so noise sensitivity is not challenged,
                as a competitor at large.

Victory over sleep assists the fragility of discovery,
      assists the stagecoach of delivery,
      assists the waggon load of assortments,
      assists the whistle of a train for the attracting of attention.

Victory over sleep cannot veer to the left or to the right,
      cannot sag down onto a chest,
      cannot be involved in the flipping of an egg,
             some bacon,
             or a piece of bread,
             within the frying pan of breakfast,
               with its wakeup call at last.

Victory over sleep does not push or shove,
      does not relinquish nor fail in observation,
      does not recount and get a different answer,
      does not recycle and expect a better result,
          within the practical and retained until approved,
             to be signed off as being up to specification,
          as attributed to the night where consistency is important,
                and a rash is not.

Victory over sleep can be lead by the hand of God,
      can be first aroused by the voice of God,
      can be fulfilled by following the directions of God,
      can be assisted by the nursemaids of God,
      can be within the equilibrium of God,
          where certainty both validates and measures,
          the call upon resources within the finality of completion,
             with on-going success."

Nursing End-time Losses

And I hear Jesus saying,
"Nursing end-time losses is not a source of sympathy.

Nursing end-time losses do not see them gravitate to the sympathetic,
    do not see them soften with a smile,
    do not see them with a handclasp in a bed.

Nursing end-time losses is not a medical condition.

Nursing end-time losses is in the world of extremism and of vilification,
    of blame and denial,
    of lies and truth,
    of investment and of fraud,
    of sequences and impounding.

Nursing end-time losses has care for end-time funds,
    has care for decreasing value,
    has concern for the potential loss resulting,
        or for the practical loss sustained,
        and now missing from the count.

Nursing end-time losses will be common at the end,
    will be common with the approaching of uncertainty,
    would be best to cut and run,
    with the profits as established,
    in a time of high scale movement,
        up the investment ladder,
    with some stupidity required for the registering of a loss.

Nursing end-time losses should not be very great,
    should be the net result of a specific time frame,
    of the end-time movements as liquidity again becomes the king,
        within the field of resource management at large.

Nursing end-time losses is a sing-song without a chorus,
    is a no-go for investment as uncertainty approaches while
        the way is down,
    as uncertainty is thought to prevail on trumping,
    while the waiting for a movement of renown,
        as destined to go down in history,
    with the rewarding of all who placed their trust in a continuation,
        as the job is not yet finished,
    as the wise will foresee the end-result with the recovery
        of the losses,
    on an upward gradient which rewards the wise and the trusting,
    as to the intent of many,

who are fed-up with the majority as called to serve,
who behave like little children in achieving nothing worth
the commenting,
as they follow the chief goat,
as they do not want to give up and go home,
until they're seen to have left the fields in tatters,
as dismembered broken and deserted when it is too late,
and the stable door is open,
and the horse is still there in the stable,
in readiness and good health,
for another trip around the track.

Nursing end-time losses is soon to be a thing of the past,
is soon to be wiped out by recovery,
on the uptick of time as set for the decision making,
is soon to mark a party at which no-one wishes to attend,
at which there is an agreement that it is manned,
by those well past their use-by dates,
as agreement has been dragged apart,
as stupidity has approached the biased guards for more,
as the liars and the fraudsters are meeting their past due
of accountability,
for the wasted opportunities and the loss of truth within the party,
where the lying is endemic,
where the concepts are not only impractical but also unwanted,
by those who know the truth and are not indoctrinated,
by those who wondered how a party could come to be like this,
where both joy and jubilation are no longer in the showroom,
of the children who are soon to be told to pack their bags to go home,
from the showroom where the blisters are to get their heads to heal;
so common sense can experience a transplant of new growth,
which it thoroughly deserves,
from within a party which honours the integrity of Freewill.

Nursing end-time losses are not the be-all of survival,
are not the chasers after security,
are not the careful and considerate.

Nursing end-time losses feeds upon itself,
creates an environment of losing even more,
yet will not free the hands to action.

Nursing end-time losses is not the thing to do,
       has no basis for doing such unless a raw recruit,
       has no spark of knowledge which will frown and stop a loss developing,
       has no gift of knowledge which can see the prospect for advancement,
              soon coming to fruition,
       has no other home address where meaningful advice resides,
         where it can be sought without fear of intimidation or of need,
         where it can leave in righteousness a funding pathway to the stars.

Nursing end-time losses can bring bitterness,
          both to the mouth and to the stomach.

Nursing end-time losses can just see them running around in circles,
          doing nothing but getting giddy as they soon fall over,
             and it's too late to rest.

Nursing end-time losses marks a beginner not knowing the way forward,
          not understanding the basics of investing,
          not following the advice of wise counsel,
             or a mentor established in the sector,
              known to be of interest.

Nursing end-time losses are often stupid enough to sit and watch them,
              increase by the day,
     to hug them tight and hope for the better,
     to watch and wait,
     to still take no limiting action of imposing a stop-loss order.

Nursing end-time losses can creep up to expand very quickly,
         when the market plunges on bad news,
       as the naïve then sell at the bottom,
       so they have supplied the bargains of the day,
         as they miss-out on recovery,
         as they frown and get upset,
         at their own lack of knowledge,
         when coupled with the fear to act."

My Content Study Aid

_____

_____

_____

_____

_____

Praying for The Coming

And I hear Jesus saying,
"Praying for the coming must be within The Will of God.

Praying for the coming must be within the timing of God.

Praying for the coming must be within the locality of God.

Praying for the coming has a decided effect;

confirms the willingness of support,
confirms the degree of preparation,
confirms the landing place of new life.

Praying for the coming does not sidestep authority,

does not sidestep the reality,
does not offer instructions as to how it should be done.

Praying for the coming is placing a request,

is ensuring the support is practical and current,
is offering an invitation open to acceptance.

Praying for the coming slots the past into the present,

lines up the presentations to the elite,
seconds the coming of authority in all its fullness of glory
and of power released.

Praying for the coming is a mind-sweep of The Earth,

is the updating of the clock of time,
is the establishing of the thrones of God,
is the instructional album now available to My Kingdom people:

the committed and the loving,
the verified and the waiting,
the learning and the preparing:
as families and singles,
as clusters and as enclaves,
as gatherings and churches,
as recorders and the faithful,
as kingdoms and of nations,
as the governed and the lawless,
as listed and included—

from around The Earth of both man and God.

Praying for the coming arouses the sanctified of God,

arouses the justified of God,
arouses the redeemed of God,
arouses the communion takers and the communities
as known to God,
arouses the fluent as the speakers in,
the interpreters of,

together with the thought transferors:
as to soon become the dominant means of communication,
within the tongues of heaven.

Praying for the coming is best with precision and conciseness,
as mixed within the sincerities of faith and truth.

Praying for the coming has no need for the diarrhoea of the tongue,
has no need for attempting to be the catch-all,
of the relevant phrases in the surrounding of divinity.

Praying for the coming can be short and brief,
can be an acknowledgement of remembrance,
can be a finger in the pie,
can be the short changing of selection.

Praying for the coming progresses when encountering the informed and the caring,
the committed and the enthusiastic,
the searchers and the finders.

Praying for the coming is a measure of belief,
of commitment to a happening,
of a result where justice is installed,
where accountability is examined for liability within the folds of life.

Praying for the coming can be from a pregnant mother-to-be,
can be from an expectant father-in-waiting,
can be from their friends and family who know their way to God.

Praying for the coming asserts a claim to God,
inserts a responsibility fast coming to a head,
expects a day full of excitement and reward.

Praying for the coming spreads calm into what may well be the unknown,
and the nervous,
into what may be encountered and overcome,
into what may be handed to the mother to be cuddled to her breast.

Praying for the coming is a form of gratitude released,
is a form of thanks expressed with sincerity of existence,
is a sense of appreciation for the gift of God as maturity approaches,
as earnestness exists with tremors to the fore,
for an anxious father awaiting affirmation,
who knows not what to do,
other than to sit upon a chair.

Praying for the coming has an end in sight,
has all preparations complete and readied,
for acceptance of a new born child.

Praying for the coming covers all and sundry,
        includes the tried and true,
        meets with the challenge of waiting,
           for due process in progression along the road to birth.

Praying for the coming has both a start and an end,
        has a reward for waiting to see the end result,
          cleaned and wrapped in the first coverings from the world.

Praying for the coming comes to fruition,
        has a lot to see and do,
        has a new noise to become accustomed to,
            from the alive and moving,
            from the birthed and growing,
            from a child given the task of exploration,
              in its new world of brightness,
              encountered for the first time,
              with eyelids running practice trials,
                of what they can achieve.

Praying for the coming,
        in a second sense,
          is really at an end,
        where success does breed success,
        with a new born child of great value,
        now transferred to a mother's arms,
        as the father with a twinkle in his eye looks on in appreciation,
              of what he will soon be holding,
          with a welcoming smile to the world of giants.

Praying for the coming in the first sense is far from over or complete.

Praying for the coming will find and await The City of the promise,
           The City of return,
         The City of belonging in which He walked and taught and strode,
        to limp to fall to die and to return as now planned,
           unblemished and mature now in outlook and intent,
        as responsibilities with wonders await the coming of the new day,
         with the kingdom for His people of the covenants with God.

Praying for the coming can assist in informing the uninformed,
         in declaring the undeclared,
      is settling on the coming change in governance with the entry to eternity,
            wherein the scales of justice are balanced once again,
              for the to-be-the-sequestered and the judged,
           while Freewill accountability is settled very quickly,
             with neither error nor appeal to mercy,
            which was not shown to others at the time."

Help Within Attendance

And I hear Jesus saying,
"Help within attendance varies with the task,
          varies with the level of responsibility,
          varies with success or otherwise.

Help within attendance is not a ricochet from the moon,
          is not a second guess at pinning a tail on a donkey,
          is not a sequence of prime numbers.

Help within attendance is something quite special,
          speaks of medical aid within an ambulance,
          speaks of medical aid upon a race track of the cars,
          speaks of first aid at a game of football.

Help within attendance shutters all the windows,
          discovers help within the cyclones and the hurricanes,
          rescues the flooded and dismayed with boats or ladders,
               set for the cruising of the streets and homes,
          rescues beach swimmers from the water when in difficulty:
               with the surf the currents or the rips.

Help within attendance guards the organ transplants for both the temperature,
               and the time.

Help within attendance is the newsman on the phone.

Help within attendance is the doctor at the race track meeting of the horses.

Help within attendance is when present at a posting,
          within a possible life threatening situation,
          where injuries are possible,
          and are likely to need attention.

Help within attendance has fire engines requested for a battle,
               with the flames and smoke,
               of houses or of factories or of bush fires,
               in the forests and the scrub,
               where the smoke or flames can overcome,
               and when the help is in very urgent need.

Help within attendance soothes the feelings of a mother,
               in the seeking of safety for a child,
          holds fast to the prospect of an injury when a car collides,
          hastens to the side of someone motionless,
               and spreadeagled on a grass verge,
               where the unfortunate has been thrown;
          peers down into a chasm,

where the vehicle with the driver,
have both gone over the edge,
to be hidden in the native bush,
somewhere down below.

Help within attendance is waiting at an airport,
is waiting at the beaches of popularity,
with lifeguards on their viewing platforms,
is waiting at the ambulance bays of hospitals,
with trolleys at the ready,
for the injured and the maimed,
as collected from the roads and streets and homes.

Help within attendance can be summoned via the telephone,
can be summoned on an alarm button issuing specific instructions,
can be sent to situations of extremism,
where death or severe injury is likely to follow,
in the presence of the guns or knives,
or of marital disagreements carried to extremes.

Help within attendance seeks the very best,
with knowledge and application skills,
as endowed and found capable,
and with a willingness to serve.

Help within attendance sometimes catches up with the mountaineers,
subjected to a slip or fall or a stumble on a rock,
or supported by a rope after a wild fall,
with bouncing off the rocks,
to then be hanging limply in the air.

Help within attendance can be an accident at home,
where something sharp has not gone where expected,
and has let some blood escape.

Help within attendance can sometimes be without a task,
when arriving at a crash site of an aircraft,
either large but mostly small,
where all are deceased,
and beyond the help on offer.

Help within attendance can be out late at night,
or all through the night,
as followers of the mess left by drunken drivers,
either as a dare or race across the city,
where the lights go red but the speedsters do not stop,
and the innocent join in the cry for help.

Help within attendance are sometimes robbed,
for tablets or for liquids or for needles,
are sometimes knocked unconscious,
are sometimes exposed to the helper being victimised,
for no other reason than the call to drugs.

Help within attendance sometimes sees demand outstripping supply,
sometimes the seasons see increasing numbers of sporting stations,
seeking manning for prompt attention to the players,
when the play is halted by a whistle,
for the players on the ground not immediately getting up.

Help within attendance can be limited to first aid kits,
loaded with bandages and pain killers,
and water for the rinsing or to ease the swallowing.

Help within attendance seldom has the time for cameras,
seldom has the need to study what it was,
rather would see it in the reality of the present,
with a relaying of its history to date.

Help within attendance can save both life and limbs,
can prevent the cripples of tomorrow,
from arising from the injured of today,
can assist in moving the wheelchairs back into the shadows.

Help within attendance should be both speedy and essential,
where contact sports are played with strong intent;
with concentration in the run down to a conflict,
likely to be broached.

Help within attendance has the eyeball on potential injuries,
as they first approach and then recede,
into an off-the-field-of-play decision,
as a willing substitute willingly takes the position,
just made vacant in the line-up of the battle,
hardened warriors of both commitment and determination,
who can see a golden trophy nearly in their grasp,
to fit into a cabinet of pride or a shelf on high,
when on display as a souvenir of a war well won."

My Content Study Aid

_____

_____

_____

Trucks Delivering

And I hear Jesus saying,
"Trucks delivering through the night as well as through the day,
   keep commerce alive and well,
   keep commerce responding to demand,
   keep commerce restocking off-takes to the reserves for either sale or use,
      or just delivering items according to the schedule for the trip.

Trucks delivering have rest stops periodically,
     for comfort or a top-up of the appetite.

Trucks delivering don't like encountering delays or detours on the route,
    where truck time is valuable and needs to be accounted for,
       in the manifest of delivery.

Trucks delivering call in at the way stations where they are often expected,
      because of frequency of passing through.

Trucks delivering can have refuelling stops as well,
    where fuel can be pumped in the hundred's of gallons,
      with apportionment to accounts.

Trucks delivering like to continue with the journey without unexpected delays,
   which are best made up and overcome,
   so costs incurred are realized but restrained by apportionment,
     on the time sheets as recorded.

Trucks delivering appreciate listening to long playing audiotapes of books,
      of interest,
      of things not known before,
    as the hours are assisted to tick by,
    within the cabs deployed.

Trucks delivering keep to the schedules of cross-country driving,
   do not dissipate their time on random stops,
     without a qualifying reason.

Trucks delivering can have two drivers alternating,
   as each in turn is sleeping on the bed within the cabin,
   in accordance of complying with the resting periods,
     as required and annotated.

Trucks delivering know their routes from experience,
   know their routes with the stops along the way,
   know the routes as affected by the weather,
     in stretching to the snow bound.

Trucks delivering are not inconsiderate users of the roads,
   are not careless in their driving,
   are not churlish in that which they encounter on their routes.

Trucks delivering are prepared for unexpected emergencies,
   for spare tyres and the means of replacement,
   for breakdowns in the sensitive filters of both engine air
       and fumes,
   and of electrical connections for the lighting and the playback,
    of those items designed as holders of attention,
    all subject to the pounding of the roads,
    with their composite wear and tear.

Trucks delivering may encounter flood waters with extensive detours,
   may encounter livestock escaped from their holding areas,
    and found browsing on the roading berms,
   may encounter areas where there are power outages,
    with traffic lights temporarily out of action.

Trucks delivering have stops to check their loads,
   to ensure straps are both relevant and tight,
    and nothing is astray or dangerous,
    while the brake lights remain effective.

Trucks delivering have hill climbs and descents,
   where the gears are used with certainty of application,
    for both speed and pulling power,
   as the engine revs on changes,
   as well as on rebuilding speed of travel or of braking.

Trucks delivering are moving both mass and weight,
   in two trailers of connection,
   are not easily stopped when an emergency is seen,
    with something in the headlights,
    which requires avoidance at a much lower speed,
    with braking into a partially vacant lane,
    where sheer size demands both attention,
     and the ultimate right-of-way.

Trucks delivering cannot have tired drivers driving beyond their permitted time,
    of access to the roads,
   cannot have sleepy eyes peering through the rain,
   cannot have headlights on the blink,
   cannot have stones thrown up creating chips,
    with the potential for serious harm from a crazed windscreen,
    with a corresponding loss of vision in a flash.

Trucks delivering have professionals at the wheels,
> are experienced with the momentum,
>> and the stopping distances,
> are aware of the engine braking and of that applied to wheels,
> are aware of the weather impact on the roading surfaces,
> are aware of the wind strength,
>> and its effect on straight-line driving,
> are aware of the sun and its positioning,
>> and of how reflections can bedazzle with a distraction,
>>> which could prove fatal in its application.

Trucks delivering can be seen as the steam-rollers of the roads,
>> which are used to winning arguments,
>>> however small or large;
> where the cab is high and out of reach,
> where only legs are left exposed unto collisions,
>> of both might and thoughtlessness,
> where passers of stupidity do not recognize the size,
>> as they choose a high speed pass,
>>> and then immediately brake to pull back into line,
> where the practical available stopping distance is immediately
>>>> cut in half,
> but the actual stopping distance remains as it was before,
> but now has safety halved as well with avoidance nigh impossible,
>> because of the stupidity of the other users of the road.

Trucks delivering have a responsibility as users of the roads,
> have a responsibility to drive with all due care,
>>> in the fulfilment of the hope,
>>> of returning home alive and well,
>>> to both spouse and family.

Trucks delivering are exposed to all types of weather,
>>> with the varying density of vehicles,
>>> which impose their own restraints,
>>> both to speed and to passing capabilities.

Trucks delivering are not the see-saws of the playground,
> should not be those who call the curtain down upon a life,
>>> because of another's lack of care,
> with the skid marks left as the sole evidence of foolishness at large,
>> whereupon a wheel chair has now been brought into service,
>> which was previously unnecessary and quite undesirable."

Change in Governance

And I hear Jesus saying,
"Change in governance will impact on The Earth,
    will change the aspects of survival,
    will change the influences now coming to significance.

Change in governance is as a result of a procurement standing free,
    as a result of a semblance of curtailment,
    no longer meeting with acceptance,
    when thought is applied,
    as a result of promises long upheld for activation,
    whose time is finally approaching with relevance and expectation.

Change in governance arises with a change in both type and style,
    in both freedom and justice as sought
    for installation,
    in both righteousness and truth,
    where supposed alternatives are frowned on,
    in both health and happiness in a breakout,
    of the rewards for long term Faith and Grace:
    both meeting their approaching end-time of existence.

Change in governance is bringing Accountability to The Throne of Administration,
    to the fields of Justice and of Equality in functioning;
    to The Throne of Light where Righteousness prevails,
    within a close proximity to The Mercy Seat upon The Bema,
    to everyone's delight and satisfaction with the end result;
    to The Throne of Expectation,
    to the fields charged with the upholding of the future,
    as set for achievement and for growth.

Change in governance seeks the very best in the removing,
    of the waste and the collusion in the pot of sin,
    as it is seen to whither and to fade into an ignoble absence,
    from the present and the promised.

Change in governance sees the faces and the voices selectively changed,
    with the new ideals as they advance for both installation
    and implementation,
    right across the shores the plains and the mountains of The Earth,
    which previously where bounded by differing levels of behaviour,
    non of which were or are acceptable to the entity of inheritance,
    coming into power and authority,
    which shall not be deposed.

Change in governance is wrought,
    either commonly by the will of man,
    or divinely by The Will of God.

Change in governance supersedes the shamefulness of the past,
>> for the glory seen to be attached to the new way forward.

Change in governance dispenses with the rotten kernels,
>> as evidenced in extending through,
>>> all the governing flesh of man,
>> where life has no value in the womb,
>> while money contaminates all it touches or descends upon.

Change in governance can turn the world around,
>>> to run under a much better form of control,
>> where beauty and fairness welcome every day,
>> where pain and suffering and hunger are no longer,
>>> the results arising from the driver of greed,
>>> which inhibits the niceties of man,
>>> which sees such acting as the multipliers
>>>> of the atrocities of man.

Change in governance is about to be a world-wide phenomenon,
>> where the iniquity of man will neither,
>>> be practised nor acceptable,
>> at the table of discussion in seeding future motivation.

Change in governance will have a soft hand employed when it touches on the life of man,
> will note the variation in the approach to life,
> will note the consternation,
>> as a rearguard attempts to bring,
>>> a fresh fight into an arena,
>>> from wherein they have long since lost the right,
>>>> to express either an opinion,
>>>> or the declaration of a right,
>>> when attempting to whip up the arena of lost causes,
>>> from what would seem to be a long time ago,
>> when barbarism launched its attacks upon the all and sundry,
>> as genteelism and sophistication faded from the scene,
>>> where activity was destructful and to the point,
>>> where grace could not exist.

Change in governance can soon see everything changing for the better,
>> can soon see guns no longer being carried,
> can soon see guns being committed to their funeral pyres within the cities' squares.

Change in governance is a happy time for friends as fresh memories are developed,
>>> as fresh friends come to a party,
>> as reliable friends come to join in the scope of possibilities,
>> where friendship is dominant and love is to the fore.

Change in governance gives new meanings to the words,
       in common usage,
    gives new hope for a resurrection of times past,
       within the fields of churches,
    gives new enlightenment upon the meaning of Revival,
       as it extends across The Earth,
      to be out of reach of the satanic forces,
       still hell bent on capturing the souls of man.

Change in governance can see happiness and smiles reaching:
    out across the sunrises and the sunsets,
    out across the oceans and the seas,
    out across the lakes and the rivers,
     where people have settled on the shores and banks,
     where folk are now settling with friendship to the fore,
    as companionship within morality puts shine upon relationships,
     with active invitations to learn of Righteousness with Truth,
      and how the two can combine,
      into a welding of a relationship with God:
        in all His glory,
       and of that which He has planned,
        for the committed of God,
     with the polishing of the spirit and the soul of man,
      as he learns to live in surroundings,
      as approved by God,
       with an eye unto eternity and the generosity,
       of an active Freewill within the full fluency achieved,
       for The Pentecostal Tongues of God's people,
        upon the tongues of heaven,
    when thought transference comes into play,
    as Eternity rings the bells,
    as Satan is gathered up,
    as evil slides into recess,
    as the gardens of God are showcased to all able to visit,
     and to understand what the centuries contain,
       in the measuring of the future without time,
       as time truly becomes the servant of man,
        in the coming and the going,
        and the just is."

My Content Study Aid

Appendix

The Nine End-time Psalms of God
or as The Nine End-time Homilies of God

	Pages	Total Words
1. GOD Speaks of Return and Bannered	418	90,840
2. GOD Speaks to Man on The Internet	498	126,434
3. GOD Speaks as His Spirit Empowers	272	68,205
4. GOD Speaks to Man in The End-time	248	62,358
5. GOD Speaks in Letters of Eternity	236	56,766
6. GOD Speaks to His Bridal Presence	326	78,183
7. GOD Speaks to His Edifice	512	126,890
8. GOD Speaks of Loving His Creation	280	70,658
9. GOD Speaks Now of a Seal Revealed	124	24,561

Scribal Note: These may probably be better known by man in his naming as 'The End-time Homilies of God - in being 'Religious discourses which are intended primarily for spiritual education rather than doctrinal instructions'.

My Content Study Aid

_____

_____

_____

_____

_____

_____

Journaling & Notes (1)

Journaling & Notes (2)

About The Scribe

Updated 15th April 2020
Anthony is 79, having been married to his wife, Adrienne, for 56 years. They have five married children: Carolyn, Alan, Marie, Emma and Sarah and fourteen grandchildren: Matthew & Ella; Phillipa & Jonathan; Jeremy, Ngaire & Trevor; Jake, Finn, Crystal & Caleb; Bjorn, Greta & Minka.

Anthony was raised on a dairy farm in Springston, Canterbury, NZ in the 1940s. He graduated from Canterbury University, Christchurch, NZ with a B.Sc. in chemistry and mathematics in 1962. He was initially employed as an industrial chemist in flour milling and stock food linear programming applications.

These used the first IBM 360 at the university for determining least cost stock food formulations and production parameters. Later he was involved in similar applications on the refining side of the oil industry in Britain, Australia and New Zealand. This was followed by sales and managerial experience in the chemical industry.

The family moved to a Bay of Plenty, NZ, town in 1976 when Anthony took up funeral directing, as a principal, expanding an initial sibling partnership until the close of the century. Anthony acquired practical experience in accounting, business management, and computer usage (early Apples— including The Lisa).

Upon retiring from active funeral directing in 2000 and selling his interests, he then commenced the promotion and the writing of funeral management software for the NZ funeral environment. Rewarded with national success in NZ, with his son also expanding recently into Australia, he has now retired, in 2007, from the active management of that interest, as he quits it entirely in 2020. He lives near some of his family in Hamilton NZ.

Anthony was brought up in the Methodism of his father until his mid-teens, his mother's side was Open Brethren. He is Christian in belief within an Apostolic Pentecostal Charismatic framework of choice (since the 1990s) having been earlier in the Mormon church for several years. Thereafter he was in the Baptist denomination followed by finding a home within the NZ Apostolic (Acts) church movement.

He and his wife, who has visited a number of Asian countries, have been to India in 2011, 12, 13, 16 and 18 on The Lord's tasks and have witnessed and participated in many miracles which befall His People and The Multitudes.

His forbears William Henry Eddy and Margaret Jane Eddy, née Oats, emigrated to New Zealand from Gulval, Cornwall, England in 1878 on a sailing ship, with a very slow passage time of 79 days, and with their three month old infant child, Margaret Anne, dying 21 October 1878 from Congestion of the brain on board the Marlborough while en route to NZ. The Marlborough sailed London 19 September 1878, via Plymouth 26 September 1878, and arrived Lyttelton 14 December 1878 with 336 assisted immigrants. His grandfather, Alfred Charles Eddy, then but three years old, together with an older brother aged four, obviously survived the trials of the sea voyage to become a part of a family with a further eleven New Zealand born siblings all living to maturity.

The Four Companion End-time Flowers of God

	Pages	Total Words
10. GOD End-time Updates Ancient Alien History	310	84,011
11. GOD End-time Updates His Call to The Multitudes	166	46,152
12. GOD End-time Updates The Bride of My Son	180	47,267
13. GOD End-time Updates The Guardianship of Friends	280	82,847

Four Synopses of The Flowers of God

Book Ten 'God End-time Updates Ancient Alien History' delves into the distant past of Flying Saucers with Alien strangers cross- and interbreeding to generate Neanderthals, and where the discovered new element of Moscovium disintegrates over time into an antigravity fuel, which enables flying saucers to fly the way they do, and where ancient knowledge tells of the extermination of the dinosaurs because of being predators. The current situation, with crop circles and Flying Saucers with real live Aliens, brings history up to date.

Book Eleven 'God End-time Updates His Call to The Multitudes' here The Lord Jesus speaks throughout The Earth— to all who would prepare for an ongoing life with Him. He is reaching out to have The Multitudes come to an understanding and awaits a response in answer to the question of the thoughtful: Why is The Freewill of man of such importance to God? Why is The Freewill of man such a determinant of the ultimate destiny of man? Why is The Freewill of man either respected or honoured by God? Why is The Freewill of man 'Honoured' by his movements within the new covenant?

Book Twelve 'God End-time Updates The Bride of My Son' as dictated by The Father. The Father loves and enfolds as He chooses to bring before The people of The Lord all those who are close to His Heart especially as the wisdom of the centuries has been nurtured in the heavens, is often obvious when spoken, raises eyebrows at the thoughts revealed, silences while matters are considered as to the best way forward. The wisdom of the centuries is a gift from God, is an enlightening of speech, is the victory of expression. The wisdom of the centuries is an expansion of vocabulary.

Book Thirteen 'God End-time Updates The Guardianship of Friends' with eighty six divinely selected scrolls dictated by Jesus: where The Curtain Call of God stimulates: in growth, in Faith, in righteousness, in expression, in quests, in being friendly and inviting. It affirms the value: of being under The Faith Field of Mortality, the confirmation of The Righteous Field of Morality, the requested availability of The Cleansing Field of Grace, the necessity of Seeking The Field of Preparation, The gifts of My Spirit as on The Day of Pentecost, the benefit of attaining fluency in The Heavenly Gift of Tongues, access to the given opportunity to select: the destiny of choice as the goal of life, to be so set in Faith for Freewill Activities— with righteousness prevailing as the destiny is assured. It closes out the time of Grace, opens up the time of Mercy at The Bema Seat.

CPSIA information can be obtained
at www.ICGtesting.com
Printed in the USA
BVHW012321240321
603031BV00049B/1293